Spiritual Gifts
What Can Only Come From The Holy Spirit

Judah Veritas

© 2026 by Judah Veritas

The right of Judah Veritas to be identified as the author of this work has been asserted by him in accordance with the Copyright, Designs, and Patents Act 1988.

Published by Ascend Publishing LLC

All rights reserved. No part of this publication may be reproduced, stored in a retrieval system, or transmitted in any form or by any means – for example, electronic, photocopy, or recording – without the publisher's prior written permission. The only exception is brief quotations in printed reviews.

ISBN-13: 979-8-9926324-6-0

Unless otherwise indicated, Scripture quotations are from the New King James Version.

Scripture taken from the New King James Version®. Copyright © 1982 by Thomas Nelson. Used by permission. All rights reserved.

Scripture quotations taken from the (NASB®) New American Standard Bible®, Copyright © 1960, 1971, 1977, 1995, 2020 by The Lockman Foundation. Used by permission. All rights reserved.

Scripture has been italicized to distinguish it from the author's thoughts. Brackets in Scripture indicate the author's descriptors. Scripture that contains bold font is intended to highlight the author's emphasis.

No part of this publication may be reproduced or transmitted in any form or by any means, electronic or mechanical, including photocopy or recording of any information storage and retrieval system without prior permission in writing from the publisher.

This book is dedicated to those who desire everything from the Holy Spirit and are willing to go to any lengths to have Him fulfill the Will of the Heavenly Father, after being born again and covered by the Blood of the Lord Jesus Christ.

A Special Thanks To My Wife,

You are the reason my journey into spiritual gifts began. As soon as we got married, God blessed me with a multitude of other spiritual gifts.

Thank you for imparting to me the gift of tongues and for being equally yoked with me in deliverance and spiritual warfare.

You are the godliest woman I know.

I love you.

"There are diversities of gifts, but the same Spirit."

– 1 Corinthians 12:4 NKJV

"But to each one of us grace was given according to the measure of Christ's gift. Therefore He says: 'When He ascended on high, He led captivity captive, And gave gifts to men.'"
    – Ephesians 4:7-8 NKJV

"As each one has received a gift, minister it to one another, as good stewards of the manifold grace of God."

– I Peter 4:10 NKJV

Introduction

"There are diversities of gifts, but the same Spirit."
— *1 Corinthians 12:4 NKJV*

Spiritual gifts are gifts that can only come from the Holy Spirit.

This may sound obvious on the surface, but unfortunately, due to a multitude of false prophets and false teachers, people believe they can be taught spiritual gifts. Of course, this is not the case since spiritual gifts can only come from God Almighty.

It is important to perceive the distinction between *being taught a* spiritual gift and someone *teaching how to* use it. People can help us understand our gift, and there are certain ways that we can increase the gift through practice, but it is important to understand that the gift itself only comes from God. For example, no one is taught the gift of tongues. They either have the gift or they do not.

Only the Holy Spirit brings the increase in the gift. Practicing our gift brings greater understanding and awareness. Like lifting weights at a gym, there will be growth. However, this growth can only happen at the pace of the Holy Spirit. For those of us who have the discerning of spirits, we may begin with seeing demons in people's eyes, but we ourselves are not ready to peer into the spiritual realm and see demons in the manifestation that they are (more to come on these matters).

When we are born again, we know we only need the Holy Spirit to teach us our spiritual gift. However, God will bring those who are part of the Body of Christ, and they can be helpful in our spiritual walk and journey.

Regardless of how God chooses to teach us our spiritual gift, we must understand that people are not the end-all be-all. If we are left alone in a season of isolation, we can be certain that we are not alone. We have the Holy Spirit when we have truly put our faith and trust in Jesus Christ as Lord and Savior and genuinely repent of our sins.

"'But the Helper, the Holy Spirit, Whom the Father will send in My name, He will teach you all things, and bring to your remembrance all things that I said to you'" (John 14:26 NKJV).

"These things I have written to you concerning those who *try to* deceive you. But the anointing which you have received from Him abides in you, and you do not need that anyone teach you; but as the same anointing teaches you concerning all things, and is true, and is not a lie, and just as it has taught you, you will abide in Him" (1 John 2:26-27 NKJV).

When we depend on the Holy Spirit to teach us the gift that has come from Him, He will do so initially, gradually, and continually.

"But one and the same Spirit works all these things, distributing to each one individually as He wills" (1 Corinthians 12:11 NKJV). The Holy Spirit is entirely in charge of who gets what gift, how many gifts each person possesses, and the increase of each gift.

For Paul to write on each gift of the Spirit, he himself had to possess each spiritual gift. Paul had the authority to write on each gift of the Holy Spirit because he himself received and was acquainted with each gift. By knowing this truth, we should be motivated to ask God for all the spiritual gifts.

There is nowhere in Scripture that reveals *what* we have been given is *all* we can receive. When it comes to God, there is always something new, and there is always an increase. It may not happen immediately (I prayed for years for the gift of tongues and did not receive it until six years later), but eventually, if we persevere and pray in faith without doubting, we can expect great and mighty blessings to occur.

If Paul possessed all the spiritual gifts, we could as well. This is a truth that is of the utmost importance to understand. We all have a calling and purpose, but the blessing of the spiritual gifts is to make us wiser, more discerning, loving, bold, and courageous.

By failing to pray for other gifts and an increase in our current gift(s), we will miss out on much. We will end up on that Final Day seeing all that God was willing to do, but due to distraction, entertainment, and prioritizing lesser matters, we did not receive what could have been given.

It is imperative that we press into the Truths of Scripture and understand more about Who God is. We must not only understand what He has already done, but what He is willing to do. In between these realities, we must seek to find what He is currently doing. As we learn, we must press in all the more to desire the realities, gifts, blessings, and matters of the Holy Spirit.

"But the natural man does not receive the things of the Spirit of God, for they are foolishness to him; nor can he know *them*, because they are spiritually discerned" (1 Corinthians 2:14 NKJV). Any "Christian" who continually mocks the gifts of the Holy Spirit most likely does not have the Holy Spirit.

If someone has the Holy Spirit, even if they do not understand the gifts of the Spirit, they will not deny them. Why? The Holy Spirit always confirms the Scriptures, never mocks, scoffs, or denies Them.

If someone is continually denying spiritual gifts, then it is most certainly not the Holy Spirit; and if it is not the Holy Spirit, then it is not just coming from an unclean spirit within the person – it is coming from the person themselves! Once more, as 1 Corinthians 2:14 (NKJV) states, "the natural man does not receive the things of the Spirit of God, for they are foolishness to him".

Never be ashamed if self-proclaimed Christians mock you (a true born-again believer) for your gifts. Simply because someone does not understand an aspect of Scripture does not mean there is an error in the Word of God in what It *teaches*. The error is in the person, and it is always important to seek God to make sense of what we know is in the Word of God and is Truth, but what we have yet to learn, grow in, and discover.

God is Infinite, and we will always be growing in Him. Likewise, His Word continues to unravel deeper revelations as time passes.

Those stuck in libraries reading more about men than God's Word will believe that it is impossible to receive greater revelations of God. Some may say, "The gifts were for back then, but they are not for now." This is folly, and it shows a lack of seeking God and quickly believing the thoughts and viewpoints of man.

A general principle: If it is in the Word, do *not* dismiss it. If the Word declares it, do *not* deny it.

Spiritual gifts are needed now more than ever. With people depending on artificial intelligence, answers from the internet, and partaking in occult and witchcraft activity, we need to "come boldly to the throne of grace, that we may obtain mercy and find grace to help in time of need" (Hebrews 4:16 NKJV).

Spiritual gifts are a means to edify us and the Body of Christ, rebuke and correct, warn and protect, and help us to stand bold and strong.

When God speaks and reveals the future through spiritual gifts, we can rest in peace. When God gives us the gift of tongues, it can bring edification to ourselves. When He blesses us with wisdom in all matters, life becomes easier. When we prophesy, we bring a word in due season. When God gives us a word of knowledge, we can know exactly what is to occur or what lies in the hearts of men.

When true healing and the working of miracles occur, people cannot deny the God of Heaven and Earth. When faith comes forth, we can move mountains. When discerning of spirits is activated, we can know the true intentions of individuals and the demons that are affecting their character and personality and need to be cast out. When the interpretation of tongues is known, we can peer into and know the deep and hidden things of God's Perfect, Sovereign Will.

It is time to advance in the gifts we have been given. It is time to put aside the books of those who placed their own ideology above sound Biblical Theology. Those men will be held accountable for suppressing, grieving, and quenching the Spirit. We, however, shall move forward –

not in our own understanding, but by the speaking, directing, guiding, and counsel of the Holy Spirit.

The spiritual gifts are known and activated all throughout the Holy Bible. We need only partake in seeking where these gifts were manifested and ask God to enlighten us with these Divine truths that are meant to aid us in our walk with the Lord Jesus and edify the Body of Christ.

Deception is at an all-time high, and we need the Holy Spirit now more than ever. May He bless each one of us with greater portions of His gifts. May He grant us the desires of our hearts that are in accordance with the Heavenly Father's Will. May He bless all the saints with a humble heart to steward well all the spiritual gifts.

It is time to rise in the Power of the Holy Spirit, believing the Word of God entirely and moving forward in boldness, confidence, and assurance that Christ is with us to the very end of the age (Matthew 28:20).

God in Heaven, the Trinity, Father, Son, and Holy Spirit, Who oversees all things, Who rises above all, is beyond all, and Who can do all things easily and effortlessly, You are the God Who is not bound by human reasoning and logic, by man's thoughts or imagination, or space and time. You transcend all things, and You rule and reign Sovereign over all. O God, we pray that You would bless us with understanding more about Your Word and receiving deeper revelations of Thee. Give us a spirit of wisdom and revelation to grow in the knowledge of You and receive understanding. Make us saints who are discerning. Bless Your saints who will remain humble and steward well Your gifts from the Holy Spirit, and may the Spirit Himself forever increase our gifts to be used for Your Glory. God, we are not our gifts, though many may preach as if we were. Our gifts are meant to be used for good and not evil. The gifts of the Spirit are meant to bring edification to the Body of Christ and give You Glory. Keep us from exalting ourselves with what You give. Bless us with hearts of humility, continually, that we may steward well all You give. For You are Life, and our lives are all about loving You, knowing You, serving You, and bringing You honor and glory. May Your Name be exalted high above the Heavens and the Earth forevermore. May we place You in the proper place within our hearts and minds at the very place You already are, for You alone are the Immortal, Invisible, Eternal God, Whom no man has seen in full nor can see in full. Dominion, Power, and Glory be Yours forevermore. May Thy Holy Will be done on Earth as it is in Heaven. In Jesus' name, Amen.

Imperative Principles to Understand About the Gifts of the Holy Spirit

"*But to each one of us grace was given according to the measure of Christ's gift. Therefore He says: 'When He ascended on high, He led captivity captive, And gave gifts to men.'*"
– *Ephesians 4:7-8 NKJV*

There are some very important principles to understand about the gifts of the Holy Spirit that we will review briefly.

To begin, it is absolutely crucial to understand that the gifts of the Spirit only come from the Holy Spirit. "There are diversities of gifts, but the same Spirit" (1 Corinthians 12:4 NKJV).

The predominant spiritual gifts that we see throughout Scripture are mentioned and found in 1 Corinthians 12:7-10 (NKJV), which states:

"But the manifestation of the Spirit is given to each one for the profit *of all:* for to one is given the word of wisdom through the Spirit, to another the word of knowledge through the same Spirit, to another faith by the same Spirit, to another gifts of healings by the same Spirit, to another the working of miracles, to another prophecy, to another discerning of spirits, to another *different* kinds of tongues, to another the interpretation of tongues."

The other gifts we shall review in this book are located throughout Scripture, but are not mentioned in 1 Corinthians 12 (these being dreams, interpretation of dreams, visions, interpretation of visions, revelation, discernment, joy, and encouragement). The gifts mentioned in 1 Corinthians 12:7-10 are manifested through these other gifts, but a differentiation between them will be explored in the following chapters.

Spiritual gifts are not taught but given as the Holy Spirit chooses. "But one and the same Spirit works all these things, distributing to each one individually as He wills" (1 Corinthians 12:11 NKJV). Of course, those who receive a similar gift as us from God can be taught *how to use* the gift. However, they are *not taught the gift*. They can only receive it from the Holy Spirit Who does so as He wills.

As mentioned, but for the sake of iteration, gifts can coincide with others. Some gifts complement others (either from two separate people, as my wife's gift of interpretation of visions works well with my gift of visions).

Spiritual gifts can also overlap with others. Depending on the ones you have, the gifts make you synesthetic. Someone may receive visions, but these visions are meant to be a proclamation through a prophetic word. Sometimes, a prophetic word receives a word of knowledge about someone they just met. The gifts can overlap and can accomplish much in the Power, Wisdom, and working of the Holy Spirit in us.

This leads us to our next point – spiritual gifts can only work in accordance with God's Will when it is God's Spirit working through us. Without God's Holy Spirit, the gifts are given and obtained but not used for God.

This is also a great segue to understand that each person is born with a certain spiritual gift. This spiritual gift can be used by those who are not born-again, but again, it is not for God's Will when they do so. There are those who do not yet know God and possess a strong prophetic gift of sensing and understanding future or present realities. This is not due to divination or witchcraft. They were given the gift by God and may even be interested in Christianity, but have not yet taken the full step of faith in the Lord Jesus Christ and repentance of sin to receive the Holy Spirit and become born again.

Initial gifts are therefore given at birth and can be used before becoming born-again; however, they can be used only up to a certain point. It is the Holy Spirit Who brings the increase with each gift.

"But earnestly desire the best gifts. And yet I show you a more excellent way" (1 Corinthians 12:31 NKJV). When we go to God requesting the best gifts, we go to Him desiring *all* the gifts.

If all gifts are from the Holy Spirit, they are equal in value. Though there may be differentiation in this life, insofar as what we perceive, each is valuable.

"If the foot should say, "Because I am not a hand, I am not of the body," is it therefore not of the body? And if the ear should say, "Because I am not an eye, I am not of the body," is it therefore not of the body? If the whole body *were* an eye, where *would be* the hearing? If the whole *were* hearing, where *would be* the smelling? But now God has set the members, each one of them, in the body just as He pleased. And if they were all one member, where *would* the body *be?*" (1 Corinthians 12:15-19 NKJV).

Just as each person of the Body of Christ is different, yet equally important, so are the spiritual gifts. When we desire all the gifts and continue to pray to God, He most certainly can give us all the spiritual gifts. Is it possible to receive them all on a moment's notice? Yes, however, God typically gives the gifts at different points throughout our lives, if that is something we continue to seek throughout our lives. Some of the gifts I received have a difference of a couple of months or a few years in receiving them.

We should seek to possess all the gifts. Nonetheless, if we do not, it is not that God favors one over another. Each has their function within the body and God distributes as He Wills. If He sees fit that a person should have one gift and another have all the gifts, that is by His Own discretion of knowing what lingers within the heart, what a person's future will be, their position that God has anointed them for within the Body of Christ, so on and so forth.

Another point to consider is that God is in charge of when gifts are *active* and when they are *dormant*. When they are dormant, it is for

Divine reasons. We have not lost the gift. "For the gifts and the calling of God *are* irrevocable" (Romans 11:29 NKJV). When a gift of the Spirit is given, it is given and cannot be lost. However, we would like to address this point further, as individuals may sometimes believe they have lost the gift. No, that does not occur. Someone who has the gift of tongues will always be able to speak in tongues. Just because they transfer to their native tongue does not mean they have lost the gift.

I will share a brief testimony (which we will cover in more detail in the appropriate chapters). When God first gave me the gift of discerning of spirits, I was seeing spirits continually in people's eyes. During this time, however, I felt like I was not receiving any fresh 'revelation' from God. I put revelation in quotations because the revelation was receiving the gift of discerning of spirits and learning how to steward and wield it at that time.

What I meant by 'revelation' is that I was not receiving extra insight into God, His Nature, Being, Attributes, and Characteristics. It has been a life journey of mine to know God as much as possible in this life. There are moments when God reveals a tremendous amount of revelation. At other times, months pass, and it seems I am not getting anything.

During this time when I was worried, "I lost the gift of receiving revelation from God", my Wife encouraged me. She said all was well and reminded me of Romans 11:29. I eventually rested in that and knew God would speak at a certain time again and give me greater revelation of Who He was.

Fast forward roughly six months, and within the span of a few weeks, God opened the floodgates and gave me roughly two hundred attributes never written about God. I am excited to share that the first two volumes of this multi-volume series can be found under the title of *The Infinite Omni: The Unending All Behind All Things*.

I say this because we are finite. We cannot handle the entirety of the gifts all at once. If I received the revelation God was gracious enough to share about Himself and His Attributes, all during the same time of understanding and discerning the spiritual realm and demons in people, I would become exhausted and reach a point of mental overload.

God has His reasons for why one gift lies dormant and another seems more prominent. Truly, "To everything *there is* a season, A time for every purpose under heaven" (Ecclesiastes 3:1 NKJV).

Expounding on the point that we cannot lose the gift further, it is important to note that, although you cannot lose your gifts, we can refrain from a fuller measure or portion of them. As we age, it is important that we mature spiritually. Many people have remained the same for twenty years after they first became Christians. This is alarming, as we are called to mature and endure. If someone is staying the same, then they are a slave to their own complacency and lack of growth.

Likewise, it is with our spiritual gifts. We may have a gift, but if we do not steward it well, live in sin, refuse to repent to God, and do not listen to the counsel of the Lord, then we will not have an increase in the gift. We will hinder the growth that the Holy Spirit was willing to bring about by our own perpetual selfishness and sinfulness.

Truly, everything given by God can increase. The Holy Spirit can continue to increase each spiritual gift with each passing day, but it is our responsibility to listen to His speaking, directing, and what the Word of God is instructing us to do.

With these basic principles understood about spiritual gifts, it is now time to begin our journey of growth into the spiritual gifts – what they are, their function, how they are to be used and performed, and the blessing of trusting in the Holy Spirit to work the gift through us.

May God grant you the desires of your heart, according to His Will, all the days of your life. May you dwell in the House of the Lord forever as you become born-again, keep in step with the Spirit, and seek nothing but the Will and Glory of God.

God in Heaven, the Creator of the physical and spiritual, Who brought forth the seen from the unseen, Who is the only One Who declares what is and it comes to be, Who alone does all things effortlessly and is willing to do more for man than what man can ask, Your Ways are not our ways and Your Thoughts are not our thoughts. O Blessed Trinity, draw us into Thy Love, Grace, and Holiness. May we stand in awe at the One Who died and rose again, the Lord Jesus Christ. God, we seek You for greater wisdom and discernment behind spiritual gifts. As we move forward, make known to us the gift You have given us. Teach us to steward it well for Your Glory. God, if we find favor in Your sight, bless us with more gifts, that we may be of greater use to the Kingdom of God. You do not need us, God. Nonetheless, we know You love us and allow us to be part of Your Divine plan. May we fulfill the work You have called us to while it is still day. Cleanse our minds, restore our hearts, and renew a right spirit in us that we may live for You. We submit and surrender all to You, Lord God, desiring nothing but Your Name to be glorified. May Thy Holy Will be done on Earth as it is in Heaven. In Jesus' name, Amen.

The Gift of the Word of Wisdom

"*For to one is given the word of wisdom through the Spirit.*"
– 1 Corinthians 12:8 NKJV

Wisdom is the ability to move forward and handle present situations in the best, most efficient manner.

Knowledge provides us with information, whereas wisdom is the ability to use that information effectively.

There is no wisdom without God. All wisdom is derived from Him, and any wisdom given by man has first been bestowed, allotted, and permitted by the Holy One of Israel.

"For the LORD gives wisdom; From His mouth *come* knowledge and understanding; He stores up sound wisdom for the upright; *He is* a shield to those who walk uprightly; He guards the paths of justice, And preserves the way of His saints" (Proverbs 2:6-8 NKJV).

Many people perceive having a great deal of knowledge and information as a form of wisdom. This predominantly occurs within school systems, among those with degrees, and in the world. This, of course, is not bad, but it is not wisdom.

Wisdom is stored up for those who are upright and found righteous under the Blood of the Lord Jesus Christ. Until God comes, man cannot possess godly wisdom; only worldly intellect remains.

When we begin to understand this reality, we will see that "the foolishness of God is wiser than men, and the weakness of God is stronger than men" (1 Corinthians 1:25 NKJV). God is not literally weak and foolish, but for the sake of understanding, the "lowest part" of Him is greater than the highest heights man can possess.

Ironically, the "lowest part" of God coincides with the Unending Peak of all He *Is*. Since He was not created, He, therefore, had no starting point to arrive at a literal "ultimate." He is forever Boundless and Transcends the borders of all that is and all that shall ever be.

"Great *is* the LORD, and greatly to be praised; And His greatness *is* unsearchable" (Psalm 145:3 NKJV). "Great *is* our Lord, and mighty in power; His understanding *is* infinite" (Psalm 147:5 NKJV).

As we begin to meditate on Who God truly is and all He can do (for more on Who God is, see my books *Ineffable Attributes: Understanding the Inconceivable Characteristics of God* and *The Infinite Omni: The Unending All Behind All Things*), we will begin to assess the foolishness of why we do not go to Him in all things and request of Him His Wisdom.

"If any of you lacks wisdom, let him ask of God, Who gives to all liberally and without reproach, and it will be given to him" (James 1:5 NKJV). To receive wisdom in specific areas of life and in particular circumstances and situations, we must ask God for wisdom, and He will provide it to us. This is a promise from God toward His people; however, this is not the gift of wisdom.

The gift of wisdom given by the Spirit of Wisdom is the ability to provide wise counsel that can only come directly from God Almighty.

Men can teach systems to build businesses, and professors can answer questions that have been asked throughout history. However, true, Godly wisdom can only come from God Himself.

When we have the gift of wisdom, we will be those who give the correct answer in due season. "A man has joy by the answer of his mouth, And a word *spoken* in due season, how good *it is!*" (Proverbs 15:23 NKJV). When we operate in the gift of wisdom, we will always have an answer ready that comes from God. This occurs because we are merely vessels and temples of the Holy Spirit.

When we are not grieving or quenching the Holy Spirit, He flows more fully. Not only does He give us the gift, but He works out the gift through us. Of course, in a season of backsliding, the gift may not be as profound and operate to the heights it could if we were walking in obedience. Nonetheless, this does not mean that we will lose the gift. "For the gifts and the calling of God *are* irrevocable" (Romans 11:29 NKJV).

What is important to understand is that perpetual sin or a rough season *suppresses* the full potential of our gift, but it does not mean we *lose* the gift.

Sadly, many move forward in the gifts of the Spirit and become so familiar with the gift that they begin to depend on it rather than on God. This, in turn, becomes a *subtle idol*.

Subtle idols often begin as something originally intended for good. However, when we begin to rely on the gift rather than God, we put what is *from* God ahead *of* God Himself. This is cause for disaster to follow and a distancing of the Presence of the Holy Spirit. Not that He Himself leaves our vessels, but His Presence and Power begin to subside. We begin to use the gift given by God on our own, and there will not be an increase in power, amazement, wonder, and glory for God through the gift, due to us not seeking the Holy Spirit.

This is why it is imperative that we not only request God's wisdom, but also ask that He wield, speak, and operate that wisdom through us by the Might, Strength, and guidance of the Holy Spirit.

Let us take the story of Noah. Noah was given wisdom on how to build something that had never been built before. He, in some sense, was the first man to become an entrepreneur. To build what no eye had seen or mind imagined.

Noah was given the spirit of wisdom, but he depended on God daily to guide him in the next step. Genesis 6:13-22 (NKJV) reveals:

> "And God said to Noah, "The end of all flesh has come before Me, for the earth is filled with violence through them; and behold, I will destroy them with the earth. Make yourself an ark of gopherwood; make rooms

in the ark, and cover it inside and outside with pitch. And this is how you shall make it: The length of the ark *shall be* three hundred cubits, its width fifty cubits, and its height thirty cubits. You shall make a window for the ark, and you shall finish it to a cubit from above; and set the door of the ark in its side. You shall make it *with* lower, second, and third *decks*. And behold, I Myself am bringing floodwaters on the earth, to destroy from under heaven all flesh in which *is* the breath of life; everything that *is* on the earth shall die. But I will establish My covenant with you; and you shall go into the ark—you, your sons, your wife, and your sons' wives with you. And of every living thing of all flesh you shall bring two of every *sort* into the ark, to keep *them* alive with you; they shall be male and female. Of the birds after their kind, of animals after their kind, and of every creeping thing of the earth after its kind, two of every *kind* will come to you to keep *them* alive. And you shall take for yourself of all food that is eaten, and you shall gather *it* to yourself; and it shall be food for you and for them." Thus Noah did; according to all that God commanded him, so he did."

We received a condensed version of what occurred, but God continued to instruct Noah over the course of many decades. We don't see the specifics of every little detail of the Ark, which reveals that God was with Noah, giving him a spirit of wisdom to understand how to build it.

Many times, God will do one of two things: He will either give you a future vision but not the steps to get there, or He will give you the next steps but not tell you where He is taking you. God does this based on our personalities, circumstances, what we can handle, the need to grow specific virtues in us, and the like.

For Noah, God told him what to do and what he was making, without Noah truly understanding what an "Ark" was and what the finished product would exactly look like. This is where the need to seek God continually arose, and the need to operate in the gift of wisdom. For wisdom is knowing how to work off of information given and doing what is necessary for the next step.

Noah did not sit there and experiment and say, "Well, I wonder if this would work. Let me try this next step." No, as far as we are concerned, God gave him step-by-step instructions. Noah did not have to experiment because of God's gift of wisdom and God's willingness to come alongside him and help him build the Ark throughout the coming decades.

In Genesis 41:33-36 (NKJV), we find Joseph saying to Pharaoh (after interpreting his dream):

> "'Now therefore, let Pharaoh select a discerning and wise man, and set him over the land of Egypt. Let Pharaoh do *this,* and let him appoint officers over the land, to collect one-fifth *of the produce* of the land of Egypt in the seven plentiful years. And let them gather all the food of those good years that are coming, and store up grain under the authority of Pharaoh, and let them keep food in the cities. Then that food shall be as a reserve for the land for the seven years of famine which shall be in the land of Egypt, that the land may not perish during the famine.'"

Although I have written extensively on Joseph in my book, *Theology of Work*, and how God prepared and led him, we see that Joseph knew the exact statement that needed to be said after he interpreted Pharaoh's dream. Joseph could have easily left it by just interpreting the dream. He could have given Pharaoh what he wanted, but instead, Joseph spoke in a way that brought to Pharaoh's attention the next steps.

Joseph did not just exercise his gift of interpreting dreams (which we will review in later Chapters); Joseph used his gift of wisdom to tell Pharaoh the next best step.

How many times do we speak with others and not know much about them? How many times have individuals spoken to us and not shared anything of value? As we grow (and hopefully all of us do) in maturity, we will begin to reflect and learn not just to leave conversations as they are. We will seek to provide value and next steps.

How many times has a man or woman been interested in another, finally got the conversation going, and then failed to take the next step (such as asking for their number or planning a coffee date)? Of course, all of this should be done based on whether the Holy Spirit is leading us or not. We don't just want to play the dating game the way the world does. Instead, we want to do what is right in God's eyes and trust Him to bring us our future spouse and make us aware when that moment comes.

The point we are simply trying to make is that rather than leaving conversations at a "goodbye," we must always strive to provide action steps. It could be at the end of evangelizing or praying for someone, "Now, I would encourage you to begin reading the Book of John. It is short, and it takes a couple of minutes to read One Chapter. If you do this with an open mind and heart and ask that God would reveal Himself to you through His Word, He will." This leads someone not just to feel temporarily loved by being prayed over or feeling seen by someone willing to share the Gospel message with them. Instead, they can now move forward on their own, knowing the next steps and what must be done.

This is the power of the gift of wisdom. It guides not only oneself (by the Holy Spirit's leading) but also helps guide others to the next steps. The gift of wisdom is not bestowed upon those who are lazy in the faith and are unwilling to follow through. No, God gives wisdom to those who will receive it, act on it, cherish it, and continue to seek Him for His guidance and counsel and a greater portion of the gift.

Again, God will give wisdom if we ask (James 1:5), but the *gift of wisdom* is given to those whom God knows are "go-getters" and do not want to be wise for the sake of *ego*. Instead, they seek wisdom to operate throughout life with a sound mind, helping others, growing in God, and understanding more about Who He Is and what He desires from them within a specific season.

What kind of wisdom is the gift of wisdom? James 3:17 (NKJV) declares, "But the wisdom that is from above is first pure, then peaceable, gentle, willing to yield, full of mercy and good fruits, without partiality and without hypocrisy." Any wisdom that boosts ego, causes others to stumble in pride, and makes one have a greater sense of themselves (rather than God in them) is not true wisdom but is earthly and demonic.

"Who *is* wise and understanding among you? Let him show by good conduct *that* his works *are done* in the meekness of wisdom. But if you have bitter envy and self-seeking in your hearts, do not boast and lie against the truth. This wisdom does not descend from above, but *is* earthly, sensual, demonic" (James 3:13-15 NKJV).

Often, wisdom lies not in the answers given, but in the *questions* asked. When the right questions are asked, greater answers will follow (when wisdom is found in both the one asking a question and the one giving the answer).

What is so beautiful about wisdom is that it can lead people to an answer by asking them a question and then giving them the answer. This can all come from one person, and it is strategically done to prompt others to think before responding. At other times, it is to ask them questions they cannot answer so that we may assist them with the answer and bring forth greater value. This is especially true when asking deeper-level questions about God, rather than merely repeating questions within seminaries. Again, this is not bad, but those who operate from a seminary will many times miss out on revelations given by the Holy Spirit (more on this in the Chapter on the gift of revelation).

"When they had come to Capernaum, those who received the temple tax came to Peter and said, "Does your Teacher not pay the temple tax?" He said, "Yes." And when he had come into the house, Jesus anticipated him, saying, "What do you think, Simon? From whom do the kings of the earth take customs or taxes, from their sons or from strangers?" Peter said to Him, "From strangers." Jesus said to him, "Then the sons are free. Nevertheless, lest we offend them, go to the sea, cast in a hook, and take the fish that comes up first. And when you have opened its mouth, you will find a piece of money; take that and give it to them for Me and you"" (Matthew 17:24-27 NKJV). Throughout His Life, Jesus spoke words of Truth, Wisdom, and Love. There was never a sentence uttered that was not full of one of these attributes.

In the passage above, we see Christ asking a question and giving an answer. He gave Peter time to reply and answer, and Peter had no follow-up questions for Jesus after the answer. This is the effect of wisdom, as it leaves people to give an answer without knowing what will be said afterward. However, those who operate in the gift of wisdom will speak knowing what is to occur or what answer will be given, which will lead others to a greater truth and revealment of a particular aspect of reality.

Wisdom is often found in the art of listening. Many people hear and nod their heads, but if you were to take the time to ask them, "Are you following?" or "What have you understood thus far?" they would reveal that they were not really listening because what we were saying was of no importance to them! This is especially true for those who are entirely dependent on wealth, fashion, and connections as their identity, rather than in Christ.

When we learn to listen, we will gain wisdom. This wisdom can be spoken and received even by a poor man. Ecclesiastes 9:13-15 (NKJV) declares, "This wisdom I have also seen under the sun, and it *seemed* great to me: *There was* a little city with few men in it; and a great king came against it, besieged it, and built great snares around it. Now there was found in it a poor wise man, and he by his wisdom delivered the city. Yet no one remembered that same poor man" (Ecclesiastes 9:13-15 NKJV).

Wisdom is not loud. Often, it is quiet and easily overlooked. Wisdom is found within humble hearts, and the proud of heart have no such gift as wisdom. They may be knowledgeable about multiple or particular areas of life, but that is not wisdom. Wisdom is only given by God, and the gift of wisdom is exercised through the vessels of those who are born again and have received the gift from the Heavenly Father.

Although Moses is a pillar saint in all of Scripture, he was not above seeking wise counsel from others. In Exodus 18:17-23 (NKJV), Moses listens to the instruction of Jethro, his father-in-law:

> "So Moses' father-in-law said to him, 'The thing that you do *is* not good. Both you and these people who *are* with you will surely wear yourselves out. For this thing *is* too much for you; you are not able to perform it by yourself. Listen now to my voice; I will give you counsel, and God will be with you: Stand before God for the people, so that you may bring the difficulties to God. And you shall teach them the statutes and the laws, and show them the way in which they must walk and the work they must do. Moreover you shall select from all the people able men, such as fear God, men of truth, hating covetousness; and place *such* over them *to be* rulers of thousands, rulers of hundreds, rulers of fifties, and rulers of tens. And let them judge the people at all

times. Then it will be *that* every great matter they shall bring to you, but every small matter they themselves shall judge. So it will be easier for you, for they will bear *the burden* with you. If you do this thing, and God *so* commands you, then you will be able to endure, and all this people will also go to their place in peace.'"

What did Moses do? He didn't neglect to hear this wisdom that came with rebuke and correction. Instead, Exodus 18:24 (NKJV) reveals that "Moses heeded the voice of his father-in-law and did all that he had said."

We see another instance in which Elisha did not need to go to God and pray about what to do. Instead, since he was already walking with God and very close to Him, through his gift of wisdom, he knew exactly what to do with the situation that was given. He knew the question to ask, the instruction to give, and what the end result would be. 2 Kings 4:1-7 (NKJV) states:

"A certain woman of the wives of the sons of the prophets cried out to Elisha, saying, "Your servant my husband is dead, and you know that your servant feared the Lord. And the creditor is coming to take my two sons to be his slaves." So Elisha said to her, "What shall I do for you? Tell me, what do you have in the house?" And she said, "Your maidservant has nothing in the house but a jar of oil." Then he said, "Go, borrow vessels from everywhere, from all your neighbors—empty vessels; do not gather just a few. And when you have come in, you shall shut the door behind you and your sons; then pour it into all those vessels, and set aside the full ones." So she went from him and shut the door behind her and her sons, who brought the vessels to her; and she poured it out. Now it came to pass, when the vessels were full, that she said to her son, "Bring me another vessel." And he said to her, "There is not another vessel." So the oil ceased. Then she came and told the man of God. And he said, "Go, sell the oil and pay your debt; and you and your sons live on the rest.""

This is the beautiful reality about all the gifts of the Spirit, but in this case, about the gift of wisdom: it is not dependent on whether or not we have prayed right before. The effectiveness of the gift is determined by the amount of time we spend with God and in His Presence, prior.

If we consistently make God a priority each day, beginning and ending our day in prayer, revealing to Him that He is our First Love, our gifts will be automatically operated and stewarded by us through the inner working of the Holy Spirit. We won't have to say to someone who asks us a question, "Just give me one moment. I need to pray for 30 minutes, and I'll get back to you." No, many times, the answer will roll right off our tongue, and we will look back later and say, "How did I know to say that in that moment? There is no way that was me. That was all You, Holy Spirit. Thank You."

After hearing two harlots bicker and complain about a particular son being their own baby before King Solomon, we see him respond in 1 Kings 3:24-28 (NKJV) with the following:

> "Then the king said, "Bring me a sword." So they brought a sword before the king. And the king said, "Divide the living child in two, and give half to one, and half to the other." Then the woman whose son *was* living spoke to the king, for she yearned with compassion for her son; and she said, "O my lord, give her the living child, and by no means kill him!" But the other said, "Let him be neither mine nor yours, *but* divide *him*." So the king answered and said, "Give the first woman the living child, and by no means kill him; she *is* his mother." And all Israel heard of the judgment which the king had rendered; and they feared the king, for they saw that the wisdom of God *was* in him to administer justice."

The gift of wisdom will be used in places of authority. The ability to respond without hesitation and know that it is the right thing to do is how those of wisdom operate.

Those with the gift of wisdom are not gossipers, slanderers, or liars. They desire the Truth and nothing less. When a ruler truly possesses the gift of wisdom, they will be recognized for handling more complex matters (just as Moses did in Exodus 18:26).

The gift of wisdom always knows the appropriate way to deal with matters, and also gives assurance to others about what God is doing and thinking. This, in some relation, coincides with the gift of the word of knowledge (as many of the gifts have certain portions of overlap). We see this clearly in Acts 27:21-26 (NKJV):

> "But after long abstinence from food, then Paul stood in the midst of them and said, 'Men, you should have listened to me, and not have sailed from Crete and incurred this disaster and loss. And now I urge you to take heart, for there will be no loss of life among you, but only of the ship. For there stood by me this night an angel of the God to Whom I belong and Whom I serve, saying, 'Do not be afraid, Paul; you must be brought before Caesar; and indeed God has granted you all those who sail with you.' Therefore take heart, men, for I believe God that it will be just as it was told me. However, we must run aground on a certain island.'"

Men were fearful for their lives, but Paul assured them that they were not going to die. He knew, actually, what to say and how to say it. Paul knew the appropriate time to rise up and declare what was to occur and how he saw an angel. In wisdom, he discerned the state of the men and what to say to calm them and give them assurance. He did this by incorporating the angel and what the angel had declared to him.

Another aspect of the word of wisdom coming into play is evident in no more than 1-2 sentences that pierce the soul, convict the heart, and leave men speechless. Those who have a heightened gift of the word of wisdom are those who can say much in a few words. Take Jesus' reply found at the end of John 8:3-7 (NKJV) toward the men who brought him a woman caught in adultery:

> "Then the scribes and Pharisees brought to Him a woman caught in adultery. And when they had set her in the midst, they said to Him, "Teacher, this woman was caught in adultery, in the very act. Now Moses, in the law, commanded us that such should be stoned. But what do You say?" This they said, testing Him, that they might have *something* of which to accuse Him. But Jesus stooped down and wrote on the ground with *His* finger, as though He did not hear. So when they

continued asking Him, He raised Himself up and said to them, 'He who is without sin among you, let him throw a stone at her first.'"

What happens to the men during this "mic-drop" moment? "Then those who heard *it*, being convicted by *their* conscience, went out one by one, beginning with the oldest *even* to the last. And Jesus was left alone, and the woman standing in the midst" (John 8:9 NKJV).

Those who wield the gift of the word of wisdom will shock the masses with their sharp, direct, wisdom-filled sentences.

Sometimes, the most powerful statements are not those that take five minutes to declare. They are those that come at a moment's notice and are done in 1-2 sentences, and bring conviction to the consciences of men.

If you have the gift of the word of wisdom, use it wisely. For "Wisdom *is* better than weapons of war" (Ecclesiastes 9:18 NKJV). "How much better to get wisdom than gold! And to get understanding is to be chosen rather than silver" (Proverbs 16:16 NKJV).

Let us all seek God for a greater increase in wisdom that we may be as "Joshua the son of Nun" who "was full of the spirit of wisdom" (Deuteronomy 34:9 NKJV). Let us be men and women "of good reputation, full of the Holy Spirit and wisdom" (Acts 6:3 NKJV).

May God bless us with the gift of wisdom to be used to edify, rebuke, exhort, and encourage both believers and unbelievers alike. For "The words of the wise are like goads, and the words of scholars are like well-driven nails, given by one Shepherd" (Ecclesiastes 12:11 NKJV).

"To God our Savior, Who alone is wise, *Be* glory and majesty, Dominion and power, Both now and forever. Amen" (Jude 1:25 NKJV).

God in Heaven, Who alone is the Uncreated Creator and All-Wise God, You alone are Wisdom and give wisdom as Thou sees fit. God, may we live lives worthy of Your call. Give us the wisdom and strength to follow Your Voice, heed Your Word, and be led by Your Spirit. Holy Spirit, make our paths straight. Speak through us words that are fitting for every occasion and season. Keep us from being impatient and hasty in our speech. Help us to be good listeners toward others, making them feel validated, appreciated, and loved. Give us the right words in all seasons to help others. God, we ask that You would increase the gift of the word of wisdom in those of us who have been blessed to receive the gift. God, if others do not have it and seek it, honor their requests as You see fit. May they be filled with a natural heart of humility to prepare themselves for receiving the gift. We love You, O Almighty God, Who alone is the Sovereign Immortal and can do no evil or wrong. May Thy Perfect Will be done, forever and always. Lead us by the Spirit of Wisdom and Truth. In Jesus' name, Amen.

The Gift of the Word of Knowledge

"*To another the word of knowledge through the same Spirit.*"
– 1 Corinthians 12:8 NKJV

The gift of the word of knowledge is an enhanced ability to discern. It is the ability to hear God directly and know when He speaks.

This gifting works in a variety of ways from the Holy Spirit. This word of knowledge allows people to know the hearts of individuals, what is happening in the present, conversations that are occurring when one is not present, what someone is thinking, what will happen if circumstances and situations do not change, and the future.

All of this is directed by the Holy Spirit, and He shares whatever it is that the Heavenly Father Wills to share. "For what man knows the things of a man except the spirit of the man which is in him? Even so no one knows the things of God except the Spirit of God. Now we have received, not the spirit of the world, but the Spirit Who is from God, that we might know the things that have been freely given to us by God" (1 Corinthians 2:11-12 NKJV).

The Holy Spirit is One of the Three in the Holy Trinity. The Being of God contains Three Persons; namely, the Heavenly Father, the Son (the Lord Jesus Christ), and the Holy Spirit.

When we grow in understanding Each Person of the Trinity, we will begin to understand deeper realities.

No carnal man can understand the things of the Spirit. The "natural man does not receive the things of the Spirit of God, for they are foolishness to him; nor can he know *them,* because they are spiritually discerned" (1 Corinthians 2:14 NKJV).

When we speak of the gifts of the Spirit, there will be those who automatically scoff. When this occurs, we must understand that "A proud *and* haughty *man*—"Scoffer" *is* his name; He acts with arrogant pride" (Proverbs 21:24 NKJV). When proud men mock the things of the Spirit, we should not feel down and discouraged. Instead, we must see that scoffers merely reflect the lack of spiritual knowledge. They cannot obtain truths and realities outside of their physical senses, for they cannot perceive, understand, or wield what only God can bring forth, give, and make known.

Therefore, we must never let people discourage us when we share the gifts of the Spirit and what God has given us. Their mockery is a revealment of their lack of knowledge and their unwillingness to truly submit to God. They choose to limit God or dismiss Him and His Word entirely. To do this is a grave error, and unless there is repentance, devastation awaits.

Continuing with the gift of the word of knowledge, Daniel 2:27-28 (NKJV) speaks of how "Daniel answered in the presence of the king, and said, 'The secret which the king has demanded, the wise men, the astrologers, the magicians, and the soothsayers cannot declare to the king. But there is a God in heaven Who reveals secrets, and He has made known to King Nebuchadnezzar what will be in the latter days. Your dream, and the visions of your head upon your bed, were these'".

We will discuss more on this particular Chapter of Daniel toward the end of the book in "The Gift of Dreams" and "The Gift of the Interpretation of Dreams". For now, we are focused on the reality that it is God Who Wills to give the gift of knowledge to whoever He chooses and to make known whatever knowledge He desires to disperse.

In the passage above, Daniel is the only one who "cracked the code" and could discover the king's dream and its interpretation.

Imagine you hold a position of high stature, and you are called to both know and interpret a particular substance of information that is secluded from all people except that person. Imagine the pressure that lies at stake. How many people could actually do this? The short answer is none apart from God Almighty.

Truly, God alone "*is* the God of gods, the Lord of kings, and a revealer of secrets" (Daniel 2:47 NKJV). No one could even begin to speak about what someone dreams, since dreams are a particular realm accessible only to the individual who had the dream and to God. There is no one else on this Earth or in the spiritual realm who can discern dreams. Only God could give such information.

This reveals that demons, sorcerers, astrologers, and the like do not have access to our dreams. Instead, demons can only influence our state of dreaming (we will cover this topic in more detail in the relevant chapters).

For now, it is important to understand that the word of knowledge is given to those who seek God and are sensitive to the Holy Spirit.

"When Jesus had said these things, He was troubled in spirit, and testified and said, "Most assuredly, I say to you, one of you will betray Me." Then the disciples looked at one another, perplexed about whom He spoke. Now there was leaning on Jesus' bosom one of His disciples, whom Jesus loved. Simon Peter therefore motioned to him to ask who it was of whom He spoke. Then, leaning back on Jesus' breast, he said to Him, "Lord, who is it?" Jesus answered, "It is he to whom I shall give a piece of bread when I have dipped it." And having dipped the bread, He gave it to Judas Iscariot, the son of Simon. Now after the piece of bread, Satan entered him. Then Jesus said to him, "What you do, do quickly"" (John 13:21-27 NKJV).

The Lord Jesus knew who would betray Him before it occurred. He knew all along. Not just because He was the Godman but because of the Heavenly Father, and the Holy Spirit within Him.

It is interesting to note that, as far as we know, Jesus was in an entirely different sphere, possessing knowledge and wisdom throughout his entire life. In Luke 2:41-47 (NKJV), we find:

Jesus' "parents went to Jerusalem every year at the Feast of the Passover. And when He was twelve years old, they went up to Jerusalem according to the custom of the feast. When they had finished the days, as they returned, the Boy Jesus lingered behind in Jerusalem. And Joseph and His mother did not know *it;* but supposing Him to have been in the company, they went a day's journey, and sought Him among *their* relatives and acquaintances. So when they did not find Him, they returned to Jerusalem, seeking Him. Now so it was *that* after three days they found Him in the temple, sitting in the midst of the teachers, both listening to them and asking them questions. And all who heard Him were astonished at His understanding and answers."

As the Lord Jesus grew older, "Jesus increased in wisdom and stature, and in favor with God and men" (Luke 2:52 NKJV). The Lord Jesus was always wise, discerning, and knowledgeable, but it is very interesting that miracles did not begin for Him until He turned age thirty and was baptized and received the Holy Spirit.

To perform holy acts of God, it takes the Spirit of God to guide us into specific works. Of course, there are demonic works that cause certain supernatural activity, but if it is a holy act and done out of love and goodness, we can be sure that the Holy Spirit must be within us before holy miracles and signs manifest (John 2:11).

In coming to all of this, we understand that the Holy Spirit *must* be present. When Jesus knew that Judas would betray him, it was not simply because Jesus was Lord and Savior. It was not simply because He is the God-man. He had the Holy Spirit and was always attuned to the Voice of the Heavenly Father since Jesus is One of the Three in the Trinity.

We are reviewing all of this because many times, people may conclude, "Well, that was Jesus. I don't have the ability or authority to do what He did. That's just for Him." This viewpoint is short-sighted and narrow-minded and combats the Word that we claim we believe!

We are not superheroes, but the Holy Spirit in us brings forth giftings that can only come from God. The Lord Jesus Christ declared, "'Most assuredly, I say to you, he who believes in Me, the works that I do he will do also; and greater *works* than these he will do, because I go to My Father'" (John 14:12 NKJV). Though much could be written on this passage, it is wise to go in child-like faith and understand that Christ not only declares and allows us to do what He did but to do it in greater measure! This is all by the Holy Spirit.

When we begin believing the Word of God, we will begin to take God at His Word and witness miracles. We will see and receive what only God can bring forth and give.

It is a tremendous blessing to know that when we are born again, there are no limits to the Holy Spirit. We need to move beyond denominational beliefs that suppress the Holy Spirit and bring God down to our level. To do so is to have a low view of God, and a low view of God is the root of all our problems today.

When we pray and ask God to give us the gift of the word of knowledge, He will do so and reveal that which He knows is current or will happen to protect us.

There have been many times in my life when God has revealed the future. This future has been revealed through visions, a prophetic word, a still, small voice of the Holy Spirit, discernment, and an inner knowing.

I used to believe it was just discernment, and I had an ability to perceive what *might* happen. As I have grown up, I have always had a discernment and a sense of knowing about certain events. My wife will attest to this, but there have been many instances of caution and warning that I have mentioned, and when they were not heeded, the events I predicted happened exactly as I had declared.

I am not sharing this to boast or brag, but to make you aware that this is a reality that God brings about. My wife has the same gift, but it is different. Her word of knowledge typically pertains to present situations, but it also extends to the future.

I cannot speak of how many times we have sat down at restaurants, and my wife has prayed for a word of knowledge for the waiter or waitress (something that will encourage and remind people that God sees them). When this occurs, these events forever change their lives.

I have witnessed many people break down crying at what she had to say. My wife shares something that she could not have known otherwise. Other times, it is a Scripture that directly speaks to what they are going through in their lives. "A man has joy by the answer of his mouth, And a word *spoken* in due season, how good *it is!*" (Proverbs 15:23 NKJV).

It was incredible when I first began to witness this, but over time, I have become accustomed to it and am no longer surprised that this is how God chooses to work through her gifting. I find it incredibly amazing, and her gift only continues to increase.

At other times, she will claim to hear conversations others are having. These people are out of the city or out of state! When we meet up or speak with them, what she hears is exactly what gets said at those gatherings or phone calls! If they don't outright say what my wife heard, how certain people *behave* around us reveals what God revealed to her.

Again, this gift can only come from God, and often what my wife hears is the result of praying. When she wants to give a word of knowledge to someone, she will pray for it. Of course, there are times when she does not pray, and God blesses her with insight.

The word of knowledge is a gift meant to point people to God and as a means of preparation and warning. It is intended for good, not to expose others for personal gain. It is an excellent gift from the Holy Spirit that should not be used for evil, exploitation, defamation of reputation, gossip, or slander. Anyone who remains in a state of these will not be blessed with the gift nor wield it. God does not give His gifts to manipulators and those who are power-hungry and want to control people.

The Lord Jesus was always aware (at the times He needed to be) of what lingered in men's hearts. Take the Disciples wondering who would be the greatest amongst themselves in Luke 9:46-48 (NKJV):

> "Then a dispute arose among them as to which of them would be greatest. And Jesus, perceiving the thought of their heart, took a little child and set him by Him, and said to them, 'Whoever receives this little child in My name receives Me; and whoever receives Me receives Him Who sent Me. For he who is least among you all will be great.'"

Jesus perceived what was in the hearts of the Disciples even before anything occurred! We see this again with the Pharisees in Matthew 12:22-30 (NKJV):

"Then one was brought to Him who was demon-possessed, blind and mute; and He healed him, so that the blind and mute man both spoke and saw. And all the multitudes were amazed and said, "Could this be the Son of David?"

Now when the Pharisees heard *it* they said, "This *fellow* does not cast out demons except by Beelzebub, the ruler of the demons."

But Jesus knew their thoughts, and said to them: "Every kingdom divided against itself is brought to desolation, and every city or house divided against itself will not stand. If Satan casts out Satan, he is divided against himself. How then will his kingdom stand? And if I cast out demons by Beelzebub, by whom do your sons cast *them* out? Therefore they shall be your judges. But if I cast out demons by the Spirit of God, surely the kingdom of God has come upon you. Or how can one enter a strong man's house and plunder his goods, unless he first binds the strong man? And then he will plunder his house. He who is not with Me is against Me, and he who does not gather with Me scatters abroad."

It is rather interesting that many times, spiritual gifts are used in the ministry of deliverance. This is an important reality to note: When it comes to spiritual matters, it takes spiritual discernment and giftings. Without the proper gifts of the Spirit, we cannot detect when the Enemy is on the move.

Is it any wonder why many people are sitting in the pews, unable to discern the Enemy? When he is moving? When he is speaking? When he is deceiving?

The moment demons are dismissed is the moment they excel. The moment spiritual gifts go unaccredited is the moment the Enemy goes undetected. When people, denominations, pastors, and particular groups deny spiritual gifts, they deny the means of detecting the Enemy. When this occurs, devastating consequences are sure to follow.

It is, therefore, a doctrine of demons to deny demons. In a like manner, it is of the Enemy to deny that which comes from the Spirit. For the Holy Spirit gives, reveals, illuminates, and compels us toward that which is of Him. If we dismiss it behind, "Well, I wasn't taught that way," "I didn't grow up hearing anything about that," or "That's good for you, but not for me," we are going to prevent any ability to properly discern the Enemy and see that the underlying cause behind a multitude of problems is not surface level, but spiritual matters that require getting to the root.

Spiritual gifts are meant to bring a proper diagnosis, not one based on what is perceived with worldly eyes. It takes the gifts of the Spirit, and the Spirit working through us with the gifts, to help us understand the underlying problem. Of course, not everything is spiritual. However, many aspects are spiritual, and the word of knowledge is one of the gifts in which God speaks directly to the person who has it. This instills a confidence that cannot be earned or learned, but is rather graciously given by the Heavenly Father, through Christ, and by the Holy Spirit to those made in His image.

"Now when He was in Jerusalem at the Passover, during the feast, many believed in His name when they saw the signs which He did. But Jesus did not commit Himself to them, because He knew all *men,* and had no need that anyone should testify of man, for He knew what was in man" (John 2:23-25 NKJV).

When we begin to succeed and excel from a worldly standpoint, we will grow in both those who support us and our work for God and those who despise us, only wanting to be near us to puff up their own stature and ego. This occurs for the sole purpose of bragging before men that which is by way of *association* but is not truly an intimate *relationship*.

As Jesus performed miracles and signs, many believed in Him. However, He did not become waivered by them, seek to please them, or be influenced by them because He knew what was in their hearts. "Then the LORD saw that the wickedness of man *was* great in the earth, and *that* every intent of the thoughts of his heart *was* only evil continually" (Genesis 6:5 NKJV).

When we have the gift of the word of knowledge, not only do we see what lingers within people's hearts (as God brings forth discernment and expertise), but we also are able to hear conversations. The exercising of my wife's gift is found in this manner, just as it was with Elisha. 2 Kings 6:8-12 (NKJV) reveals the gifting of this Prophet of the Lord:

"Now the king of Syria was making war against Israel; and he consulted with his servants, saying, "My camp will be in such and such a place." And the man of God sent to the king of Israel, saying, "Beware that you do not pass this place, for the Syrians are coming down there." Then the king of Israel sent someone to the place of which the man of God had told him. Thus he warned him, and he was watchful there, not just once or twice. Therefore the heart of the king of Syria was greatly troubled by this thing; and he called his servants and said to them, "Will you not show me which of us is for the king of Israel?" And one of his servants said, "None, my lord, O king; but Elisha, the prophet who is in Israel, tells the king of Israel the words that you speak in your bedroom.""

It is quite interesting that the king of Syria believed there to be a spy in his camp when, in actuality, God gifted his servant, Elisha, to hear the conversations that were occurring in his bedroom in private!

It is vital that we speak only what is edifying and encouraging. When people plot evil and intend to do things that are contrary to God, God has full authority to expose wickedness, sinfulness, and treachery. He brings it to the attention of those He deems worthy to hear and will steward well the information He gives. Then, He brings further instructions on how to proceed with the information. This would be followed by the gift of words of wisdom, where wisdom will move one in the direction they should go based on the information that was given.

Truly, it is a dangerous matter to speak ill of others and wish them harm. God will bring the words they say, the thoughts they think, and what lingers within their hearts to those with the gift of words of knowledge and expose them.

Not only will they be exposed, but God does this to warn His people of what others are plotting. With the ability to have this sort of gift truly comes great responsibility, as God is no respecter of persons (Romans 2:11) and will even reveal matters of kings to His people who possess this gift.

When we review another story of Elisha, we find that He was given a word of knowledge (which can sometimes come through a vision). This vision is almost as if words reveal a picture, and the picture is made known by the words. Like reading a book and imagining what the words convey, so the word of knowledge can reveal certain imagery that God gives, so that the picture, event, place, color of people's hair, location, room, and other pertinent details are made known.

My wife also has this portion of the gift, and I believe it is her greatest gift. She will describe certain events to me, her clients, and others around her. What she describes is what happened. People will say, "You are exactly right. It was there", "They look just like that," "They say that all the time," or "It happened exactly as you stated!" It is quite remarkable, and it is a revealment of what we see in 2 Kings 5:20-27 (NKJV):

> "But Gehazi, the servant of Elisha the man of God, said, "Look, my master has spared Naaman this Syrian, while not receiving from his hands what he brought; but *as* the LORD lives, I will run after him and take something from him." So Gehazi pursued Naaman. When Naaman saw *him* running after him, he got down from the chariot to meet him, and said, "*Is* all well?"
>
> And he said, "All *is* well. My master has sent me, saying, 'Indeed, just now two young men of the sons of the prophets have come to me from the mountains of Ephraim. Please give them a talent of silver and two changes of garments.' "
>
> So Naaman said, "Please, take two talents." And he urged him, and bound two talents of silver in two bags, with two changes of garments, and handed *them* to two of his servants; and they carried *them* on ahead of him. When he came to the citadel, he took *them* from their hand, and stored *them* away in the house; then he let the men go, and they departed. Now he went in and stood before his master. Elisha said to him, "Where *did you go,* Gehazi?"
>
> And he said, "Your servant did not go anywhere."
>
> Then he said to him, "Did not my heart go *with you* when the man turned back from his chariot to meet you? *Is it* time to receive money and to receive clothing, olive groves and vineyards, sheep and oxen, male and female servants? Therefore the leprosy of Naaman shall cling to you and your descendants forever." And he went out from his presence leprous, *as white* as snow."

Prophets are a danger to the camp of the Enemy. Ironically, until God permits something to occur, Prophets remain untouchable. Their lives cannot be taken, and they are God's servants; arrows in His Hand to send fiery darts into the camp of the Enemy.

This is why Prophets are often not killed (immediately) but are rejected. If this rejection is taken to heart, it can discourage them and make them want to give up on living. This, in turn, can further tempt them to act on their emotions. Since the Enemy cannot take them out because God is not allowing them, the Enemy thinks of different alternatives (ex: overdose in drugs).

The road of a true Prophet (not these "YouTube Prophets"), but a Prophet appointed by God Almighty Himself, will experience tremendous opposition, affliction, and rejection from man. This occurs because of the immense call on their lives. They are bold, courageous, and willing to go where God leads. While others would rather please man, true Prophets of God are concerned with wielding well all He gives and delivering the message He wants them to speak in truth and love. They do all things willingly. The Enemy hates this and does what he can to abolish them from fulfilling God's plan.

As we see with Elisha, his heart went with Gehazi. God made it known to Elisha exactly what occurred. The word that Elisha was given was further made known by the precise circumstance. Elisha proceeded to speak on how "the man turned back from his chariot to meet" Gehazi (2 Kings 5:26). Elisha could not have known this other than by the revealment of God Almighty Himself.

A person's history can also be revealed through the gift of the word of knowledge. This is not to have a twisted view of an individual, but to properly move forward with the knowledge that has been given.

God also often gives a general word of knowledge, but keeps specifics hidden. We see this in 2 Kings 4:27 (NKJV): "Now when she came to the man of God at the hill, she caught him by the feet, but Gehazi came near to push her away. But the man of God said, "Let her alone; for her soul *is* in deep distress, and the Lord has hidden *it* from me, and has not told me." The man of God knew she was in deep distress; however, God refrained from revealing *why* at that moment.

Many times, we don't need to know the *why*. At other times, and with many individuals who have the gift, people cannot help but speak out about the why that is revealed. Many people do not monitor their lips and, therefore, cannot be trusted with knowledge that only God can reveal. We must let this truth shed light on how we deal with knowledge. Do we speak about anything and everything we hear, as if it were our own? Or are we a vault that can be trusted with any information?

When Christians begin to embrace and understand these giftings, they will be among the most excellent counselors and therapists. They will understand most aspects (if not everything) behind why someone is feeling the way they do. Of course, people do not need to be counselors and therapists. This can occur without a degree, as God has proven time and time again that He uses the foolish things of the world to confound the wise (1 Corinthians 1:27). God does not need degrees to further along His Will; only a humble, submissive, genuine heart for Him and the willingness to go the length and distance that He is leading and directing.

Let us take John 4:16-18 (NKJV) as our example of a word of knowledge on someone's past: "Jesus said to her, "Go, call your husband, and come here." The woman answered and said, "I have no husband." Jesus said to her, "You have well said, 'I have no husband,' for you have had five husbands, and the one whom you now have is not your husband; in that you spoke truly.""

Eventually, the woman figures out Who Jesus is, as He reveals Himself to her in John 4:26. However, before she finds out that Christ is the Messiah, "The woman said to Him, 'Sir, I perceive that You are a prophet'" (John 4:19 NKJV).

Truly, many Prophets of God possess the gift of word of knowledge. It is meant to reveal the Power of God and instill the fear of the Lord into people, cities, and nations. Only then does God want the fear of Him to lead to His Love. It is by fearing Him that we repent and accept His Grace and Mercy. It is by accepting His Grace and Mercy that we want to love Him for all He has done and continues to do as we walk in reverence for Who He is.

Truly, God speaks mouth-to-mouth to those with the gift of the word of knowledge. 1 Samuel 9:17-20 (NKJV) reveals this in greater measure:

"So when Samuel saw Saul, the LORD said to him, "There he is, the man of whom I spoke to you. This one shall reign over My people." Then Saul drew near to Samuel in the gate, and said, "Please tell me, where *is* the seer's house?"

Samuel answered Saul and said, "I *am* the seer. Go up before me to the high place, for you shall eat with me today; and tomorrow I will let you go and will tell you all that *is* in your heart. But as for your donkeys that were lost three days ago, do not be anxious about them, for they have been found. And on whom *is* all the desire of Israel? *Is it* not on you and on all your father's house?"

This is truly a remarkable encounter, and a huge revealment of the power and authority true Prophets of God carry.

When we first read this Scripture, we see that the Lord spoke to Samuel. This, of course, is not the Lord being physically present and speaking to Samuel. It is a dialogue that occurs as God speaks, without the human eye seeing or the ear discerning what is being said (we will cover this notion in more detail as we examine the gift of visions).

When Saul comes to Samuel, he asks for the *seer*. Notice that this is the only dialogue they have had. There was no prior contact. As Samuel answers him, he not only declares that he is the seer, but he goes on further to reveal to Saul exactly who he is in the presence of and what Samuel can do by the might and power of God's Spirit.

Samuel reveals to Saul that the following day, he is going to reveal everything in Saul's heart. Talk about intimidation! Not only does he use the gift of prophecy of what is to occur (what he will do in the future) through a word of knowledge (about what is in Saul's heart), but he further reveals his gift by telling Saul of past occurrences. Samuel spoke of the donkeys that had been lost for three days.

Finally, if this wasn't enough, God then spoke to Samuel about Saul's future identity, revealing what he would become – the one who would reign over God's people. God revealed all this the moment Saul approached Samuel, and Samuel made known the past, present, and future to Saul in a brief and concise dialogue.

When a Prophet speaks, we would do well to listen. When someone predicts and reveals what could only be known by God and us, we should treat them with the utmost respect – not because of who they are, but because of how close God walks with them. God has given them gifts for specific reasons, and if someone who *truly* has the gift of the word of knowledge tells us what our purpose is when we find our identity in Christ, we will do well to give a listening ear.

Truly, this gift is of the Lord, and He reveals whatever He desires.

How then does God speak? In many ways, and speaking in many tones. The word of knowledge He gives to those who possess the gift is all the same.

For encouragement, it can come in the way of a person revealing how God has "'reserved seven thousand in Israel, all whose knees have not bowed to Baal, and every mouth that has not kissed him'" (1 Kings 19:18 NKJV).

A word of knowledge can also provide guidance on where to go and a person's location. 1 Kings 21:17-18 (NKJV) makes this evident:

> "Then the word of the Lord came to Elijah the Tishbite, saying, 'Arise, go down to meet Ahab king of Israel, who *lives* in Samaria. There *he is*, in the vineyard of Naboth, where he has gone down to take possession of it.'"

Note in the Scripture above that Elijah not only gives the location, but the reason why Ahab is there! Not only is the physical understanding of where Ahab is had, but also the discernment as to *why* he is there. Only God can reveal the *why*, since He alone discerns the thoughts and intentions of the heart (Jeremiah 17:10, Hebrews 4:12).

Maybe it's a foretelling, as we see in 1 Kings 20:22 (NKJV): "the prophet came to the king of Israel and said to him, 'Go, strengthen yourself; take note, and see what you should do, for in the spring of the year the king of Syria will come up against you.'" Not only can a word of knowledge be a foretelling, but also an instruction within the foretelling. 1 Samuel 10:1-7 (NKJV) states:

> "Then Samuel took a flask of oil and poured *it* on his head, and kissed him and said: "*Is it* not because the Lord has anointed you commander over His inheritance? When you have departed from me

today, you will find two men by Rachel's tomb in the territory of Benjamin at Zelzah; and they will say to you, 'The donkeys which you went to look for have been found. And now your father has ceased caring about the donkeys and is worrying about you, saying, "What shall I do about my son?" ' Then you shall go on forward from there and come to the terebinth tree of Tabor. There three men going up to God at Bethel will meet you, one carrying three young goats, another carrying three loaves of bread, and another carrying a skin of wine. And they will greet you and give you two *loaves* of bread, which you shall receive from their hands. After that you shall come to the hill of God where the Philistine garrison *is*. And it will happen, when you have come there to the city, that you will meet a group of prophets coming down from the high place with a stringed instrument, a tambourine, a flute, and a harp before them; and they will be prophesying. Then the Spirit of the Lord will come upon you, and you will prophesy with them and be turned into another man. And let it be, when these signs come to you, *that* you do as the occasion demands; for God *is* with you."

God not only brings a word of knowledge for *foretelling*, but also a word of *forewarning*. Just look at 1 Kings 14:1-5 (NKJV):

"At that time Abijah the son of Jeroboam became sick. And Jeroboam said to his wife, "Please arise, and disguise yourself, that they may not recognize you as the wife of Jeroboam, and go to Shiloh. Indeed, Ahijah the prophet *is* there, who told me that *I would be* king over this people. Also take with you ten loaves, *some* cakes, and a jar of honey, and go to him; he will tell you what will become of the child." And Jeroboam's wife did so; she arose and went to Shiloh, and came to the house of Ahijah. But Ahijah could not see, for his eyes were glazed by reason of his age. Now the Lord had said to Ahijah, "Here is the wife of Jeroboam, coming to ask you something about her son, for he *is* sick. Thus and thus you shall say to her; for it will be, when she comes in, that she will pretend *to be* another *woman*.""

Even within a word of forewarning, God also will give knowledge behind the reason why He does something (or in this case, does not offer something), which may seem "unfair". Isaiah 22:11-14 (NKJV) reveals:

> "You also made a reservoir between the two walls
>> For the water of the old pool.
>> But you did not look to its Maker,
>> Nor did you have respect for Him who fashioned it long ago.
>> And in that day the Lord God of hosts
>> Called for weeping and for mourning,
>> For baldness and for girding with sackcloth.
>> But instead, joy and gladness,
>> Slaying oxen and killing sheep,
>> Eating meat and drinking wine:
>> "Let us eat and drink, for tomorrow we die!"
>> Then it was revealed in my hearing by the Lord of hosts,
>> "Surely for this iniquity there will be no atonement for you,
>> Even to your death," says the Lord God of hosts."

At other times, God will bring a word of future victory yet to come. 1 Kings 20:28-30 (NKJV) declares:

> "Then a man of God came and spoke to the king of Israel, and said, "Thus says the Lord: 'Because the Syrians have said, "The Lord *is* God of the hills, but He *is* not God of the valleys," therefore I will deliver all this great multitude into your hand, and you shall know that I *am* the Lord.' " And they encamped opposite each other for seven days. So it was that on the seventh day the battle was joined; and the children of Israel killed one hundred thousand foot soldiers *of* the Syrians in one day. But the rest fled to Aphek, into the city; then a wall fell on twenty-seven thousand of the men *who were* left. And Ben-Hadad fled and went into the city, into an inner chamber."

God will also send someone with a word of knowledge to speak a strong word, not just correction, but a warning of impending destruction. "Then he said to him, 'Thus says the Lord: 'Because you have let slip out of *your* hand a man whom I appointed to utter destruction, therefore your life shall go for his life, and your people for his people'"" (1 Kings 20:42 NKJV). Truly, "I know that whatever God does, It shall be forever. Nothing can be added to it, And nothing taken from it. God does *it*, that men should fear before Him" (Ecclesiastes 3:14 NKJV).

Let us live appropriately and walk humbly before God. Let us seek Him for clean hands and a pure heart to steward well the gift of the word of knowledge. God will give it to those who will use the gift for His Glory and not to harm, gossip, or slander.

If any of these sinful desires linger at all within someone's heart, the gift will not be given. If one possesses the gift and continues down the path of deception, manipulation, and control, using it for selfish motives and to tear others down, there will be unparalleled consequences.

Let us use all that God gives for His Glory, and let us remember that to do so appropriately, we must seek God's Spirit to use the gifts of the Spirit that have been given to us.

When God knows we will be humble with the gift, and He gives it, we will be as the priest in Judges 18:5-6 (NKJV):

> "So they said to him, 'Please inquire of God, that we may know whether the journey on which we go will be prosperous.'
>
> And the priest said to them, 'Go in peace. The presence of the Lord *be* with you on your way.'"

We will not only hear from the Lord, but we will be inquired by others to see what God has to say, specifically, for those who are not hearing His Voice. If God desires to reveal what is sought, He will do so, either directly or through His vessels. This is the way God chooses to speak, and it is up to Him whether it is through Him, directly, or one of His saints.

Bless the Holy Name of the Lord Jesus Christ, for He alone is the Son of God, the Word Who spoke and brought forth all things into existence.

God in Heaven, Who is Omniscient and All-Understanding, Who perceives all events and knows what is to occur before it happens, Who knows what lingers within the hearts of men and instantly knows all intentions and motives of the heart, Who knows those who are truly for You and those who are against You, Who loves all and is calling all to partake in fellowship with Thee through the Blood of Christ and by the Spirit, You alone are the Living God, the Maker and Creator of all that exists, has been, and is to be. God, we worship and praise Thee! We exalt Thy Holy Name far above the Heavens. You are High and Lifted Up! You dwell in Unapproachable Light and inhabit eternity. O Great and Mighty Ruler, Thy Holy Light pierces through all darkness. None is hidden, but all is exposed before You, to Whom we must give an account. Help us to live upright, holy, and blameless lives before Thee. We love You, Lord God, and we ask that You help us steward well the gifts You have given us. If we are found humble in Thy sight, bless us with the gift of the word of knowledge that we may help the Body of Christ and lead others to You. For You alone know what is done in darkness, and You reveal what Thou decides to bring forth. You alone, O God, bless Your saints with greater revealment of Thy Might and Splendor. God, we worship You, the Great Alpha and Omega, the Beginning and the End. May Thy Will be done, forever and always. In Jesus' name, Amen.

The Gift of Faith

"*To another faith by the same Spirit.*"
– 1 Corinthians 12:9 NKJV

There are multiple gifts of faith. The first and foremost is the faith to believe that God exists.

"For since the creation of the world His invisible *attributes* are clearly seen, being understood by the things that are made, *even* His eternal power and Godhead, so that they are without excuse, because, although they knew God, they did not glorify *Him* as God, nor were thankful, but became futile in their thoughts, and their foolish hearts were darkened" (Romans 1:20-21 NKJV).

The focus of this book is not on Apologetics. Therefore, we will leave the proof of the existence of God to be in accordance with the Scripture above. Anyone can clearly look around, take some time to think logically, and come to the rational conclusion that God exists.

Once we accept that God exists, we move on to faith in the One True God. "'I *am* the Lord, and *there is* no other; *There is* no God besides Me. I will gird you, though you have not known Me, That they may know from the rising of the sun to its setting That *there is* none besides Me. I *am* the LORD, and *there is* no other'" (Isaiah 45:5-6 NKJV).

When we understand that there can only be One God, we then must seek to figure out *Who* He Is. God can give us the faith to believe in His Son, the Lord Jesus Christ. As we sincerely place our faith and hope entirely in Him and not in our good works, and we genuinely repent of our sins, we fulfill the call of God that He desires of every man and woman.

"For this *is* good and acceptable in the sight of God our Savior, Who desires all men to be saved and to come to the knowledge of the truth. For *there is* one God and one Mediator between God and men, *the* Man Christ Jesus, Who gave Himself a ransom for all, to be testified in due time" (1 Timothy 2:3-6 NKJV). "The Lord is not slack concerning *His* promise, as some count slackness, but is longsuffering toward us, not willing that any should perish but that all should come to repentance" (2 Peter 3:9 NKJV).

Once we have the faith to believe in Who the One True God is (the Trinity – the Father, the Son (the Lord Jesus Christ), and the Holy Spirit), we can then begin to receive the gift of faith, which comes by the Holy Spirit.

This faith that can only be given, instilled, activated, and exercised by the Holy Spirit is that which moves mountains! Matthew 17:14-21 (NKJV) reveals this in greater understanding:

> "And when they had come to the multitude, a man came to Him, kneeling down to Him and saying, "Lord, have mercy on my son, for he is an epileptic and suffers severely; for he often falls into the fire and often into the water. So I brought him to Your disciples, but they could not cure him."
>
> Then Jesus answered and said, "O faithless and perverse generation, how long shall I be with you? How long shall I bear with you? Bring him here to Me." And Jesus rebuked the demon, and it came out of him; and the child was cured from that very hour.
>
> Then the disciples came to Jesus privately and said, "Why could we not cast it out?"

So Jesus said to them, "Because of your unbelief; for assuredly, I say to you, if you have faith as a mustard seed, you will say to this mountain, 'Move from here to there,' and it will move; and nothing will be impossible for you. However, this kind does not go out except by prayer and fasting."'"

The Holy Spirit gives us the faith to perceive that there are spiritual enemies at work in a multitude of sicknesses, diseases, character flaws, bad habits, addictions, compulsions, and feelings of enslavement and being compelled to continue in what is harmful, hurtful, and damaging.

Of course, not everything is a demon or unclean spirit. "For the flesh lusts against the Spirit, and the Spirit against the flesh; and these are contrary to one another, so that you do not do the things that you wish. But if you are led by the Spirit, you are not under the law" (Galatians 5:17-18 NKJV).

We are called to be led by the Spirit. However, when we are habitually and continually doing, thinking, or partaking in the very thing we are praying and desiring to get away from, and we do not have freedom, it is because there is a hidden Enemy secretly enslaving, destroying, and wreaking havoc and destruction in our lives.

"For we do not wrestle against flesh and blood, but against principalities, against powers, against the rulers of the darkness of this age, against spiritual *hosts* of wickedness in the heavenly *places*" (Ephesians 6:12 NKJV). It takes faith from the Holy Spirit to discern this reality. Not everything is a demon, and in like manner, not everything is of the flesh.

"Be sober, be vigilant; because your adversary the devil walks about like a roaring lion, seeking whom he may devour" (1 Peter 5:8 NKJV). When we begin to discern that just as the Devil roams, and so do his legions of demons and unclean spirits, we will be better equipped for spiritual warfare and casting out the very entities that are severely hindering our walk with the Lord.

The Disciples could not cast out the demon because they lacked the faith to believe that God's Power was greater than the demon who was throwing the child into the fire and water (Matthew 17:15). The Lord

Jesus gets frustrated by their lack of faith and ends up rebuking the demon out of the man's son.

Demons are huge mountains in the way of many people's lives. Some think it is due to trauma or psychological makeup that makes people act a certain way. Though this can be true or sometimes partially correct, people who do not see with spiritual eyes cannot discern that a continually repeated offense and sinful habit, that people have tried to get out of, but cannot, is a demon.

When a married couple is born-again and a spouse continues to look at pornography, they most likely have a demon enslaving them to the very thing they want to depart from! If a man continues to place career over family and continually wants to make more money, there could be a spirit of "ego" (which is tied to the spirit of "Lucifer" as seen in Isaiah 14 (we are not referencing Satan himself regarding this spirit, but the *function* the spirit brings forth)), "greed", or "pride".

If a spouse continually lacks empathy and wants their way, there is most certainly a demon of "Leviathan", "Jezebel", or a "religious" spirit. When a woman is continually contentious and sowing division and strife, it is most likely a demon of "Jezebel", "accusation", "division", or, if divorce runs in the family, a spirit of "divorce" that needs to be cast out in the name of Jesus!

When we begin operating in the faith to believe the entirety of God's Word, we will start to see life as it is in greater measure. We won't just operate on what is seen, but on what is unseen. "By faith we understand that the worlds were framed by the Word of God, so that the things which are seen were not made of things which are visible" (Hebrews 11:3 NKJV). The greatest exercising of faith and aspects of life are found in that which remains unseen.

When we believe God to perform miracles and move the mountains in our lives, He will do so according to His Will and timing. We are trusting in Him Who we cannot see, knowing He will bring forth a miracle we have *yet* to see, but which will occur in the future.

Toward the end of this Chapter, we will end with the hallmarks of faith from those throughout Scripture (as found in Hebrews 11). For now, we want to examine what the instillation of faith from the Holy Spirit can do to an individual when God gives it in greater measure.

"Then David said to the Philistine, 'You come to me with a sword, with a spear, and with a javelin. But I come to you in the name of the Lord of hosts, the God of the armies of Israel, whom you have defied. This day the Lord will deliver you into my hand, and I will strike you and take your head from you. And this day I will give the carcasses of the camp of the Philistines to the birds of the air and the wild beasts of the earth, that all the earth may know that there is a God in Israel. Then all this assembly shall know that the Lord does not save with sword and spear; for the battle is the Lord's, and He will give you into our hands'" (1 Samuel 17:45-47 NKJV).

It is truly remarkable to consider the story of David and Goliath and observe that David showed no fear. When faith comes in its fullest measure, there is not an ounce of fear, only boldness. There is no focus on what man sees, but on Who God *Is*. When faith comes forth, it comes as a mighty current, making a person blind to circumstances and situations. A person finds comfort and complete trust in God when the gift of faith arises from within them by the working of the Holy Spirit.

David was not concerned about how many men Goliath had killed, Goliath's height, weight, strength, armor, weapons, or skill set. David was concerned about only one matter: declaring what God was *going* to do through him to overcome the obstacle that stood in his way!

When we learn to have this sort of faith, we are not going to walk around each day in anxiety and fear. We will not walk and operate in fear of man. For we know that "The fear of man brings a snare, But whoever trusts in the LORD shall be safe" (Proverbs 29:25 NKJV).

We must ask and declare to ourselves, "For do I now persuade men, or God? Or do I seek to please men? For if I still pleased men, I would not be a bondservant of Christ" (Galatians 1:10 NKJV). "Anxiety in the heart of man causes depression" (Proverbs 12:25 NKJV). When we give in to anxiety from individuals, circumstances, finances, relationships, and the Enemy, we open ourselves up to depression.

Depression occurs not just from a multitude of reasons (selfishness, disobedience, loss of a loved one, traumatic experiences) – depression occurs from being in a perpetual state of anxiety. If we begin to focus on externals and let them make us anxious, we give in to the Enemy and, indirectly, tell God, "You are not Great enough to overcome these impossible odds stacked against me." Inadvertently, we tell God, "My circumstance is greater than You."

We must begin to seek God and ask Him for the faith that was found in David and the Prophets of old! When we do, we will see God show up in mighty ways. If we do not, we will live a life not pleasing to God. "But without faith *it is* impossible to please *Him,* for he who comes to God must believe that He is, and *that* He is a rewarder of those who diligently seek Him" (Hebrews 11:6 NKJV).

God has given me this gift ever since I can remember. It was something that furthered me along in life, though I was combated many times by those whom I loved the most.

I cover more of this in other books, but very briefly, it is important to note that there were times and seasons in my life where I did not know what was going to happen, but God came through, and He gave me the faith to trust He had a plan!

When I was promised a starting spot on my college soccer team, I tore my ACL and meniscus (for the second time) on my same knee during a pre-season game. As soon as I went down, I immediately said, "God, I don't know why You allowed this to happen, but I am trusting You through this. I know You are going to help me and have a plan for me." When I tore my ACL and meniscus the first time (junior year in High School), it never fully healed – despite my being rigorous in my rehab and recovery! The second time, however, God brought complete healing.

There were times when I had $30 to $80 left in my bank account. As I was trying to build my startup, my parents kept telling me I needed to get a job. As I would go apply, I heard God say, "I have something for you. You don't need to apply." Now, some people are lazy and don't want to seek employment. This is not a result of that, but in hearing the *Voice* of God clearly and directly.

As my bank was closing in on zero dollars, I received a call from a Church family friend at the time. He checked in on my startups and then asked if I wanted to join him in building his business. I said yes, and God provided a way during that season in my life.

After breaking hearts and getting my heart broken, multiple women showed interest. I had not had a girlfriend, and I've only had one other, outside of my now beautiful and amazing wife, Jackie Veritas. As I continued to grow older throughout my 20s, I felt constant pressure from individuals, even to the point where, because I didn't have my first girlfriend until 27, even family members thought I was homosexual! I refused to go on dates unless I saw an absolute confirmation or potential.

For those who know the story of my ex, that was a counterfeit sent by the Enemy who pretended to be what I wanted but revealed her true colors over time. As I refused to date all those years, I knew God had someone for me. Why? I gave it entirely over to Him! I prayed in such a way that I said, "God, I give this situation entirely over to You. I pray that I would have a God-story of You bringing my future spouse and me together. Until then, I am going to work on preparing myself and doing what You desire of me." It took a lot of faith to declare that, and, like anyone, there were moments when I felt lonely. Nonetheless, I waited on Him, and through a YouTube video recommended of my now-wife, we talked and found out we were 40 minutes apart.

I invited her to my Bible study and took her on a date to an Italian restaurant, where we were fully transparent about what God saved us from and what He is helping us through. In the next 1-2 weeks, we covered everything – from how to raise a family, a healthy family dynamic, the role of a husband and wife, Theological viewpoints, conversations around our past with others, promiscuity, addictions that used to be but God delivered us from... anything you can think of, we practically covered all of those and all the essentials in those first 1-2 weeks!

Fast forward, and we got married in 3 ½ months. God gave peace all the way through for both of us, leading up to the day of our eloping. This was God's plan *for us*. I had faith and continually prayed, "God, make it known to me when she is the one for me, and then I will put forth the work. Until then, I will do what You desire of me as I wait on You." This served me wonderfully, and God showed up in a mighty way!

In all realms of life – career, relationships, and finances, God blessed me with the faith to believe that would not stunt Him from moving, but would show me the Might and Magnificence of God's Goodness, Love, Grace, and Mercy to work and move on behalf of a sinner such as

I! If He can do that for me and bless me with the gift of faith, He can do the same for you.

It is essential to note that this gift of faith is not constant, but rather like a muscle, it must be exercised and developed. There were seasons in my life where those closest to me put me down, said vicious things, and did not believe I heard from God, much less believed in me. In all these cases, though I was battered and discouraged, God showed up. He not only blessed me with the most naturally beautiful woman who loves Him more than she loves me, but He blessed me with a wife who has never doubted or lacked belief in me.

God has worked through her to resurrect my confidence in God's Provision in business and finance. Truly, it is amazing what can occur when you trust in God and surround yourself with the right people. Truly, it is depressing and destructive when the Enemy works through those closest to you to derail, discourage, distract, and bring you to a place where you lose confidence in yourself and in God.

When this is continually occurring, it is to reveal two magnificent truths: God has much more for you, and He is allowing this to happen to reveal that truth and have you press in and find your satisfaction solely in Him, Who cannot lie and cares for you. Two, He is revealing to you that these individuals are not part of His long-term vision for you. It does not mean you have to cut them off entirely, but it means they will not accompany you for the rest of your journey through life. Just as Jesus had many disciples before there were just the Twelve (John 6:66-71), and just as He never stayed in one place for too long around the same people, so it is for us who have been called to a greater purpose for the Glory of God.

In all seasons, realms, aspects, realities, needs, and wants in life, have faith in God. Jesus Himself declares, "'Most assuredly, I say to you, he who believes in Me, the works that I do he will do also; and greater *works* than these he will do, because I go to My Father. And whatever you ask in My name, that I will do, that the Father may be glorified in the Son. If you ask anything in My name, I will do *it*'" (John 14:12-14 NKJV).

Is there something you want that is not sinful and not for self? It has been placed within you by Him Who alone can bring the answer. Do not be afraid to pray. Know that with every prayer in the Name of Jesus, it is received and done in the manner He sees fit. The revealment of it being received and done demands time, but do not be so distraught by the need to wait. For "those who wait on the LORD Shall renew *their* strength; They shall mount up with wings like eagles, They shall run and not be weary, They shall walk and not faint" (Isaiah 40:31 NKJV).

Let us examine some stories from the Bible that reveal great and mighty faith. Daniel 3 tells the story of three men who would not bow to the image made by King Nebuchadnezzar. This made the king furious! Daniel 3:13-15 (NKJV) declares:

> "Then Nebuchadnezzar, in rage and fury, gave the command to bring Shadrach, Meshach, and Abed-Nego. So they brought these men before the king. Nebuchadnezzar spoke, saying to them, '*Is it* true, Shadrach, Meshach, and Abed-Nego, *that* you do not serve my gods or worship the gold image which I have set up? Now if you are ready at the time you hear the sound of the horn, flute, harp, lyre, *and* psaltery, in symphony with all kinds of music, and you fall down and worship the image which I have made, *good!* But if you do not worship, you shall be cast immediately into the midst of a burning fiery furnace. And who *is* the god who will deliver you from my hands?'"

Due to their unwillingness to go along with the king's desires, Daniel 3:16-18 (NKJV) reveals how "Shadrach, Meshach, and Abed-Nego answered and said to the king, 'O Nebuchadnezzar, we have no need to answer you in this matter. If that is the case, our God Whom we serve is able to deliver us from the burning fiery furnace, and He will deliver us from your hand, O king. But if not, let it be known to you, O king, that we do not serve your gods, nor will we worship the gold image which you have set up.'"

What ends up happening when they are thrown into the fiery furnace? "Then King Nebuchadnezzar was astonished; and he rose in haste *and* spoke, saying to his counselors, "Did we not cast three men bound into the midst of the fire?" They answered and said to the king, "True, O king." "Look!" he answered, "I see four men loose, walking in the midst of the fire; and they are not hurt, and the form of the fourth is like the Son of God"'" (Daniel 3:24-25 NKJV).

By Shadrach, Meshach, and Abed-Nego's faith, Christ showed up and prevented the fire from touching a hair on their head! This is the power of the gift of faith. When it is instilled within us by the Holy Spirit, we will have the boldness to know that God will take care of us when we are threatened for our faith in Christ. We will stand boldly and courageously and will not cower in the darkness. As this occurs, faith arises, the presence of the Holy Spirit is enhanced tremendously, and Christ comes to be beside us! We cannot be touched when we are filled with faith. Even if we are to die for our faith, we will rise and live again, eternally, in Heaven!

O, may God give us the faith that says "No" to darkness without hesitation. May God bless us with the gift of faith that does not fear what man can do, but fears the God of Abraham, Isaac, and Jacob. The One Who alone is Immortal, Invisible, and can do all things easily and effortlessly!

There will be times in life that seem impossible, but if we have faith in God, we will see the impossible. "And Peter answered Him and said, "Lord, if it is You, command me to come to You on the water." So He said, "Come." And when Peter had come down out of the boat, he walked on the water to go to Jesus" (Matthew 14:28-29 NKJV). When we have faith in Christ not just for salvation and the covering of our sins, but also for the power to perform and the ability to partake in what only He can do, we will begin to see miracles.

Faith is the rudder that moves the ship of miracles! Without faith, we will not see God perform the miraculous. Without faith, we will not be those who are blessed to be found involved in the miracle. Only by faith will we see mountains moved, be saved from darkness and harm, and perform what can only be done by God. When faith is in us, the Holy Spirit will flow through us. Then, and only then, will we receive a greater portion of the Holy Spirit and witness what we never thought could be possible.

"But when Paul had gathered a bundle of sticks and laid them on the fire, a viper came out because of the heat and fastened on his hand. So when the natives saw the creature hanging from his hand, they said to one another, "No doubt this man is a murderer, whom, though he has escaped the sea, yet justice does not allow to live." But he shook off the creature into the fire and suffered no harm" (Acts 28:3-5 NKJV). When the gift of faith arises, we will be confronted. The Enemy will double down and attempt to squander our faith.

Especially when others begin speaking ill of us and believing that our suffering is due to some hidden sin, though, when we are walking in faith and obedience and are being perpetually attacked, this truth does not apply. So long as we do not have hidden sin, people will be wrong in their assumptions. They will speak evil of us and say, "They must be going through this because they have done much wrong." The hearts of these individuals begin to become Pharisaical in nature. As this occurs, they wrongly assume and can cast gloom on the hearts of those being attacked.

However, we have the power to shake off the Enemy and not endure suffering. Though we may be buffeted like a man in a boxing match, we will not go down. Although we feel the strike within the spiritual fight, we will not give up. We will stand firm to the very end, not in our might, but in the Power of the Holy Spirit. Then, we will see that our adversity was not a means to eternal suffering, but a means to grow and stretch us. As we navigate the adversity the Enemy seeks to derail and inflict upon us, we will grow in greater faith, being readily able to see future mountains move and greater miracles occur in our lives.

"Now when Jesus had entered Capernaum, a centurion came to Him, pleading with Him, saying, "Lord, my servant is lying at home paralyzed, dreadfully tormented." And Jesus said to him, "I will come and heal him." The centurion answered and said, "Lord, I am not worthy that You should come under my roof. But only speak a word, and my servant will be healed. For I also am a man under authority, having soldiers under me. And I say to this one, 'Go,' and he goes; and to another, 'Come,' and he comes; and to my servant, 'Do this,' and he does it." When Jesus heard it, He marveled, and said to those who followed, "Assuredly, I say to you, I have not found such great faith, not even in Israel!"" (Matthew 8:5-10 NKJV).

The greatest faith is believing that God can do what only He can do, and that we do not need to see Him do it to believe or know it can be done. The centurion knew this, and Jesus was amazed at his faith. Jesus did not say, "I am amazed. Give me a few days, and it will be done." No, the Lord Jesus Christ did it in that very hour! "Then Jesus said to the centurion, "Go your way; and as you have believed, *so* let it be done for you." And his servant was healed that same hour" (Matthew 8:13 NKJV).

I have seen this in my life, time and time again. When I have prayed to God to change the heart of an individual —to make them open to receiving deliverance or to soften their heart to accept the Gospel message —He has answered. Of course, this does not happen every single time for specific reasons that God knows, such as a hardened heart toward Him in others or a wrong use of a person's free will. However, I have had many encounters where God has answered!

We must know that God can perform within the hour that which we seek. We need the faith to believe that He can and will do so. If it takes some time, we must not get discouraged. When we pray, each time we must have faith that it will occur that very hour. If Christ can heal someone who is not even in the exact location where He walked this Earth, then He Who rules and reigns far above the Heavens and Earth can do anything at a moment's notice. Truly, "Blessed *are* those who have not seen and *yet* have believed'" (John 20:29 NKJV).

Truly, God is the One "Who gives life to the dead and calls those things which do not exist as though they did" (Romans 4:17 NKJV). He alone is the One Who Isaiah 61:1-3 (NKJV) declares:

"'The Spirit of the Lord GOD *is* upon Me,
    Because the LORD has anointed Me
    To preach good tidings to the poor;
    He has sent Me to heal the brokenhearted,
    To proclaim liberty to the captives,
    And the opening of the prison to *those who are* bound;
    To proclaim the acceptable year of the LORD,
    And the day of vengeance of our God;
    To comfort all who mourn,
    To console those who mourn in Zion,
    To give them beauty for ashes,

The oil of joy for mourning,
The garment of praise for the spirit of heaviness;
That they may be called trees of righteousness,
The planting of the LORD, that He may be glorified.'"

This is the One Who the woman believed in when touching Christ's clothing in Mark 5:25-34 (NKJV):

"Now a certain woman had a flow of blood for twelve years, and had suffered many things from many physicians. She had spent all that she had and was no better, but rather grew worse. When she heard about Jesus, she came behind *Him* in the crowd and touched His garment. For she said, "If only I may touch His clothes, I shall be made well." Immediately the fountain of her blood was dried up, and she felt in her body that she was healed of the affliction. And Jesus, immediately knowing in Himself that power had gone out of Him, turned around in the crowd and said, "Who touched My clothes?" But His disciples said to Him, "You see the multitude thronging You, and You say, 'Who touched Me?'" And He looked around to see her who had done this thing. But the woman, fearing and trembling, knowing what had happened to her, came and fell down before Him and told Him the whole truth. And He said to her, "Daughter, your faith has made you well. Go in peace, and be healed of your affliction.""

One touch from Christ by our faith heals broken hearts, delivers demons, restores the soul, renews the mind, uplifts the spirit, and makes the body whole! This woman, who struggled for twelve years, would instantly be healed by the clothes of Christ. Imagine Christ Himself touching us directly! If the woman had the faith to believe that His clothes could bring healing while He walked this life, how much more healing will come from Him in His resurrected, Immortal body—reaching down and touching us from Heaven!?

One of the last stories we want to examine with tremendous faith is that of a man known for his faith in God: Elijah.

There is a reason Elijah was one of the two permitted to visit Jesus when He walked this Earth. Luke 9:28-31 (NKJV) states:

"Now it came to pass, about eight days after these sayings, that He took Peter, John, and James and went up on the mountain to pray. As He prayed, the appearance of His face was altered, and His robe *became* white *and* glistening. And behold, two men talked with Him, who were Moses and Elijah, who appeared in glory and spoke of His decease which He was about to accomplish at Jerusalem."

While Moses was known as a humble man, Elijah was renowned for his faith. These are amongst the two most outstanding dispositions one can possess here in this life. To be a humble man who possesses faith is to wield a tremendous amount of God's Power, Presence, and giftings. A man of humility will never seek to become prideful. A man of faith moves mountains. Combine those two beautiful realities, and you have someone who can go toe-to-toe against the Devil in the Might and Strength of the Holy Spirit and not waver.

Let's examine the story of tremendous faith from Elijah, which led to a victorious win on Mount Carmel. Elijah had challenged the prophets of Baal to see whose God was the real one. 1 Kings 18:17-24 (NKJV) begins with a dialogue between the wicked King Ahab and the Prophet of the Lord, Elijah:

"Then it happened, when Ahab saw Elijah, that Ahab said to him, "*Is that* you, O troubler of Israel?"

And he answered, "I have not troubled Israel, but you and your father's house *have*, in that you have forsaken the commandments of the LORD and have followed the Baals. Now therefore, send *and* gather all Israel to me on Mount Carmel, the four hundred and fifty prophets of Baal, and the four hundred prophets of Asherah, who eat at Jezebel's table."

So Ahab sent for all the children of Israel, and gathered the prophets together on Mount Carmel. And Elijah came to all the people, and said, "How long will you falter between two opinions? If the LORD *is* God, follow Him; but if Baal, follow him." But the people answered him not a word. Then Elijah said to the people, "I alone am left a prophet of the LORD; but Baal's prophets *are* four hundred and fifty men. Therefore let them give us two bulls; and let them choose one bull for themselves, cut it in pieces, and lay *it* on the wood, but put no fire *under it;* and I will prepare the other bull, and lay *it* on the wood, but put no fire *under it.* Then you call on the name of your gods, and I will call on the name of the Lord; and the God who answers by fire, He is God."

So all the people answered and said, "It is well spoken.""

Elijah challenges four hundred and fifty prophets versus himself. It is a matter of faith in who worships the true God. Elijah is so confident because he walked with the Lord that he continues by mocking the prophets of Baal as they seek their "god" to call down fire upon the bull. 1 Kings 18:26-29 (NKJV) states:

"So they took the bull which was given them, and they prepared *it,* and called on the name of Baal from morning even till noon, saying, "O Baal, hear us!" But *there was* no voice; no one answered. Then they leaped about the altar which they had made. And so it was, at noon, that Elijah mocked them and said, "Cry aloud, for he *is* a god; either he is meditating, or he is busy, or he is on a journey, *or* perhaps he is sleeping and must be awakened." So they cried aloud, and cut themselves, as was their custom, with knives and lances, until the blood gushed out on them. And when midday was past, they prophesied until the *time* of the offering of the *evening* sacrifice. But *there was* no voice; no one answered, no one paid attention."

The prophets of Baal attempted everything, but no one answered. This is what happens when people follow after the wrong god. Secretly, they follow what their heart desires, and if the Enemy is permitted, he will grant them their heart's desires. When it comes to the challenge of Who God is, however, the Lord Jesus Christ always comes forth in a mighty way. Never will God share His Glory with another "god", for there is no such thing. He alone is the Living, One True God.

Now, it comes to be Elijah's turn. He not only goes forth with the challenge he set, but he himself goes alone against the four hundred and fifty prophets and requests that they make it harder for his bull to be lit on fire. Three times he tells them to dump water on the bull! 1 Kings 18:30-35 (NKJV) reveals this in greater measure:

> "Then Elijah said to all the people, "Come near to me." So all the people came near to him. And he repaired the altar of the LORD *that was* broken down. And Elijah took twelve stones, according to the number of the tribes of the sons of Jacob, to whom the word of the LORD had come, saying, "Israel shall be your name." Then with the stones he built an altar in the name of the LORD; and he made a trench around the altar large enough to hold two seahs of seed. And he put the wood in order, cut the bull in pieces, and laid *it* on the wood, and said, "Fill four waterpots with water, and pour *it* on the burnt sacrifice and on the wood." Then he said, "Do *it* a second time," and they did *it* a second time; and he said, "Do *it* a third time," and they did *it* a third time. So the water ran all around the altar; and he also filled the trench with water."

The stage is set – either Elijah is bluffing, or he knows Who His God is and he rests in full assurance that the Lord will answer him and put all the men to shame. 1 Kings 18:36-39 (NKJV) declares:

> "And it came to pass, at *the time of* the offering of the *evening* sacrifice, that Elijah the prophet came near and said, "LORD God of Abraham, Isaac, and Israel, let it be known this day that You *are* God in Israel and I *am* Your servant, and *that* I have done all these things at Your word. Hear me, O LORD, hear me, that this people may know that You *are* the LORD God, and *that* You have turned their hearts back *to You* again." Then the fire of the LORD fell and consumed the burnt sacrifice, and the wood and the stones and the dust, and it licked up the water that *was* in the trench. Now when all the people saw *it,* they fell on their faces; and they said, "The LORD, He *is* God! The LORD, He *is* God!""

In one request, Elijah prays before God, exalting Him and asking that God would turn the hearts of all who were about to witness what He would do back to Him—a short, direct prayer, filled with complete faith and confidence in God. At a moment's notice, God performed the impossible, not because of days of fasting beforehand. It was not because Elijah had spent hours in prayer each day over the past months to prepare for that particular day. Though these principles are fundamental to the faith, what led to an incredible miracle was one principle: faith.

God can fill us with faith and even increase it! This is what he did for Elisha: he granted him a double portion of the spirit of Elijah (2 Kings 2:9-18). This exemplified the faith he received to perform signs, wonders, and miracles by the Power of God.

Let us review the mighty saints of the Holy Scriptures and ask that God would instill in us a double portion of their faith. Hebrews 11:4-12 (NKJV) declares:

> "By faith Abel offered to God a more excellent sacrifice than Cain, through which he obtained witness that he was righteous, God testifying of his gifts; and through it he being dead still speaks.
>
> By faith Enoch was taken away so that he did not see death, "and was not found, because God had taken him"; for before he was taken he had this testimony, that he pleased God. But without faith *it is* impossible to please *Him,* for he who comes to God must believe that He is, and *that* He is a rewarder of those who diligently seek Him.
>
> By faith Noah, being divinely warned of things not yet seen, moved with godly fear, prepared an ark for the saving of his household, by which he condemned the world and became heir of the righteousness which is according to faith.
>
> By faith Abraham obeyed when he was called to go out to the place which he would receive as an inheritance. And he went out, not knowing where he was going. By faith he dwelt in the land of promise as *in* a foreign country, dwelling in tents with Isaac and Jacob, the heirs with him of the same promise; for he waited for the city which has foundations, whose builder and maker *is* God.
>
> By faith Sarah herself also received strength to conceive seed, and she bore a child when she was past the age, because she judged Him faithful Who had promised. Therefore from one man, and him as

good as dead, were born *as many* as the stars of the sky in multitude—innumerable as the sand which is by the seashore."

Hebrews 11:17-35 (NKJV) continues:

"By faith Abraham, when he was tested, offered up Isaac, and he who had received the promises offered up his only begotten *son*, of whom it was said, "In Isaac your seed shall be called," concluding that God *was* able to raise *him* up, even from the dead, from which he also received him in a figurative sense.

By faith Isaac blessed Jacob and Esau concerning things to come.

By faith Jacob, when he was dying, blessed each of the sons of Joseph, and worshiped, *leaning* on the top of his staff.

By faith Joseph, when he was dying, made mention of the departure of the children of Israel, and gave instructions concerning his bones.

By faith Moses, when he was born, was hidden three months by his parents, because they saw *he was* a beautiful child; and they were not afraid of the king's command.

By faith Moses, when he became of age, refused to be called the son of Pharaoh's daughter, choosing rather to suffer affliction with the people of God than to enjoy the passing pleasures of sin, esteeming the reproach of Christ greater riches than the treasures in Egypt; for he looked to the reward.

By faith he forsook Egypt, not fearing the wrath of the king; for he endured as seeing Him Who is invisible. By faith he kept the Passover and the sprinkling of blood, lest he who destroyed the firstborn should touch them.

By faith they passed through the Red Sea as by dry *land*, *whereas* the Egyptians, attempting to do so, were drowned.

By faith the walls of Jericho fell down after they were encircled for seven days. By faith the harlot Rahab did not perish with those who did not believe, when she had received the spies with peace.

And what more shall I say? For the time would fail me to tell of Gideon and Barak and Samson and Jephthah, also *of* David and Samuel and the prophets: who through faith subdued kingdoms, worked righteousness, obtained promises, stopped the mouths of lions, quenched the violence of fire, escaped the edge of the sword, out of weakness were made strong, became valiant in battle, turned to flight the armies of the aliens. Women received their dead raised to life again."

Let us strive to be those who walk in confidence, assurance, and complete trust and faith in God Almighty to perform the miraculous, strengthen us amid adversity, aid us in stewarding well what comes in the season of prosperity, the belief that moves mountains, the wisdom to depend and seek Him in all matters, and to live on fire for Him by the Power, Presence, and Wisdom of the Holy Spirit. If this is what we desire, then we must make it our aim to be as Abraham according to Romans 4:16-25 (NKJV):

"Therefore *it is* of faith that *it might be* according to grace, so that the promise might be sure to all the seed, not only to those who are of the law, but also to those who are of the faith of Abraham, who is the father of us all (as it is written, "I have made you a father of many nations") in the presence of Him whom he believed—God, who gives life to the dead and calls those things which do not exist as though they did; who, contrary to hope, in hope believed, so that he became the father of many nations, according to what was spoken, "So shall your descendants be." And not being weak in faith, he did not consider his own body, already dead (since he was about a hundred years old), and the deadness of Sarah's womb. He did not waver at the promise of God through unbelief, but was strengthened in faith, giving glory to God, and being fully convinced that what He had promised He was also able to perform. And therefore "it was accounted to him for righteousness."

Now it was not written for his sake alone that it was imputed to him, but also for us. It shall be imputed to us who believe in Him who raised up Jesus our Lord from the dead, who was delivered up because of our offenses, and was raised because of our justification."

God in Heaven, Who instills in man the faith to believe in Thee, to trust Thee, and to believe that You are for us and not against us, You are Him Who rules from generation to generation. God, we know You place us in positions many times where there is nowhere to go and no one to trust but You. It is in these moments where Your miraculous Power comes forth! You alone bring healing, deliverance, and restoration. You alone make up for the years the locust has eaten. O God, we bless You and we seek You. Grant us the desires of our hearts and help our unbelief. Give us the child-like faith that moves mountains. May we live lives that reveal Who You are and what You can do. By faith, we believe that You Are and You can do exceedingly and abundantly above all we ask or think. Lead us to pray big prayers in faith. Lead us to believe in more than what we see. Grant us the gift of faith that will believe You are working and preparing the way, even when we cannot see it in our physical realm. We bless You, Almighty God, Sovereign Ruler, and Lord of the Heavens and Earth. May Thy Will forever be done. In Jesus' name, Amen.

The Gift of Healings

"*To another gifts of healings by the same Spirit.*"
– 1 Corinthians 12:9 NKJV

The gift of healing is just that – the ability to supernaturally heal in the Power of the Holy Spirit.

Throughout Scripture, we see that God not only mends hearts and saves souls, but He also heals physical ailments in this life.

It is essential to recognize that God does not heal everyone. Of course, we are aware of this, but we don't necessarily understand why it is the case.

In a very simplistic answer, it is because God allows evil only if it will ultimately work out for the greater good. He does not answer everyone for various reasons, including what might happen in the future and what is going on in a certain individual's heart.

We all have a cross to bear. Even though there are demons related to certain illnesses (as seen in Mark 1:30-31), we also know that the Lord declared to Moses, "'Who has made man's mouth? Or who makes the mute, the deaf, the seeing, or the blind? *Have* not I, the Lord?'"

(Exodus 4:11 NKJV). Yet, every person who is deaf or blind is not a result of God's will. Sometimes, it is from a demon.

"When Jesus saw that the people came running together, He rebuked the unclean spirit, saying to it, 'Deaf and dumb spirit, I command you, come out of him and enter him no more!'" (Mark 9:25 NKJV). When we understand that God has His reasons and some ailments are related to demons, we begin to realize that everything is either done or permitted by God to work out a greater good.

We could discuss this matter further, but that is not the point of this book. For now, we want to focus on the gift of healing and understand that healing can truly happen to our physical bodies. God can perform miracles. We need to have faith that He will, as we repent of our sin, and desire for God to move in a mighty way. Not only desiring, but believing!

I used to have problems with my hip alignment. I visited three chiropractors over several years. They provided temporary relief but not long-term sustainment. As a result, I continued to experience hip misalignment.

As we will review later on in the Chapter on "The Gift of Discerning of Spirits", I also had one leg that was shorter than the other. Amid these problems, no one could help me. It was not until my wife (who has the gift of healing) prayed and commanded, "Bones, ligaments, and tendons to align in Jesus' name," that I experienced the supernatural healing of God.

It is worth noting that I was not raised to believe in such things. I was actually raised to dismiss them. However, in my spirit, I believed God's Word. Even though I had never seen someone healed, I believe God could do it. Why? He brought forth the Universe from nothing by a single Word. To bring healing upon me was no significant feat. After all, all things are small before the God of Heaven and Earth. Nothing is too complicated for Him.

As I believed, I would be suppressed by the environment I found myself in. Having gone to a Calvinist College, there was never any talk about spiritual gifts (ironically, I went there, though I was never a Calvinist). I grew up my whole life around individuals who suppressed the Holy Spirit and did not believe that the gifts were for today. Where did they learn this? From their pastors. Where did their pastors learn this? From seminary.

I am not anti-seminary, but I am also not pro-seminary. There is too much suppression, dictatorship, and "my way or the highway" within a vast majority of colleges and universities. Many of them do not believe that a greater revelation of God or God's Word can come forth.

It is quite sad when meditated upon, as God desires to do more than we ask or think. Yet, if our pastor or professor tells us "Everything there is to know", we automatically refrain from believing God and His Word. We think it is men who can reveal all we need to know about God. Little do we meditate that these are men who are feeble, flawed, most likely have certain addictions to sins, and do not possess all the answers. It is only the Holy Spirit Who is Pure, Holy, and brings revelation.

Pastors and professors are good when they keep in step with the Spirit. Sadly, however, many believe spiritual maturity comes through being well-learned, reading many books written by men, and relying on human intellect. This is not the way of God, as demonstrated by whom He chose throughout the Word of God. We must never allow men to suppress the Holy Spirit – especially those who have made intellect an idol and have made intimacy with Christ idle.

I once heard a pastor say, "I went overseas, and let me tell you. I saw some things that changed my Theology." No, dear friend, it did not change *your* Theology. It changed how you were *taught* Theology. There is only *Theology*. There is no such thing as "my Theology" or "your Theology". There is simply *Theology*. If God is true and not a liar, which He is (Numbers 23:19, Hebrews 6:18, Titus 1:2), and if God is not the author of confusion or division, but of clarity and unity, then differences in Theology are not due to a misalignment of God, but of us. This is why it is imperative to seek nothing but the Truth; namely, Christ Himself, Who gives us the Truth by the speaking of the Holy Spirit from within, which we receive when we are born again.

The point of the matter regarding seminaries and men being taught their Theology by men is that multitudes are suppressing, quenching, and grieving the Holy Spirit. They set themselves up to have all the answers and, without consulting the Holy Spirit, they issue the final say. One of these is the widespread view that "the gifts of the Spirit were only for back then." Anyone who walks with God and cultivates a relationship with the Holy Spirit knows that this is entirely misleading, unscriptural, and of the flesh and devil. God never declared such a thing. In fact, His Word says the complete opposite. Since this is the case, why are we following man?

This is the realm in which I grew up my whole life, yet my spirit has always believed that God could do more and reveal more than the surface-level religiosity we see in much of America today.

As I got to know my now-wife during the courting phase, she began telling me stories about how God had healed others through her. There were only a handful of stories, as she told me that God does not heal everyone she prays for. Yet, the stories she did tell me, my response was always, "I have never seen anyone healed before, but I know God can do it. I believe it, and I know He did it through you, even though I have not witnessed the gift of healing."

God healed people's broken hands, pulled calf, headaches, lower back pain, and more through my wife. I know God will continue to enhance her gifting as time goes on, as it is not her, but the Holy Spirit working through her.

When we begin to see that these gifts are the Holy Spirit's doing, we will delight in the Lord and be more able to accept the gifts of the Spirit when they are foreign to us. To believe that it is merely humans is faulty thinking and will most certainly lead one to forsake the gifts. When one has the maturity, wisdom, and discernment to recognize that we are vessels through which the Holy Spirit can work, we will become more open to the reality of spiritual gifts.

Fast forward to my wife and me being married, God has moved through her in a variety of ways. Though it is embarrassing to admit, it is important to address it for what God can do. All throughout my life, I had bowel problems. It wasn't easy to use the restroom, and I would spend hours sometimes each day in the bathroom trying to go. Of course, to be productive, I would work in there as well.

Even in our marriage, I would be in the restroom for 2-3 hours a day! It was agonizing and tormenting. Though some may say there are worse problems in life, there most certainly are, but this, for me, was extremely tormenting.

Imagine every day feeling the need to use the restroom but being unable to do so. Imagine that as soon as you leave the bathroom, the feeling would come again. You try to go again, and you cannot. This was my life since the earliest I can remember.

When my wife and I chose to keep our precious girl at home with family and take a getaway weekend to a theme park, we stayed at a hotel. I attempted to use the restroom but was unable to. Eventually, my wife and I sat on the bed, held hands, and began to pray. I asked her to please pray for healing in my stomach, as it was tormenting me, having to go through this every day.

As we prayed and my wife began to speak out against any demons hindering my bowel movement in the name of Jesus, I began to burp repeatedly for the next 30-45 minutes. It was uncontrollable.

For those in deliverance ministries, it is not uncommon to have demons come out in this way. As demons can dwell within us, they also come out of us through the air many times. This is why Satan is referred to as "the prince of the power of the air" (Ephesians 2:2 NKJV). When demons are expelled from someone in the name of Jesus, they typically leave by way of yawning, burping, coughing, and sneezing. Other manifestations of demons leaving are feeling lighter, more level-headed, pain suddenly gone in the body, crying, screaming, yelling, or throwing up.

This may seem scary to many, and it can be during the first time doing deliverance. When we understand, however, that greater is the One in us than the one in the world (1 John 4:4), we know that nothing can in any wise harm us and deliverance is a blessing. It is not something to shy away from, but to press into, knowing we will feel different in our body, character, emotions, personality, and thinking.

Continuing on, I burped for 30 to 45 minutes. I am convinced that the type of manifestation reveals the depths of the root of the demon. If a demon has been present throughout the bloodline, it will most likely manifest in a very intense manner. If demons have entered through open doors throughout our lives (ex, continually looking at pornography, getting perpetually drunk, or always gossiping and slandering others), then it may be a much less severe manifestation. It all depends on the demon and the length of time it has dwelled within someone (whether they are born-again or not born-again). More to come on this in the Chapter on "The Gift of Discerning of Spirits".

Eventually, my burping ceased, and I have not had bowel problems since that day! I have been able to go when the feeling comes, and instead of being in the bathroom for hours, I am in there for minutes. Praise God for His healing power through my wife and simultaneously delivering me from a tormenting demon that was dwelling in my digestive system!

This may sound radical to those not acquainted with these types of truths, but we are not trying to appease man but live in the Power, Might, and awesome wonder of God! It is no wonder the realities of the Spirit are foolishness to man, for man can only believe and perceive what he sees and what is in the physical. It takes the Holy Spirit to bring spiritual enlightenment to our minds on Divine Truths that God has spoken and revealed through His Word.

Now that we have a solid understanding that the gift of healing is just as active today as it was in the past, it is essential to briefly address and call out false teachers. There are many who (for the sake of not going down a rabbit trail, I will not mention) pretend to have the gifts of healing. This was evident in the 20th century, but has always been the case in each generation, as *"there is* nothing new under the sun" (Ecclesiastes 1:9 NKJV).

Many of these individuals have been seen on television and have hired actors and actresses to play their part and pretend they were healed. Others request money before someone receives healing (which is entirely unbiblical). Some film YouTube videos that typically focus on "healing people's legs," which is done by being taught the art of slowly pulling and pushing each leg into a specific position (nothing more than a placebo effect due to visual deception).

Those who have actually needed healing have also come to present themselves before certain individuals, and the staff of these men have said, "Go backstage. He will pray a 'special' prayer for you away from the audience."

Men are often deceptive, and many are con artists. We want to address this, as it is a continual reality for many. Sadly, many do not open their spiritual eyes because they are not led by the Holy Spirit. They therefore go anywhere there is a lot of rucus and noise, but where there is no Holy Ghost Fire!

As you walk with the Spirit and cultivate a living relationship with Him, you can always tell when the Holy Spirit is in something and when He is not. Sadly, many "healing ministries" consist of wolves in sheep's clothing, seeking to profit off the backs of slaves and the naïve, all while they prosper and compile an abundance through deceptive means. May God give each of us discernment regarding these types of individuals (for more on understanding who is of God and who is not, see my book *Unraveling Deception: Discerning Darkness*).

For those who truly have the gift of healing, however, they do not do it for show, but out of the abundance of love from their heart. They don't need to be seen. Instead, they want God glorified. They don't request payment; they simply exercise the gift. The gifts of the Spirit are gifts meant to bless others and worship God, and those who truly have the gift of healing desire to take it extremely seriously, lest they fall into a pit and take all the glory and credit for themselves.

"And behold, a leper came and worshiped Him, saying, "Lord, if You are willing, You can make me clean." Then Jesus put out His hand and touched him, saying, "I am willing; be cleansed." Immediately his leprosy was cleansed" (Matthew 8:2-3 NKJV). Instead of going to the doctor for every illness or seeking to find a solution online, why not turn to God first?

How many times have we stunted a miracle in our lives by not going to God first? How many times have we prolonged the process by not seeking God as God and approaching man as man? Of course, doctors and sound, naturopathic practices are wonderful. Of course, natural remedies and having resources and connections are helpful, but what if God wanted us to seek Him first? Instead of looking for a quick remedy when we have a typical illness, what if we said, "Lord, if You are willing, cleanse me from this sickness and make me healthy"?

Many times, God is ready to heal us. It is not to say that every prayer we pray will be answered with instant healing, but it is important to note that what we do not pray for, we will not receive.

If we want to see the healing touch of Christ (or have someone with the gift of healing pray and lay their hands on us, in the Power of the Holy Spirit), we must be willing to go to God first in all matters. Without placing Him at the forefront in all things, we will not see, live, experience, or allow His miraculous working to have a greater impact and testimony within our lives. Instead, we will do what is easy and what we think is best.

Again, it is essential to highlight the benefits of the specialized skills of certain doctors and healthcare professionals. However, we must be willing to be like the leper who came to Christ and asked Him to bring healing. God may not answer nine times we are sick (for Divine reasons), but the tenth time He answers will be an incredible testimony of the Powerful touch from Thee Almighty God!

Although we reviewed this passage in the Chapter on "The Gift of Faith," it is essential to reemphasize the power of Christ. Mark 5:25-34 (NKJV) begins with the following:

> "Now a certain woman had a flow of blood for twelve years, and had suffered many things from many physicians. She had spent all that she had and was no better, but rather grew worse. When she heard about Jesus, she came behind Him in the crowd and touched His garment. For she said, "If only I may touch His clothes, I shall be made well." Immediately the fountain of her blood was dried up, and she felt in her body that she was healed of the affliction. And Jesus, immediately knowing in Himself that power had gone out of Him, turned around in the crowd and said, "Who touched My clothes?" But His disciples said to Him, "You see the multitude thronging You, and You say, 'Who touched Me?'" And He looked around to see her who had done this thing. But the woman, fearing and trembling, knowing what had happened to her, came and fell down before Him and told Him the whole truth. And He said to her, "Daughter, your faith has made you well. Go in peace, and be healed of your affliction.""

When we pray, we must pray in faith that God will heal us. When we go to God, we must not doubt, "for he who doubts is like a wave of the sea driven and tossed by the wind. For let not that man suppose that he will receive anything from the Lord; *he is* a double-minded man, unstable in all his ways" (James 1:6-8 NKJV).

This woman believed in the Power of Christ to be healed. When we pray, we must believe in the Power of God. When we have the gift of healing, we must steward our gift in faith. Without faith, it is impossible to please God (Hebrews 11:6). If the Lord Jesus Christ said, "'Most assuredly, I say to you, he who believes in Me, the works that I do he will do also; and greater *works* than these he will do, because I go to My Father'" (John 14:12 NKJV), then we who have the gift can perform healings in the Power of the Holy Spirit. Even greater works can be done than Christ; not because of us, who we are, or what we can do, but because of the Spirit at work within us – God's Holy Spirit.

What type of works can those who have the Holy Spirit do that will be greater than Christ's? When it comes to healing, let us examine a few passages on Christ's help to others. Then, we can simply think of having a certain healing done more easily than the Lord Jesus had it done. For example, if Christ *speaks* to someone in person and they are healed, we can simply *pray* in faith from a distance (in the Power of the Holy Spirit and exercising the gift He has given), and they can be healed — even if they are in another country!

Let's begin with Mark 10:46-52 (NKJV):

> "Now they came to Jericho. As He went out of Jericho with His disciples and a great multitude, blind Bartimaeus, the son of Timaeus, sat by the road begging. And when he heard that it was Jesus of Nazareth, he began to cry out and say, "Jesus, Son of David, have mercy on me!" Then many warned him to be quiet; but he cried out all the more, "Son of David, have mercy on me!" So Jesus stood still and commanded him to be called. Then they called the blind man, saying to him, "Be of good cheer. Rise, He is calling you." And throwing aside his garment, he rose and came to Jesus. So Jesus answered and said to him, "What do you want Me to do for you?" The blind man said to Him, "Rabboni, that I may receive my sight." Then Jesus said to him, "Go your way; your faith has made you well." And immediately he received his sight and followed Jesus on the road."

Asking in faith leads Christ to perform the miraculous. What we once lacked, we can possess when God brings the healing through His saints and servants who walk faithfully with Him. Just as Christ gave sight to the blind man, the Holy Spirit, through us, can open spiritual eyes, bestow gifts, heal sicknesses, and infirmities. We need only have faith and allow the gift of the Spirit to flow fully through us, by the working of the Holy Spirit in us.

Let us review another passage of the Lord Jesus bringing forth healing. Luke 5:18-25 (NKJV) states:

> "Then behold, men brought on a bed a man who was paralyzed, whom they sought to bring in and lay before Him. And when they could not find how they might bring him in, because of the crowd, they went up on the housetop and let him down with his bed through the tiling into the midst before Jesus. When He saw their faith, He said to him, "Man, your sins are forgiven you." And the scribes and the Pharisees began to reason, saying, "Who is this who speaks blasphemies? Who can forgive sins but God alone?" But when Jesus perceived their thoughts, He answered and said to them, "Why are you reasoning in your hearts? Which is easier, to say, 'Your sins are forgiven you,' or to say, 'Rise up and walk'? But that you may know that the Son of Man has power on earth to forgive sins"—He said to the man who was paralyzed, "I say to you, arise, take up your bed, and go to your house." Immediately he rose up before them, took up what he had been lying on, and departed to his own house, glorifying God."

Sometimes, without even knowing what someone is thinking about someone else, the Holy Spirit can reveal what people think of that person. "Oh, they are always slow." "They will never amount to anything." "They don't know how to speak." "They will never go far in that sport." "They weren't meant to play." "This person always gets in the way."

In the circumstances above, there is a multitude of pain for an individual. When God gives a word of knowledge to perceive people's thoughts, He often exposes them by having someone help or speak against the very thing they are thinking.

If a crowd believes that a person will not amount to anything because they are a slow reader, have a missing limb, have some impairment in the body, or are different because something doesn't come easily due to a certain deficiency, God loves to prove those individuals wrong. God loves working through the underdog. This is why multiple born-again believers are doing God's work, even though they have missing limbs and certain ailments. God has allowed them to continue with that cross because He knew that they would make great use of it. The lives of those who steward well their ailments and sicknesses directly confront and should convict us who are completely healthy and have all bodily functions intact.

The Lord Jesus directly confronted the Pharisees without them saying a word about their thoughts. He not only amazed them within this instant, but also asked a question that brought conviction. Then, He decided to further His authority by revealing that He was the Son of Man through healing the blind man. As this occurred, He directly revealed to the Pharisees that He was Who He claimed to be; namely, the Son of God.

When we have the gift of healing, people will mock. They will say, "O yeah, you think you know and follow God. Then do (such and such)!" Ironically, this is what happened with my wife.

A young man had mocked her at a gas station. She was evangelizing to a group, and one of them had a broken hand. He said, "Well, if Jesus is God, prove it!" He proceeded to extend his hand out to my wife and said, "Heal my broken hand." My wife goes into much more detail with the story, but at that moment, she prayed in her head and said, "God, I don't have the faith for this. You are going to have to help me."

She proceeded to grab the young man's hand and said, "Bones and ligaments, I command you to repair yourself right now in the name of Jesus!" As soon as she said that, the bones clicked and went into place. The man was shocked! He started doing push-ups and said, "Are you a witch?" My wife replied, "No, I am a Christian, and this was all Jesus." He said, "Can I talk to Him?" She proceeded to share more about the Gospel and how God is ready and willing to listen at any moment.

When people mock, God will not only expose their hearts, but also put them to shame for their mockery. When we have the Holy Spirit and the gift of healing, we will perform what only God can do through us. In turn, God will shut the mouths of blasphemers, mockers, and scoffers. He will do what only He can do, and no one will be able to deny what is witnessed or done when it is done in the Wisdom, Knowledge, and Power of the Holy Spirit.

Let's look at one more example, as found in Luke 17:12-19 (NKJV):

> "Then as He entered a certain village, there met Him ten men who were lepers, who stood afar off. And they lifted up their voices and said, "Jesus, Master, have mercy on us!" So when He saw them, He said to them, "Go, show yourselves to the priests." And so it was that as they went, they were cleansed. And one of them, when he saw that he was healed, returned, and with a loud voice glorified God, and fell down on his face at His feet, giving Him thanks. And he was a Samaritan. So Jesus answered and said, "Were there not ten cleansed? But where are the nine? Were there not any found who returned to give glory to God except this foreigner?" And He said to him, "Arise, go your way. Your faith has made you well.""

Many times, when God performs miracles in our lives or answers our prayers, we quickly move on. We cease from thanking Him. We stop taking time to praise and give Him Glory. We merely accept what He does or answers and then move on as if it never happened.

This grieves the heart of God and is a sign of disrespect. All of us have done this, and I am very guilty of this from certain moments in my past. God would do something miraculous, then the next hour I would completely forget about it. When another problem would arise, I would complain and become critical. I would convince myself that God is not answering and therefore does not care. How tragic this state was, as all I needed to do in those moments was reflect on what He had already done. If I had spent more time thanking Him and bringing to mind all that He has done thus far, I would not have allowed myself to fall into a sinful mindset.

When we see some of the ways Christ performed healing, we see that in a like manner, Paul the Apostle did as well. Acts 14:8-10 (NKJV) shows us that "in Lystra a certain man without strength in his feet was sitting, a cripple from his mother's womb, who had never walked. This man heard Paul speaking. Paul, observing him intently and seeing that he had faith to be healed, said with a loud voice, "Stand up straight on your feet!" And he leaped and walked."

It is important to first note that one does not need to be an "Apostle" to have the gift of healing. The Scriptures clearly reveal that "There are diversities of gifts, but the same Spirit" (1 Corinthians 12:4 NKJV) and that "one and the same Spirit works all these things, distributing to each one individually as He wills" (1 Corinthians 12:11 NKJV). Whatever gift(s) one receives, it is the Holy Spirit's will to impart those gifts to others.

When it came to this instance of Paul healing the cripple, he perceived there was faith in the man. Without faith, nothing will occur. Even James 5:14-15 (NKJV) declares, "Is anyone among you sick? Let him call for the elders of the church, and let them pray over him, anointing him with oil in the name of the Lord. And the prayer of faith will save the sick, and the Lord will raise him up. And if he has committed sins, he will be forgiven."

This is a declarative promise from the Word of God that *if* healing is to occur (and God Wills for this to occur, and He sees more good will come from healing the person than permitting them a cross to bear cheerfully and joyfully and amazing those of the world with the willingness to praise God amid adversity), there *must* be faith. From Paul's healing of the cripple, the *recipient* needed faith. From the passage above in James, it is clear that the *person praying* or *going before God and making a declaration* must have faith. When there is faith from the one going before God and the one receiving what God can do, there is nothing that can stop the flow of God's Divine healing Power, so long as it is in His Will to do and perform what is being requested in the name of Jesus.

Notice, Paul did not touch the cripple. He merely said, "stand up straight on your feet" (Acts 14:10)! In faith, he told the cripple what to do, and God's healing power made the cripple leap up and walk.

Another instance where Paul worked the gift of healing in the power of the Holy Spirit was in Acts 28:8-9 (NKJV): "And it happened that the father of Publius lay sick of a fever and dysentery. Paul went in to him and prayed, and he laid his hands on him and healed him. So when this was done, the rest of those on the island who had diseases also came and were healed." Here, we see that Paul, this time, laid his hands on the person.

God's healing Power can occur through prayer for someone, declaring someone to do something that they cannot do with their current illness, and laying hands on someone. Now, in some denominations, they say hands should not be laid on others lest a demon enter. This is driven by a spirit of fear, not a sound mind.

When people get afraid of laying on of hands, they believe that someone else's demons can enter them. This is like saying, "If I bump someone in line at the grocery store, I am going to get their demons," or "if I introduce myself with a handshake, I am going to get this person's unclean spirits." This is not wise thinking, as if this were the case, it would not have been said, "Greet one another with a holy kiss" (Romans 16:16 NKJV) during the time of Paul. As a side note, this does not mean that single men should say this to every new girl they meet at their local Bible study!

We also see that Jesus would lay His hands on others (Matthew 9:18-26; Matthew 19:13-15; Mark 5:23; Mark 6:5; Mark 7:32-35; Mark 8:22-25; Luke 13:11-13). No demons entered Him, clearly, since He was Perfect and Pure throughout the entirety of His Life in this life.

The power is not in laying on of hands, necessarily, though this can manifest the Power of the Holy Spirit through an individual to another. God leads each according to their comfort (insofar as a woman not feeling comfortable laying hands on a man) and how He desires the gift to be exercised and performed. God is not only the Giver of the gift, but the Guider of the means of how the gift will be used.

The beautiful story found in Acts 3:1-10 (NKJV) illustrates Peter's response to a lame man. Peter did not have much to give from a worldly perspective, but from a spiritual perspective, he could do more for the man with his gifting than any amount of money. The story goes as follows:

> "Now Peter and John went up together to the temple at the hour of prayer, the ninth *hour*. And a certain man lame from his mother's

womb was carried, whom they laid daily at the gate of the temple which is called Beautiful, to ask alms from those who entered the temple; who, seeing Peter and John about to go into the temple, asked for alms. And fixing his eyes on him, with John, Peter said, "Look at us." So he gave them his attention, expecting to receive something from them. Then Peter said, "Silver and gold I do not have, but what I do have I give you: In the name of Jesus Christ of Nazareth, rise up and walk." And he took him by the right hand and lifted *him* up, and immediately his feet and ankle bones received strength. So he, leaping up, stood and walked and entered the temple with them—walking, leaping, and praising God. And all the people saw him walking and praising God. Then they knew that it was he who sat begging alms at the Beautiful Gate of the temple; and they were filled with wonder and amazement at what had happened to him."

Peter knew what He had, namely, Who He had within Him. He had the power to declare to the lame men, "Rise up and walk". This type of power only comes from the Holy Spirit blessing an individual with the gift of healing. What artificial intelligence may be able to do in the future through strengthening one's legs or replacing them does not equate to a spoken word in faith from someone with the gift of healing. No technology was needed. No amount of rehab or physical therapy helped. In a moment, a declaration was made, followed by an action. That action was performed because the healing that occurred did not just allow the man to walk; God supernaturally gave his muscles, bones, and ligaments the capacity to do what they had previously been unable to do. God gave that lame man's vessel the strength needed to begin "walking, leaping", which led him to "praising God" (Acts 3:8).

It is important to once again note that God is in charge of the means of the gift. He tells others how to use the gift and what must be done.

Often, people harbor bitterness and envy. Without knowing, they have problems with their spine and an arched back. Demons manifest in many ways. If they reside in our bodies, clearly, they have legal ground to do certain things within our bodies (such as we discussed with my bowel problems). This is important to know because, if we are called to, for example, repent of certain sins and God will then heal us, and we respond, "What? I'm not going to repent. I've done nothing wrong", then we will block the healing Power of God. We will remain bitter and envious, covering it up with our stubbornness and pride. Ultimately, God will not bring healing.

We see an example of God declaring the means by which someone would be healed. 2 Kings 5:1-14 (NKJV) gives a full exposition:

"Now Naaman, commander of the army of the king of Syria, was a great and honorable man in the eyes of his master, because by him the LORD had given victory to Syria. He was also a mighty man of valor, *but* a leper. And the Syrians had gone out on raids, and had brought back captive a young girl from the land of Israel. She waited on Naaman's wife. Then she said to her mistress, "If only my master *were* with the prophet who *is* in Samaria! For he would heal him of his leprosy." And *Naaman* went in and told his master, saying, "Thus and thus said the girl who *is* from the land of Israel."

Then the king of Syria said, "Go now, and I will send a letter to the king of Israel."

So he departed and took with him ten talents of silver, six thousand *shekels* of gold, and ten changes of clothing. Then he brought the letter to the king of Israel, which said,

Now be advised, when this letter comes to you, that I have sent Naaman my servant to you, that you may heal him of his leprosy.

And it happened, when the king of Israel read the letter, that he tore his clothes and said, "*Am* I God, to kill and make alive, that this man sends a man to me to heal him of his leprosy? Therefore please consider, and see how he seeks a quarrel with me."

So it was, when Elisha the man of God heard that the king of Israel had torn his clothes, that he sent to the king, saying, "Why have you torn your clothes? Please let him come to me, and he shall know that there is a prophet in Israel."

Then Naaman went with his horses and chariot, and he stood at the door of Elisha's house. And Elisha sent a messenger to him, saying, "Go and wash in the Jordan seven times, and your flesh shall be restored to you, and *you shall* be clean." But Naaman became furious, and went away and said, "Indeed, I said to myself, 'He will surely come out *to me,* and stand and call on the name of the LORD his God, and wave his hand over the place, and heal the leprosy.' *Are* not the Abanah and the Pharpar, the rivers of Damascus, better than all the waters of Israel? Could I not wash in them and be clean?" So he turned and went away in a rage. And his servants came near and spoke to him, and said, "My father, *if* the prophet had told you *to do* something great, would you not have done *it?* How much more then, when he says to you, 'Wash, and be clean'?" So he went down and dipped seven times in the Jordan, according to the saying of the man of God; and his flesh was restored like the flesh of a little child, and he was clean."

When Naaman heard what he needed to do to be healed, he became furious. He wanted nothing to do with the Lord's instruction through Elisha. It seemed like a foolish request and would take too long. He reasoned in his mind that surely Elisha could wave his hand over him and the leprosy would be gone. Although this could have been done, it was not the means God wanted to use for Naaman's healing.

Many times, God brings healing in a different way and at a different time than what we initially expected. He does this to both test our faith and expose our hearts. We often sing songs in Church and declare the Truths of Scripture, yet we do not live in the Truths we know and sing. This leads toward a double-minded faith, where we declare one thing, but when opportunities and circumstances arise to test our faith in God, we fold. We become angry and upset, and we say to God, "Why couldn't You just do it the way I thought and in the timeframe I believed it to occur?" In essence, we tell God, "You should have followed my thought process. I know what is best for me."

Of course, we do not know what is best for us. This has been proven by keeping long relationships with toxic people. This is revealed by our exes, whom we dated and courted. This is revealed by the consequences of our sin. We think we know what is best, and when we don't go to God, we will not receive the healing we desire. We will stunt or prolong the process. Eventually, if we become wise after being foolish, we will turn to God and not only believe in Him but also follow His instructions.

Obedience is the door to many blessings from God. If we humble ourselves, we will listen to the Word of God. Even if it seems contrary to our human senses, if the Holy Spirit is convicting and directing us, we must listen.

Eventually, through the wise counsel of his servants, Namaan listened. He did what seemed foolish. He could very well have gone grumbling and complaining. He could have said on the way, "This is foolish. I will look like an imbecile to others if they see me doing this. Dip myself seven times? I'm going to look like a kid playing in the water! This is one of the silliest instructions I have ever received. I'm a great and honorable commander. I don't have time for this!"

Through all this inner turmoil and (most likely) mumbling and complaining along the way, he showed he was willing to listen. It doesn't mean he was happy about obeying, but he nonetheless obeyed. As he followed the instruction, he became healed.

Many times, we don't want to obey. We may even obey with a poor attitude. Although this can prevent rewards in Heaven (as God looks at the heart and tests our works based on our intention, motive, and heart posture), our obedience, even when accompanied by a bad attitude, can still bring forth blessings. This, in turn, convicts us substantially and, if we are mature in the faith, leads us to repentance, for it is the goodness of God that leads us to repentance (Romans 2:4).

Let us praise God that He Himself is willing to bring healing. Let us go to Him, requesting that our heart posture and spiritual maturity be brought to where they must be to possess the gift of healing. God will grant our request in His time, provided we desire to be a blessing to others.

Many people take the gifts of God and use them for self-gain. There are a few testimonies out there about people who were accepted into Satanic circles for their "powers". When you watch the interviews of these individuals, they are very pompous and prideful. Of course, it is sad to hear of all the terrible things done to them. Praise God, they were set free and got out of those hellish circles. Nonetheless, because they do not know God, they are unaware that the gifts come from Him.

Yes, that is correct. Many of us have gifts from the Holy Spirit the moment we are born. The increase and ability to receive more gifts, however, comes from being born again, walking in obedience, and praying and seeking God for all the gifts. These individuals say they were brought in for "their powers". Little do they know that it is the gifts given by God that are meant to glorify Him, not themselves.

When people are apart from God, they do not know better. Just as the Holy Spirit gives life to the bodies of individuals who are unbelievers (as without the Holy Spirit touching them from the outside, they would cease to be), likewise is it with the gifts. "If He should set His heart on it, *If* He should gather to Himself His Spirit and His breath, All flesh would perish together, And man would return to dust" (Job 34:14-15 NKJV). Of course, the Holy Spirit is not just *outside* us, but comes to live *inside* us when we are born again by believing Jesus Christ is Lord and Savior and repenting of our sins.

Being made in the image of God grants us the ability to possess a gift of the Spirit. These "powers" are nothing more than the wrong use of a spiritual gift given by God. So long as they did not sell their soul to the Devil, the powers they believe they have, because of who they are, have actually been given to them by God, and meant to be used by God when God's Spirit lives within them when they are born-again.

May all come to know the One, True God. Let us all seek Him while it is still day. Let us praise Him for His many blessings and for His many healings! God works in and through individuals just as much as He works in and throughout the world. We must simply be open to the Holy Spirit's moving and directing. As we seek God, He will open doors no man can open. He will bless us with gifts that can only come from Him.

To God be the Glory, now and forevermore.

God in Heaven, the Great Alpha and Omega, the One Who Was, Is, and always will Be, the One Who died and rose again, the One Who blesses man with spiritual gifts undeserved, the One Who came to set the captives free, the One Who opens the ears of the deaf, gives sight to the blind, and makes the mute speak, You are worthy of worship, forevermore! You alone, O God, are the One Who loved us while we were still yet sinners. You are the One, Lord Jesus, Who died on the Cross for our sins and rose again on the Third Day. Truly, nothing is too hard for You, the One Who holds the keys to death and Hades. God, we humbly come before You, requesting that You bless us, Your children, with the gift of healing. As You are the Great Physician and heal us from our past, trauma, sin, selfishness, iniquity, transgressions, and depravity, we know that You are the One Who can heal us from our pain, sorrow, ailments, diseases, and infirmities. O Great God, bless us with the gift of healing, that Your Power may be manifested through us for Thy Glory. Keep us from becoming prideful in that which comes from You. Bless us with a natural heart of humility and a desire to persevere in prayer by faith until You answer. You are Good, and all that You do is Upright, Pure, and Holy. We bless You, O God of Heaven and Earth. May Thy Holy Will be done. In Jesus' name, Amen.

The Gift of the Working of Miracles

"*To another the working of miracles.*"
— 1 Corinthians 12:10 NKJV

The gift of working miracles is different from healing. Healing can be involved in the working of miracles, but miracles are those that only God can perform.

Now, every spiritual gift comes from God. However, when it comes to miracles, this is amongst the greatest revealment of God's Glory. It is not just a healing or a sign that occurs through us. It is not just something that is brought forth from within. Instead, it is the revealment of God Himself, externally.

When we look through the Scriptures, we see God performing many miraculous wonders. Though this seemed to be most prevalent in the Old Testament, it also occurred in the New Testament. This is one of the many areas in which Jesus Christ declares that we will do greater works than He did in the Power of the Holy Spirit (John 14:12).

Let us begin in the Old Testament, where mighty works of miracles occurred. Exodus 14:21-22 (NKJV) states:

> "Then Moses stretched out his hand over the sea; and the Lord caused the sea to go back by a strong east wind all that night and made the sea into dry land, and the waters were divided. So the children of Israel went into the midst of the sea on the dry ground, and the waters were a wall to them on their right hand and on their left."

Moses performed many miracles throughout his life. We could write a whole book just on Moses, but for the sake of discussion, we want to bring emphasis and revealment to multiple occurrences within Scripture.

The Passage clearly reveals that "the Lord caused the sea to go back by a strong east wind" (Exodus 14:21). We see that it was not Moses performing the miracle. Moses simply stretched his hand out over the sea. The Lord then did the rest.

When God performs miracles, it often begins with an initial prompting to one of God's people. As this happens, it is done by the Divine instruction of the Holy Spirit. As the Holy Spirit speaks and the declaration or action is performed, God takes care of the rest.

We see this in the story of Elijah when he stayed with the widow, and her son stopped breathing and temporarily died. Let us view 1 Kings 17:17-22 (NKJV) to unpack the story further:

> "Now it happened after these things *that* the son of the woman who owned the house became sick. And his sickness was so serious that there was no breath left in him. So she said to Elijah, "What have I to do with you, O man of God? Have you come to me to bring my sin to remembrance, and to kill my son?"
>
> And he said to her, "Give me your son." So he took him out of her arms and carried him to the upper room where he was staying, and laid him on his own bed. Then he cried out to the Lord and said, "O Lord my God, have You also brought tragedy on the widow with whom I lodge, by killing her son?" And he stretched himself out on the child three times, and cried out to the Lord and said, "O Lord my God, I pray, let this child's soul come back to him." Then the Lord heard the voice of Elijah; and the soul of the child came back to him, and he revived."

Elijah was staying at a woman's house, and immediately the son at the house became sick and ceased breathing. Elijah went to God in prayer, as he usually did, and without saying many words, requested from God an impossible task: to allow the child's soul to come back to his body.

After Elijah prays, we see that "the LORD heard the voice of Elijah; and the soul of the child came back to him, and he revived" (1 Kings 17:22).

Before tremendous miracles occur, an action is taken. Not only did Elijah pray a short, specific prayer of something impossible for man, but he also spread himself across the boy. Now, this is quite interesting, as it would be a rather unusual sight. However, Elijah, being a man of God, did what may have seemed weird: he allowed God to do what only He could do.

In this instance, we see that God wanted Elijah to be an equal part of the miracle's working. God determines the means by which the gift of the working of miracles will come forth. In this instance, God allowed Elijah to spread himself across the boy. While this was done, God did what only He could do – He placed the soul back in the boy's body.

No man on the face of this Earth can place the soul back in the body of one who is deceased. That power belongs only to God.

Miracles don't just manifest on a visual scale (as with Moses) or on a spiritual scale (as with Elijah). Miracles can also occur in time.

Time is a fantastic concept to ponder – how does it work? What dictates time? What is time? How has it been established? Why is it different throughout the world? Is it different in space? What is time like in the spiritual realm? All these questions are beautiful aspects to ponder, but it is not the point of this book. I have answered these types of questions in various books and in video format on YouTube (as of 01/24/2025).

For now, we want to see how the Lord God answered Joshua when he prayed for the sun to stand still. Joshua 10:12-14 (NKJV) states:

> "Then Joshua spoke to the Lord in the day when the Lord delivered up the Amorites before the children of Israel, and he said in the sight of

Israel: "Sun, stand still over Gibeon; And Moon, in the Valley of Aijalon." So the sun stood still, and the moon stopped, till the people had revenge upon their enemies. Is this not written in the Book of Jasher? So the sun stood still in the midst of heaven, and did not hasten to go down for about a whole day. And there has been no day like that, before it or after it, that the Lord heeded the voice of a man; for the Lord fought for Israel."

Notice that this was not a private matter (as with Elijah). This was a public request to God to do what only He could do! It takes a tremendous amount of faith to ask God for something particular that no one has ever seen done (and, in this instance, something that has never occurred after). To declare it before Israel means one of two things: there is a strong assurance that God will answer and an extreme amount of faith to make such a declaration, or Joshua is entirely mad. Of course, we know it was the former.

Again, when it comes to the gifts of healing and working miracles, they must be coupled with faith. There is no other alternative. Faith must be present to believe that God will answer.

As Joshua prayed, the sun stood still, and the moon stopped for a whole day. For 24 hours, the sun stayed shining in the same place on Earth where there would otherwise have been hours of nighttime. God answered and performed the miracle because only He is the Ruler, Creator, and Maker of the laws of nature. He alone can intervene in the fine-tuning process and perform the miracle of having the sun stand still (which means the Earth stopped its usual rotation on its axis) and having the moon stop (meaning it ceased its regular rotation around the Earth and on its axis). As a side note, Joshua 10:12-14 (NKJV) is a great passage for debunking those who, for whatever reason, believe in a flat Earth.

As God performed this miracle, He invaded the very laws He set up and created. He alone can do so because He is God! He does what pleases Him, and it was good in His sight to honor the request of Joshua. He heeded Joshua's voice, and all of Israel witnessed a miracle.

Two other stories from Elisha are found in 2 Kings. The first Scripture we will review is 2 Kings 4:1-7 (NKJV):

"A certain woman of the wives of the sons of the prophets cried out to Elisha, saying, "Your servant my husband is dead, and you know that your servant feared the LORD. And the creditor is coming to take my two sons to be his slaves."

So Elisha said to her, "What shall I do for you? Tell me, what do you have in the house?" And she said, "Your maidservant has nothing in the house but a jar of oil."

Then he said, "Go, borrow vessels from everywhere, from all your neighbors—empty vessels; do not gather just a few. And when you have come in, you shall shut the door behind you and your sons; then pour it into all those vessels, and set aside the full ones."

So she went from him and shut the door behind her and her sons, who brought *the vessels* to her; and she poured *it* out. Now it came to pass, when the vessels were full, that she said to her son, "Bring me another vessel."

And he said to her, "*There is* not another vessel." So the oil ceased. Then she came and told the man of God. And he said, "Go, sell the oil and pay your debt; and you *and* your sons live on the rest.""

In this instance, we see God again invading the scientific laws He created and allowing the oil to continue. Just as Jesus fed the five thousand with five loaves and two fish in John 6:1-14, so Elisha spoke to the widow of what to do, and God did the rest.

Miracles are exciting. They always occur by God's hand. There is nothing too hard for Him, and when we start believing He is the Miracle Worker (and not just singing about it), we will begin to see mighty moves of God within our lives and the lives of those around us.

There is nothing in Scripture that says miracles will never be. They come in different ways, and God does so by different means, but He continues to perform them! Scripture even reveals to us that *true* Apostles will have signs and wonders follow them (Acts 5:12; 2 Corinthians 12:12).

This is a general note: if someone claims and continually professes a title of the faith, they do not possess it. If they are publicly declaring, "I am Prophet (fill in the blank)" or "I am Apostle (fill in the blank)", they are not those very positions. Actually, the very fact that they claim they are quickly reveals to those of discernment that they are false. Their desire for fame or their insecurities rule them, leading them to want to become something they are not and claim a position that God has not placed them in.

This is why it is important to understand that *true* Apostles will have signs, wonders, and miracles occur. They are far and few between, but they do exist. God has His reasons for choosing whom He chooses, and we must not believe in people because of a self-proclaimed title.

People may declare themselves to be Pastors or Teachers. Though these are two of the five offices mentioned in Ephesians 4:11-12, the higher we climb up the "ladder", the titles of Prophet and Apostle are possessed by those who do not profess themselves to be as such.

Notice throughout Scripture that rarely (if ever) people came and said, "I am Prophet (fill in the blank). You must listen to me!" Everybody wants to be a Prophet and Apostle until they understand what these actually mean. Everyone is quick to claim a title but not to follow through with what it takes to live up to it.

This is why it is imperative to understand that a position is anointed when it is God-appointed. If God has not called someone to a particular office, it is out of the heart of an individual, and therefore will cease from having any power. This is all important to understand, as many will claim to be what they are not.

True Apostles will experience miraculous events throughout their lives. Acts 5:12-16 (NKJV) reveals this in greater measure:

> "And through the hands of the apostles many signs and wonders were done among the people. And they were all with one accord in Solomon's Porch. Yet none of the rest dared join them, but the people esteemed them highly. And believers were increasingly added to the Lord, multitudes of both men and women, so that they brought the sick out into the streets and laid *them* on beds and couches, that at least the shadow of Peter passing by might fall on some of them. Also a multitude gathered from the surrounding cities to Jerusalem, bringing sick people and those who were tormented by unclean spirits, and they were all healed."

At the beginning of this passage, we see that "through the hands of the apostles many signs and wonders were done among the people" (Acts 5:12). True Apostles will always have a multitude of people attest to the miraculous power of God.

Though we saw Elijah go before God in private and request that the soul be returned to the body, he was a prophet of the Lord. He was not an Apostle. Apostles not only request of God and have miracles occur in private, but also in public.

People were healed, even to the point where Peter's shadow passing by brought healing. This is not because Peter was a "super saint". It was because of the call God had for him and what God Himself was willing to do both for him and through him.

When God moves through Apostles, mighty signs and wonders are done. People are healed and risen from the dead. Signs and wonders that only God can perform are accomplished as declarations are made before a multitude of people. As we stated—and we will state again (as this point cannot be overemphasized)—it takes an incredible amount of faith to request of God, before a vast audience, what only He can do. God, however, can do so, and He will in greater measure than we ever thought.

The gift of working miracles, therefore, is not just for Apostles, but for Prophets; not just Prophets, but for anyone willing to believe that God can bless them with the gift when they request Him for it!

As with all the gifts, but most certainly with this one, God will not just give the gift of working miracles to anyone. He will only bless His saints with this gift who are honest, humble, holy, and desire nothing but to see God magnified and glorified. For God to move mountains, we must believe He is a mountain mover. For God to do miracles and to be part of the initial process of having His Glory and Power come forth, we must be in a heart posture of utmost respect, adoration, reverence, and fear of the Lord. Without doing so, we will not be given this gift.

Another story of God performing a miracle and defying the laws of nature is found in 2 Kings 6:1-7 (NKJV). It is as follows:

> "And the sons of the prophets said to Elisha, "See now, the place where we dwell with you is too small for us. Please, let us go to the Jordan, and

let every man take a beam from there, and let us make there a place where we may dwell."

So he answered, "Go."

Then one said, "Please consent to go with your servants."

And he answered, "I will go." So he went with them. And when they came to the Jordan, they cut down trees. But as one was cutting down a tree, the iron *ax head* fell into the water; and he cried out and said, "Alas, master! For it was borrowed."

So the man of God said, "Where did it fall?" And he showed him the place. So he cut off a stick, and threw *it* in there; and he made the iron float. Therefore he said, "Pick *it* up for yourself." So he reached out his hand and took it."

An axe head is nothing light. As a matter of fact, it probably sank to the bottom of the water rather quickly. Yet, Elisha did not fret. He did not say, "Well, son, go and get another job and get the money to owe them back." No, instead, just as Jesus told Peter, "'go to the sea, cast in a hook, and take the fish that comes up first. And when you have opened its mouth, you will find a piece of money'" (Matthew 17:27 NKJV), so Elisha operated as if he knew what would happen.

The average person would have said to Elisha, "What are you doing? You are wasting time. This isn't going to work. What are you trying to prove? You are crazy, that will never happen!" The beautiful aspect about Elisha is that he did not care what others thought. He operated immediately, with complete assurance that God would perform a marvelous miracle.

Elisha asks him where it fell. Once he figured out the location, he threw a stick into the water there. Eventually, the iron floated right up to the stick. This miracle, though it may seem small in comparison to others we have discussed, is like throwing a large rock into the bottom of the water and expecting it to float.

Despite every ounce of reason to suggest and know that rocks don't float, we will be amazed if a rock starts floating up to the surface. Likewise, it was with the iron. Elisha asked the man what had happened, and he quickly and confidently knew precisely what to do.

This is the beautiful reality about how God's Spirit operates. He will give us a word of knowledge and even lead, prompt, or tell us what to request, declare, or pray for before God. As He does this, He is instilling in us the faith to follow through and to go before God and request the very thing He will do. It is a win-win situation, so long as we obey, follow through, and do so in faith!

The more we begin to understand we are just vessels, the less we will stunt the Holy Spirit from performing miracles. The more we follow through with 1 Corinthians 6:20 (NKJV), "For you were bought at a price; therefore glorify God in your body and in your spirit, which are God's", the more God will move mightily through us and on our behalf!

Though we already briefly mentioned this story, let us review it in greater depth. Matthew 14:19-21 (NKJV) declares of Jesus, "Then He commanded the multitudes to sit down on the grass. And He took the five loaves and the two fish, and looking up to heaven, He blessed and broke and gave the loaves to the disciples; and the disciples gave to the multitudes. So they all ate and were filled, and they took up twelve baskets full of the fragments that remained. Now those who had eaten were about five thousand men, besides women and children."

The loaves and fish in the baskets continued to spring forth, despite there being only a certain amount of supply each basket could hold. Whenever one was taken, supernaturally from the bottom of the basket, God filled it with another.

When God brought forth the fish, it didn't take a long, ongoing process for the fish to be fully developed. Whether someone believes the Earth is old or new, it doesn't matter (so long as they believe God could have created everything in seven milliseconds if He so desired!). If God can replenish a fish taken from the basket with another fully developed fish, this shows that God can do anything in a moment. God doesn't need time for things to come to be since He is the Creator of time and can bring forth fully developed creations within less than a millisecond!

Since "The everlasting God, the LORD, The Creator of the ends of the earth, Neither faints nor is weary" (Isaiah 40:28 NKJV), He can perform anything easily and effortlessly (for more on Who God is and what He can do, see my books, *The Infinite Omni (Series)*, *Ineffable Attributes: Understanding the Inconceivable Characteristics of God*, *The*

Unknown Known: From God's Simplicity to His Infinity and *Absolute Supremacy: The Ascendency of God Almighty*).

God can do a miracle of replenishing or bringing forth an abundance at a moment's notice. God can do so at His Own discretion and by the means He so desires. Take financial blessings, for example. They are out there, and my wife and I have been blessed in different seasons of our lives. We didn't know where the rent money would come from, but we would trust God. Out of nowhere, people would message us, saying they felt led by the Holy Spirit to give us a certain amount of money.

God has done financial miracles for many individuals who believe, trust, follow, and obey Him. If it hasn't happened and we are in need, the very fact that we are still living and breathing, surviving, and have food and clothing reveals God's faithfulness. If a particular miracle hasn't happened for us, we don't need to sit and sulk and say, "Those things never happen for me." They would if a continual belief were instilled and faith in God were fostered. He *will* move in His timing when hearts are fully surrendered to Him and walking in obedience.

Similar points have been made about marriage. From single folk (which I was for almost 28 years), they will say, "Everyone else is getting married but me. God doesn't care. I'm waiting on Him, and nothing is happening." I have been there at different seasons, but I also made sure to get my own house in order, to grow in God, and prepare myself. Some people are accusing God of not moving when they themselves are not listening! There is a call to obey and repent of sin and seek Him for dominion over sin. Grace doesn't just cover our sin; God's grace empowers us to overcome sin! If we are still single and stuck in a habitual lifestyle of sin (either in the mind, heart, mouth, or other means), we cannot expect God to perform a miracle of giving us one of His children. God does not give just any one of His daughters to a man who is unwilling to lead, repent, and become spiritually mature in Him. It does not work that way.

I have seen God perform a miracle in my life through my wife. Though we have had our difficulties in our marriage (which has been predominantly due to the very thing we told ourselves in the courtship phase – spiritual warfare), she has been a tremendous blessing.

Think about this... our gifts go hand in hand together. I receive dreams and visions from God, and she has the gift of interpreting them. We both speak in tongues. I have the gift of discerning spirits; she can feel people's emotions. My word of knowledge is predominantly about the future; hers is about the present. We agree on everything Theological – and I mean, everything!

It is incredible, and something only God could have done. He performed the miracle of giving me the most natural, gorgeous, godly woman, who is a person of growth. These are the three "g's" I looked for, and any man waiting on the Lord should ask Him to perform this miracle in their lives. The wait may be long, but it is well worth it to receive from God a *godly, gorgeous* woman who is a person of *growth*.

"Then He arose and rebuked the wind, and said to the sea, "Peace, be still!" And the wind ceased and there was a great calm. But He said to them, "Why are you so fearful? How is it that you have no faith?" And they feared exceedingly, and said to one another, "Who can this be, that even the wind and the sea obey Him!"" (Mark 4:39-41 NKJV). The same God Who created the winds and the sea can control them at His Own discretion.

Some may say, "Well, that is just for the Lord Jesus. We can't do that." They would be right. We can't do such things, but the Spirit in us most certainly can bring such impossible miracles forth! Just look at the life of Elijah. "Elijah was a man with a nature like ours, and he prayed earnestly that it would not rain; and it did not rain on the land for three years and six months. And he prayed again, and the heaven gave rain, and the earth produced its fruit" (James 5:17-18 NKJV).

Truly, "The effective, fervent prayer of a righteous man avails much" (James 5:16 NKJV). Elijah was a man with a nature like ours. He was nothing special compared to us. What was performed through him was due to God being with Him! The same can be done for us if we get out of our toxic circles that box God in and want to keep life nice and tidy. When this occurs, and we begin to open our spiritual eyes and hearts to Who God is and what He can do, we will start storming the Throne day and night until He answers. We will begin to pray bigger, bolder prayers in the power of the Holy Spirit. In time, He will answer. He can bless us with the gift of working miracles!

"And Peter answered Him and said, "Lord, if it is You, command me to come to You on the water." So He said, "Come." And when Peter had come down out of the boat, he walked on the water to go to Jesus" (Matthew 14:28-29 NKJV). What we have noticed about the working of miracles is that Peter was both a *recipient* and a *performer* of miracles. The miracles were done by God, but, as we saw early in Acts 5:12-16, even Peter's shadow healed the sick. This was due to the miraculous power God gave to Peter. Of course, this could not have happened to Peter if Peter did not exist.

We continue to review these understandings, as we always want to give God the Glory. We may play a part, take on a role, or be the main person, but we are not the Ultimate Performer behind the miracles. It is God alone Who does the miracle and brings it forth.

Peter had the opportunity to walk on water with Christ. This is a mighty miracle that shows Peter's single focus on Christ. He was not initially worried about drowning or falling in the water. Instead, it was the wind that affected Peter. "But when he saw that the wind *was* boisterous, he was afraid; and beginning to sink he cried out, saying, 'Lord, save me!' And immediately Jesus stretched out *His* hand and caught him, and said to him, 'O you of little faith, why did you doubt?'" (Matthew 14:30-31 NKJV).

Peter had the faith to declare to Christ that he would call him on the water. When Peter focused on Jesus and saw what He was doing, Peter knew that Jesus could have him do the same. When we begin seeing Christ for Who He truly is, we will start to see that what He did during His time on Earth can be replicated, duplicated, performed, and done by the Holy Spirit!

When Peter stepped out of the boat, it was not the water that scared him, but the wind. How many times do we step out in faith, begin to see a miracle, and then some petty circumstance or situation offsets us? We don't see it coming because, just as a gust of wind can appear out of nowhere, so can circumstances and events.

It is important always to stay focused on God. His miracles often occur instantly. Others may happen gradually. The vital emphasis we want to make is that, however long it takes, we remain focused on God the entire time, lest we sink into despair and discouragement and receive only half a miracle.

The gift of working miracles can enable us to perform and do what we never knew how to do. Jesus grew up as a carpenter (Mark 6:3). Nowhere do we see that He was a master wine mixer. Out of nowhere, we see in John 2:6-11 (NKJV), Jesus begins His first miracle:

> "Now there were set there six waterpots of stone, according to the manner of purification of the Jews, containing twenty or thirty gallons apiece. Jesus said to them, "Fill the waterpots with water." And they filled them up to the brim. And He said to them, "Draw some out now, and take it to the master of the feast." And they took it. When the master of the feast had tasted the water that was made wine, and did not know where it came from (but the servants who had drawn the water knew), the master of the feast called the bridegroom. And he said to him, "Every man at the beginning sets out the good wine, and when the guests have well drunk, then the inferior. You have kept the good wine until now!" This beginning of signs Jesus did in Cana of Galilee, and manifested His glory; and His disciples believed in Him."

Though this is one of Jesus' "simple" miracles, it nonetheless shows us a few things. When miracles occur, we can do what we never thought we could do. Again, this is done by God, but we play a specific role in part. Two: Jesus turned water into wine. We may see something as concrete in its own right, but God can change that very thing in a moment (is this not what He has done with us who are born again and our hearts?) "I will give you a new heart and put a new spirit within you; I will take the heart of stone out of your flesh and give you a heart of flesh. I will put My Spirit within you and cause you to walk in My statutes, and you will keep My judgments and do *them*" (Ezekiel 36:26-27 NKJV).

Lastly, what people expect to be the best (either in the beginning or the middle), God performs His most significant work toward the end. When we begin to understand this, we will become excited.

Some of us may feel like our best years are behind us, even though Ecclesiastes 7:10 (NKJV) warns against this by advising us to "not say, "Why were the former days better than these?" For you do not inquire wisely concerning this." Others of us may believe that we have done absolutely nothing in our beginning years. Though we can waste our years, God can redeem the time and the years the locusts have eaten (Joel 2:25). Wherever we may fall, we may believe we had our greatest achievements in years prior. We may be a successful writer, musician, teacher, preacher, athlete, etc. God, however, is telling us that He saves the best for last! There is more to come when miracles occur.

When we have the gift of the working of miracles, we will not only live a life of continual miracles performed by God, but we will also see the miracles gradually increase. What may have started with turning water into wine is now springing forth in later years to have the faith to raise the dead!

Truly, we must never deny God, His Power, and His working. We must have faith if we are to have the gift of working miracles. We must not allow others to squander the ignited faith from within us that has been given by the Holy Spirit. Each of His gifts is meant for the greater good. We are to steward well all He gives and believe in all that He can do. It is time to stop doubting God and putting our trust in men. It is time to believe God and cease from allowing men to dictate Who God is to us. God has spoken, and we dare not limit Him.

We reviewed the following story in the Chapter on "The Gift of Faith", but we want to review Paul getting bitten by a viper in greater detail. Acts 28:1-6 (NKJV) states:

> "Now when they had escaped, they then found out that the island was called Malta. And the natives showed us unusual kindness; for they kindled a fire and made us all welcome, because of the rain that was falling and because of the cold. But when Paul had gathered a bundle of sticks and laid *them* on the fire, a viper came out because of the heat, and fastened on his hand. So when the natives saw the creature hanging from his hand, they said to one another, "No doubt this man is a murderer, whom, though he has escaped the sea, yet justice does not allow to live." But he shook off the creature into the fire and suffered no harm. However, they were expecting that he would swell up or suddenly fall down dead. But after they had looked for a long time and saw no harm come to him, they changed their minds and said that he was a god."

The working of miracles can make others appear as a "god" to those who do not know God. This is why it is of the utmost importance to remain entirely humble and meek. This state not only allows us to receive the gift of the working of miracles, but also to steward it well and give all glory to God.

Paul could have easily become inflated with pride and allowed his ego to lure these men into some agenda. Instead, Paul did not give in to their thinking that "he was a god" (Acts 28:6). Instead, just as he shook off the viper, so he shook off their thoughts, viewpoints, opinions, and admirations. Anyone who is to follow in the same footsteps with the same gifting ought to do the same.

It is fascinating that when Paul got bitten, he did not become frantic. Some of us may fear spiders and snakes, but Paul was not at all alarmed. Instead, he shook off the viper in the fire (a signification of what the Almighty Miracle Worker will do to Satan in the Lake of Fire!).

Everyone around him was curious when he would swell up or die. During this time, Paul was entirely calm and neutral. He was not concerned or worried, for He knew God was with him and God was not finished with him.

It is incredible how many people walk around each day worried about when they are going to die. Ironically, when we are born again, our death brings us forth to eternal joy and jubilation. No born-again believer should be concerned about when they die. Secondly, when we walk with God, He walks with us. He reveals deep, hidden things to us. We will know that our time has not yet come. We will have confidence that what God has declared and revealed to us will surely come to pass.

Paul knew there was more work to be done, and he was not at all concerned about being bitten by a snake. This working of miracles occurred because of the Power at work within him — namely, the Holy Spirit.

The Holy Spirit can bless us substantially, even to the point where we don't feel pain, cannot be harmed or poisoned, and can continue as if nothing happened. God has the final say with how aspects unfold throughout life, and He can intervene at any time He chooses. If we are to be bitten by a snake, run over by a car, or fall and hit our head on the pavement, we can get up and move forward as if nothing had happened.

Truly, the working of miracles is done by the Holy Spirit, not just for others, but for oneself. The Holy Spirit can keep us from getting certain diseases and illnesses. Certain sicknesses may be very contagious, but if we come across such sicknesses, we can suffer no harm.

The power of working miracles will make people who have never heard about the Lord Jesus Christ question whether we are gods. It is in that moment that we quickly say, "It is not I that you marvel, but the One within me. The Holy Spirit is the One Who performs these miracles that you revere, and He is One of the Three in the Holy Trinity. If you desire to know this God Who has given me this blessed gift, believe in Jesus Christ as Lord and Savior and repent of your sins. You will receive newness of life and understand what it is to know God and have a living relationship with Him. He desires to know you, bless you, and help you in this life. Seek Him while He may still be found."

May God give us the opportunities to evangelize. May we take hold of the opportunities and hold fast to God's promises. Let us operate in complete confidence and assurance in Who God *Is*. We can trust Him with all of our tomorrows, for He has gotten us through all of our yesterdays.

Before we close this Chapter, it is important to note that the gift of working miracles is not always for the public; it is also meant to be done in private. Sometimes, when it is done in private, it becomes public knowledge. We are not to make a spectacle of some things, as many false "Apostles" and false "Prophets" have done before and continue to do. No, true offices appointed by God are stewarded in humility. This is seen in the life of the Lord Jesus Christ in Luke 8:49-55 (NKJV):

> "While He was still speaking, someone came from the ruler of the synagogue's *house,* saying to him, "Your daughter is dead. Do not trouble the Teacher."
>
> But when Jesus heard *it,* He answered him, saying, "Do not be afraid; only believe, and she will be made well." When He came into the house, He permitted no one to go in except Peter, James, and John, and the father and mother of the girl. Now all wept and mourned for her; but He said, "Do not weep; she is not dead, but sleeping." And they ridiculed Him, knowing that she was dead.

But He put them all outside, took her by the hand and called, saying, "Little girl, arise." Then her spirit returned, and she arose immediately. And He commanded that she be given *something* to eat. And her parents were astonished, but He charged them to tell no one what had happened."

Of course, the public would know about the little girl. Nonetheless, the *exercise* of the gift of working miracles was meant only to be seen by Jesus, the Holy Spirit, and the Heavenly Father. This is why Christ put everyone outside. He was going to let the results speak about the Power of God to those who ridiculed Him, but they also were not meant to see God's Power in the moment. They would see the after-effect of what occurred. Why? God is particular in who gets to see His Glory manifested through the gifts. He does not let just anyone ascend to the Mountain of His Presence and Power in visible manifestation (as He did with Moses). Many times, people will see the results after, but lack the maturity, humility, and belief to witness what only God can do.

Again, when it comes to raising the dead, there is no need to put on a public spectacle, for those within the community who know someone is dead will believe when they see them walking. Anyone attempting to put on a show and "raising people up from the dead" on camera or on stage is not to be trusted. This was not the way of Christ, and it is not the way of those who truly have the gift.

May those who are called to more continually seek God and request Him for this gift. For we know that God declared, "'And it shall come to pass in the last days, says God, That I will pour out of My Spirit on all flesh'" (Acts 2:17 NKJV). A mighty move of God is on the horizon. Revival through repentance and revival of revelation is about to spring forth.

Let us look forward to the days ahead and press on toward the mark, finishing the race set before us, and enduring to the very end.

God in Heaven, Creator and Maker of all, Who knows what is to occur before it happens, Who is Necessary to exist for all other relaities to exist,

Who brings forth all Truth and instills in each man and woman the gift of free will to seek Thee, know Thee, and love Thee, You are the One Who reveals greater understanding of Thy Faithfulness, Might, Power, Magnificence, and Presence. O Holy Spirit, bless us with more of Your Presence in us and less of us. Show us the way that is pleasing in Your sight. Give us the strength to obey God's Word and walk in Your commands and statutes. God, we pray that You would raise men and women who will love You, serve You, and go wherever You take them. Bless this generation with men and women of You who will not compromise on Your Word. O God, if it be pleasing in Your sight, touch us and bless us with the gift of the working of miracles. We want to witness what You did in the days of old and continue to do. We want to be part of others witnessing Your Might and Magnificence. Teach us all that You desire for us to learn. Open our eyes to see, hearts to feel, and ears to hear what You are doing and speaking. We trust in You with all our days, O Sovereign Lord, Ruler of Heaven and Earth, the Most High King! May Thy Will be done. In Jesus' name, Amen.

The Gift of Prophecy

"*To another prophecy.*"
– 1 Corinthians 12:10 NKJV

Prophecy comes in three main forms: a declaration of what is to occur, a declaration of what will happen (if change does not happen or if situations remain as they are), and a call to repent.

All throughout the Old Testament, we see the Lord God speaking to His prophets. When they prophesied, it was not because of the office they had, but because of the gift God had given them.

God spoke directly to His servants (the prophets) in the Old Testament. He also spoke directly to those made in His image when the Lord Jesus lived throughout this life. Now, it is the Holy Spirit Who blesses man with the gift to prophesy and speak what comes from God.

God is not limited to speaking only through the Holy Spirit. This is made evident through those who have dreams and visions of seeing the Lord Jesus Christ (which we will review further in future Chapters). Yes, this still occurs, and all Three Persons of the Trinity are entirely permitted to do as they please, when they please.

The gift of prophecy comes through the Holy Spirit, but it is not always just the Holy Spirit speaking. Yes, the Holy Spirit speaks through us, but the receptive message can either be from the Holy Spirit Himself, the Heavenly Father, or the Lord Jesus Christ. This may sound strange to some, and the Father rarely rises to speak. Predominantly, it is the Holy Spirit and Lord Jesus Christ. However, the Heavenly Father speaks when He so desires.

This is made evident throughout the New Testament, as we rarely see the Heavenly Father speak. There were only two occurrences when the Heavenly Father spoke audibly. During Jesus' baptism, it is said, "And suddenly a voice *came* from heaven, saying, 'This is My beloved Son, in Whom I am well pleased'" (Matthew 3:17 NKJV). Another instance was the transfiguration on the Mount when Jesus spoke with Moses and Elijah. "And a voice came out of the cloud, saying, 'This is My beloved Son. Hear Him!'" (Luke 9:35 NKJV).

These are the only instances we see the Heavenly Father speak in the New Testament (insofar as speaking to a person within our physical dimension), but it is not unknown for the Heavenly Father to speak when a substantial correction is needed. If this ever occurs to you, you will know when the times are that the Heavenly Father is directly addressing you. This is what occurred to me. It only happened once, and I knew it was the Heavenly Father.

After getting married, I had a problem. I was in a state of continual discontent with my career and life. I was doing my best to work on specific projects, startups, and my job. It seemed like I was not going anywhere. I was frustrated. I wanted more. I wanted to provide for my family and couldn't understand why God wasn't blessing me financially.

There is much to the story that I unpack in much greater detail in my book, *The Realm Beyond*. For now, it is essential to know that I had a very strong ego. It was buried and hidden. I didn't profess it in the way most would, but instead it came forth when I looked at "my works" and what "I was doing," expecting God to bless me for what I was doing.

It is somewhat embarrassing to admit, but this was my internal struggle. Always asking God, "When are You going to move? It seems I am all by myself. Do You really love me? How come You are not blessing me?". There is much more to this story that you will need to explore in the other book, including external matters, multiple moves, family dynamics issues, spiritual warfare, demonic activity, the need for deliverance, and more. For now, I want to share with you what God spoke through my Wife during a night car ride.

As we were pulling into our driveway, my Wife was encouraging me and doing her best. I would get into these states of thinking that would make me so upset. I would be so discouraged and frustrated. It seemed like God was not moving or did not want to move. Just as the LORD answered Job out of the whirlwind, I know it was God Who spoke to me through my wife. Here is an excerpt from my journal, June 24, 2024:

> "God spoke through Jackie in the middle of her powerful praying. She said, "Oh, I feel like...". Immediately after, she began to speak while I was praying in tongues and she began to prophesy. This prophesying was much more powerful and firm (her prophecies are always powerful), but this one silenced me and I knew I was in the Presence of God (Who was speaking through her).
>
> I quickly stopped praying in tongues and listened to the rebuke that I rightfully deserved. God the Father spoke through Jackie saying...
>
> "Solomon received wisdom from Me because he did not desire riches, but to judge My people righteously. I then gave him riches. You want wisdom along with riches. If you want the wisdom Solomon had, you must desire it more than silver and gold. This is the heart posture you must have – you must desire to judge My people righteously. I call you to tremble at My Word and in My Presence, not your circumstances. Not your future. You must tremble at My Word and tremble at My Presence. You must seek Me with all your heart. When you seek Me you will fall upon your face before Me. My ways are not your ways. My thoughts are not your thoughts. You must seek My Will, not your will; My Vision, not your vision. I will do great and mighty things through you, My servant. Humble you are. More humble you must be."

I do not share this because I am anyone special, but to reveal to you that when God speaks, we had best listen. Jackie and I looked at each other after she prophesied and said, "Whoa, I don't know what just happened. I felt Someone take over my mouth." We both agreed that it was not just the Holy Spirit; the Holy Spirit confirmed to us that it was the Heavenly Father.

Again, I have no reason to make this up, and you are fine to disagree. I know precisely what occurred, and God is my Witness. Each Person of the Trinity can speak directly to us or through us who have the gift of prophecy. Each Person of the Trinity can share the past, present, and future. It is up to God which Person comes forth.

As we understand this truth, we move into the call to prophesy. Before looking at some of the many Biblical stories in which God's people prophesied, it is important to hear the call to seek to prophesy. 1 Corinthians 14:1-5 (NKJV) tells us what we must do:

> "Pursue love, and desire spiritual gifts, but especially that you may prophesy. For he who speaks in a tongue does not speak to men but to God, for no one understands him; however, in the spirit he speaks mysteries. But he who prophesies speaks edification and exhortation and comfort to men. He who speaks in a tongue edifies himself, but he who prophesies edifies the church. I wish you all spoke with tongues, but even more that you prophesied; for he who prophesies is greater than he who speaks with tongues, unless indeed he interprets, that the church may receive edification."

We must desire to prophesy. We must seek God and ask the Holy Spirit to bless us with this wonderful gift that is meant for "edification and exhortation and comfort to men" (1 Corinthians 14:3). This is an important verse as it reveals the means of prophesying.

The gift of prophecy is never meant to condemn, but to warn; not to instill fear, but lead one to walk in the fear of the Lord; not to bring down but to build up; not to destroy but to edify; not to discourage but to exhort; not to bring shame and guilt but to encourage and bring comfort.

When God speaks, He brings a Word in due season. Not all words will be comfortable to hear. Not all words from God will be the same by means of prophesying. There are words of correction, rebuke, and the call to repent and seek the face of God, but it is always done in love, though the love can be coupled with His anger and wrath when He is perpetually ignored and dismissed. Examples are as follows:

> "'When you beget children and grandchildren and have grown old in the land, and act corruptly and make a carved image in the form of anything, and do evil in the sight of the Lord your God to provoke Him to anger, I call heaven and earth to witness against you this day, that you will soon utterly perish from the land which you cross over the Jordan to possess; you will not prolong *your* days in it, but will be utterly destroyed.'" Deuteronomy 4:25-26 NKJV

> "And this whole land shall be a desolation and an astonishment, and these nations shall serve the king of Babylon seventy years. Then it will come to pass, when seventy years are completed, that I will punish the king of Babylon and that nation, the land of the Chaldeans, for their iniquity, says the Lord; and I will make it a perpetual desolation." Jeremiah 25:11-12 NKJV

> "Then Amos answered, and said to Amaziah: "I was no prophet, Nor was I a son of a prophet, But I was a sheepbreeder And a tender of sycamore fruit. Then the Lord took me as I followed the flock, And the Lord said to me, 'Go, prophesy to My people Israel.' Now therefore, hear the word of the Lord: You say, 'Do not prophesy against Israel, And do not spout against the house of Isaac.' "Therefore thus says the Lord: 'Your wife shall be a harlot in the city; Your sons and daughters shall fall by the sword; Your land shall be divided by survey line; You shall die in a defiled land; And Israel shall surely be led away captive From his own land.' "" Amos 7:14-17 NKJV

When we are to deliver a strong word, we must do so in humility and boldness, knowing that there is a strong likelihood we will be hated by those on the receiving end of the prophetic word. "They hate the one who rebukes in the gate, And they abhor the one who speaks uprightly" (Amos 5:10 NKJV). This is because many people are too weak to receive correction. They would rather die wrong than endure temporary rebuke, which is meant for their ultimate good.

Sometimes, God will directly tell us to be against a people or a person. Not because He was against them all along, but because the point of turning and repenting has passed. The word that is to come is for a stubborn, relentless heart that God knows is unwilling to turn. No matter what God does, this person will remain opposed to God. In turn, God will declare such things for us to speak:

"'Therefore prophesy against them, prophesy, O son of man!'" Ezekiel 11:4 NKJV

"The word of the Lord came to me, saying, 'Son of man, set your face against the Ammonites, and prophesy against them.'" Ezekiel 25:1-2 NKJV

"Moreover the word of the Lord came to me, saying, 'Son of man, set your face against Mount Seir and prophesy against it,'" Ezekiel 35:1-2 NKJV

Ezekiel 28:20-23 (NKJV) also declares:

"Then the word of the Lord came to me, saying, "Son of man, set your face toward Sidon, and prophesy against her, and say, 'Thus says the Lord God:
    "Behold, I *am* against you, O Sidon;
    I will be glorified in your midst;
    And they shall know that I *am* the Lord,
    When I execute judgments in her and am hallowed in her.
    For I will send pestilence upon her,
    And blood in her streets;
    The wounded shall be judged in her midst
    By the sword against her on every side;
    Then they shall know that I *am* the Lord.""'

To whom does God call to give such messages? Micah 3:8 (NKJV) brings the answer: "But truly I am full of power by the Spirit of the Lord, And of justice and might, To declare to Jacob his transgression

And to Israel his sin." When the Holy Spirit fully rules us, we will be filled with the Holy Spirit's desires, namely, righteousness and justice. This, in turn, will equip us to prophesy with these stronger messages as God directs and leads.

Prophecy is not for those who have hardened hearts and are power hungry. There is an art to prophesying that only the Holy Spirit can teach.

This is why we must always depend on the Holy Spirit to speak and direct the gift that He has given us. We must never attempt to speak and say, "thus saith the Lord" when He has not spoken. "'Her prophets plastered them with untempered *mortar,* seeing false visions, and divining lies for them, saying, 'Thus says the Lord God,' when the Lord had not spoken'" (Ezekiel 22:28 NKJV).

"Thus says the Lord, your Redeemer, And He Who formed you from the womb: 'I *am* the Lord, Who makes all *things,* Who stretches out the heavens all alone, Who spreads abroad the earth by Myself; Who frustrates the signs of the babblers, And drives diviners mad; Who turns wise men backward, And makes their knowledge foolishness; Who confirms the word of His servant, And performs the counsel of His messengers'" (Isaiah 44:24-26 NKJV).

How do we know if God has truly spoken and a prophecy is true? It comes to pass and God "confirms the word of His servant, And performs the counsel of His messengers" (Isaiah 44:26 NKJV). This is true of Peter speaking in Acts 2:14-18 (NKJV):

> "But Peter, standing up with the eleven, raised his voice and said to them, "Men of Judea and all who dwell in Jerusalem, let this be known to you, and heed my words. For these are not drunk, as you suppose, since it is *only* the third hour of the day. But this is what was spoken by the prophet Joel: 'And it shall come to pass in the last days, says God, That I will pour out of My Spirit on all flesh; Your sons and your daughters shall prophesy, Your young men shall see visions, Your old men shall dream dreams. And on My menservants and on My maidservants I will pour out My Spirit in those days; And they shall prophesy."

What was spoken in the Old Testament by the prophet Joel had come to fulfillment in the New Testament in Acts (and continues to this day)! What a fantastic reality to understand, that all Scripture is God breathed and will complete what It has spoken on and set forth to accomplish. Hallelujah!

Many people are running around who have witnessed what others have done, been taught by false prophets and deceptive teachers, and have taken their time studying human emotions through popular psychology. When this little human package has been developed, they begin to go around, falsely prophesying to others. These prophesies are nothing more than what people *want* to hear, not what they *need* to hear.

Common phrases you will hear are the following:

- "You are going to preach to the nations."
- "I see a mic in your hand."
- "You are going to do great and mighty things for the Lord."
- "God is going to make you rich to bless others."
- "God is going to do a miracle for you" (meanwhile, this person is living in sin and refusing to repent).

You will notice a common theme with just these few examples: "YOU". It has nothing to do with the Holy Spirit working in and through them. It merely addresses what is in the human heart and what every carnal man wants: popularity and prosperity. False prophets feed into these desires and can easily manipulate the undiscerning person. Of course, there are *true* messages within these, but many people stick to this recipe because it feeds their egos. They give the same word to many when, in actuality, it is not meant for but a few, as led by the Holy Spirit.

God has a specific word for such false prophets and counterfeit saints who bring forth a false prophetic word. Ezekiel 13:3-9 (NKJV) reveals:

"Thus says the Lord God: "Woe to the foolish prophets, who follow their own spirit and have seen nothing! O Israel, your prophets are like foxes in the deserts. You have not gone up into the gaps to build a wall for the house of Israel to stand in battle on the day of the Lord. They have envisioned futility and false divination, saying, 'Thus says the Lord!' But the Lord has not sent them; yet they hope that the word may be confirmed. Have you not seen a futile vision, and have you not spoken false divination? You say, 'The Lord says,' but I have not spoken."

Therefore thus says the Lord God: "Because you have spoken nonsense and envisioned lies, therefore I *am* indeed against you," says the Lord God. "My hand will be against the prophets who envision futility and who divine lies; they shall not be in the assembly of My people, nor be written in the record of the house of Israel, nor shall they enter into the land of Israel. Then you shall know that I *am* the Lord God.""

Those who give false prophecies are in grave danger. Greater still, those who are living in sin and giving prophetic words are seen as the wicked before God. Jeremiah 23:13-14 (NKJV) states:

"And I have seen folly in the prophets of Samaria:
  They prophesied by Baal
  And caused My people Israel to err.
  Also I have seen a horrible thing in the prophets of Jerusalem:
  They commit adultery and walk in lies;
  They also strengthen the hands of evildoers,
  So that no one turns back from his wickedness.
  All of them are like Sodom to Me,
  And her inhabitants like Gomorrah."

Truly, unhinged prophesies are dangerous. They feed on the flesh of others and draw those people into the person giving the prophecy. This, in turn, can bring devastating consequences, as the one prophesied to attaches themselves to the prophecy. If it doesn't come to fruition, the person who spoke the prophecy is seen as a liar. Prophecy is a very serious matter that should not be taken lightly.

Whoever thinks they possess this gift, let them take heed to the warning found in Deuteronomy 18:20 (NKJV): "'But the prophet who presumes to speak a word in My name, which I have not commanded him to speak, or who speaks in the name of other gods, that prophet shall die.'"

God has a righteous anger toward these false prophets and people who bring forth false prophecies. If they do not repent, they are in grave danger. May God correct and convict them, and may they have softened hearts to listen, lest they perish.

God declares to such false prophets, "'I, even I, will utterly forget you and forsake you, and the city that I gave you and your fathers, and *will cast you* out of My presence. And I will bring an everlasting reproach upon you, and a perpetual shame, which shall not be forgotten'" (Jeremiah 23:39-40 NKJV).

It would do us well to discern precisely how God feels and what He says further about those who falsely prophesy. Jeremiah 23:16-32 (NKJV) brings a strong word from the Lord:

"Thus says the Lord of hosts:
"Do not listen to the words of the prophets who prophesy to you.
They make you worthless;
They speak a vision of their own heart,
Not from the mouth of the Lord.
They continually say to those who despise Me,
'The Lord has said, "You shall have peace" ';
And *to* everyone who walks according to the dictates of his own heart, they say,
'No evil shall come upon you.' "
For who has stood in the counsel of the Lord,
And has perceived and heard His word?
Who has marked His word and heard *it?*
Behold, a whirlwind of the Lord has gone forth in fury—
A violent whirlwind!
It will fall violently on the head of the wicked.
The anger of the Lord will not turn back
Until He has executed and performed the thoughts of His heart.
In the latter days you will understand it perfectly.
"I have not sent these prophets, yet they ran.

I have not spoken to them, yet they prophesied.
But if they had stood in My counsel,
And had caused My people to hear My words,
Then they would have turned them from their evil way
And from the evil of their doings.
"*Am* I a God near at hand," says the Lord,
"And not a God afar off?
Can anyone hide himself in secret places,
So I shall not see him?" says the Lord;
"Do I not fill heaven and earth?" says the Lord.

"I have heard what the prophets have said who prophesy lies in My name, saying, 'I have dreamed, I have dreamed!' How long will *this* be in the heart of the prophets who prophesy lies? Indeed *they are* prophets of the deceit of their own heart, who try to make My people forget My name by their dreams which everyone tells his neighbor, as their fathers forgot My name for Baal.

"The prophet who has a dream, let him tell a dream;
And he who has My word, let him speak My word faithfully.
What *is* the chaff to the wheat?" says the Lord.
"*Is* not My word like a fire?" says the Lord,
"And like a hammer *that* breaks the rock in pieces?

"Therefore behold, I *am* against the prophets," says the Lord, "who steal My words every one from his neighbor. Behold, I *am* against the prophets," says the Lord, "who use their tongues and say, 'He says.' Behold, I *am* against those who prophesy false dreams," says the Lord, "and tell them, and cause My people to err by their lies and by their recklessness. Yet I did not send them or command them; therefore they shall not profit this people at all," says the Lord."

A word from God will bring encouragement, but out of the vain imaginations of the heart and mind of carnal men spring forth an abundance of useless babble and words that stroke the ego but do not come from God.

It is easy to bring an encouraging word, and sometimes that is all God will bring for the weary heart. However, those who are living in sin, refuse to repent, or need to wake up from spiritual sleep, God will bring exhortation. He will speak through those with the gift of prophecy to lead others to repent, see the error in their ways, and seek Him for assistance. We see this with Jonah. "And Jonah began to enter the city on the first day's walk. Then he cried out and said, "Yet forty days, and Nineveh shall be overthrown!"" (Jonah 3:4 NKJV).

One aspect we want to learn from Jonah is to do what God calls us to do, immediately. When it comes to prophesying in word or in writing, we are to do so and speak only what we hear. We are not meant to add to the prophetic word, nor to take away from it. If God gives us something difficult to deliver, we are responsible for moving forward exactly as He has spoken.

Now, one thing Jonah failed to do was to prophesy and bring the Word of the Lord in love. He brought forth the Truth, but there was little to no love for the people. He didn't want them to have a chance to come to know God. When God speaks and guides us, He always has us speak in love. This can be a love easily accepted or out of tough love. "For whom the LORD loves He corrects, Just as a father the son *in whom* he delights" (Proverbs 3:12 NKJV).

I am hesitant to share the following with you, as I am concerned many will attempt to replicate it. Before I share a prophetic word I had to deliver to someone (who I will leave unnamed), it is important to address a few truths.

As we see with all the gifts, the gift is concrete in its function, but the means of accomplishing it are differentiated. For some, they will hear audibly and instantly repeat what God has spoken. For others, God's Presence will fall mightily upon the person, and they will speak with authority and unction.

Some excel with the gift when given time to write. The prophecy is delivered in writing. This is where my gift of prophecy predominantly excels (though I have prophesied through speech). Writing, however, is what I currently prefer and the way God speaks to me.

When I pray for a prophetic word for someone, God always answers. He leads me to whom to pray for, and as I submit my will and mind to the Holy Spirit, He comes forth. He gives me the exact words. I don't know what the following sentence or even the next word is going to say. Yet, each time, the Holy Spirit takes over and writes through me.

This is going to sound extremely foreign to many. Others may have their concerns. The point of the matter is to go to God in prayer, allow Him to speak, and when you have the gift of prophecy, you will begin to learn the Holy Spirit's Voice all the more clearly.

God speaks, and we would do well to listen. Many times, we do not listen, and this grieves and quenches the Spirit from working through us.

If we all take time to reflect, we who are born-again know the Holy Spirit has spoken to us. "Go evangelize to that person." "Ask that person how their day is going." "Instead of watching that movie, spend time with Me in My Word." "Don't go to that party; otherwise, there will be consequences." "You need to get out of this toxic relationship. You are being abused, and it will only worsen if you stay."

We all know when God speaks when we have the Holy Spirit. It is that silent whisper, intrusive thought, or sudden knowing from God. Also, if we have had moments where we say, "That was not me speaking or giving the answer; that was all the Holy Spirit", then it is no significant feat to believe that the gift of prophecy is still for today.

Truly, if God speaks in such ways as in silence or in a still small voice, then it is not complicated or challenging to believe that He can give us the gift to prophesy and guide and lead us with what needs to be said, who it needs to be said to, and the timing of when the message should be delivered.

Too many times, people overcomplicate things and limit God. God cannot be boxed in, and it is when we begin to seek God for spiritual gifts and, above all, seek Him directly that we will learn to hear His Voice more clearly with each passing day.

Now, I am not going to tell you my whole process, as my job is not to teach you. The Holy Spirit is the Greatest Teacher, and if He blesses you with the gift to prophesy, He will lead and guide you in stewarding well the gift, how to go about using the gift, and how He will speak. Therefore, I will refrain from telling you the process that He has for me because God's Ways are not our ways. God declares, "'For My thoughts *are* not your thoughts, Nor *are* your ways My ways,' says the Lord. 'For *as* the heavens are higher than the earth, So are My ways higher than your ways, And My thoughts than your thoughts'" (Isaiah 55:8-9 NKJV).

God leads each person in the same gifting in different and unique ways. Some practices can help people grow in their gifting. These practices and the growth that comes over time are all the result of fully submitting and depending on the Holy Spirit. If we cling to the gift we have and not the One Who gave us the gift, we will surely head down a road that will lead toward destruction. We will not operate in the Spirit but in the dependency of how *we* wield our gift (when it is not ours to *wield*, but *steward*). The Holy Spirit wields us and works through us with the gift. If we attempt to do it on our own, it will not be of God, and there will be consequences.

This is a very serious matter, and too many are going around speaking empty words. "Let no one deceive you with empty words, for because of these things the wrath of God comes upon the sons of disobedience. Therefore do not be partakers with them" (Ephesians 5:6-7 NKJV).

Now, when God speaks through me, it is due to *seeking* Him, fully *surrendering* to Him, and *submitting* all to Him. On a general basis, if you can follow these three 'S's, God most certainly will speak and move through you with the gift of prophecy.

It is important to note that all prophetic words are not the same. Some will be longer than others, while others may be just a sentence or two. Some will be more difficult to deliver, some will be easier. Regardless of the word, it will always be from the Holy Spirit when we seek the Holy Spirit to speak, and it will always be Truth in love. Any deviation from this is a result of human devices, mechanisms, and schemes, and not fully trusting in the Holy Spirit.

It takes faith not only to hear, but also to proceed in confidence that we heard correctly. We are not to doubt when God speaks, for we alone are the messengers. Nothing more.

The word I am about to share with you is meant to reveal what a prophetic word can look like and what a true one from the Lord God Almighty is. Again, not all my words are like this. Some are much easier to deliver, shorter, and contain different elements and aspects (related to the past, present, or future). God is in charge of what is *declared*. We are in charge of *delivering*.

Here is a word I had to give someone, and I was nervous about it because I did not want to hurt them. Nonetheless, this is the word given to someone who is becoming lukewarm, even though they were raised in the Church. They have never really been truly born-again and are currently living in rebellion and going their own way.

Here is the prophetic word, of which I always do mine in capital letters, as it is from God – this is how He has led me to bring forth a word from Him:

"REBELLION IS AS WITCHCRAFT, CAUSE FOR CONCERN" PROPHETIC WORD FOR (ANONYMOUS) (11/07/2024)

I AM THE ONE WHO SHUTS THE MOUTHS OF THE LIONS.

I AM THE ONE WHO SPEAKS AND IT IS DONE.

I AM THE ONE WHO SAVES MAN FROM THEIR INIQUITY.

I AM THE ONE WHO CANNOT BE DEFILED.

IN ME IS NO WRONG OR EVIL.

IN ME IS THE LIGHT OF LIFE. I AM THE LIGHT OF LIFE AND THERE IS NOTHING UNLESS I FIRST SPEAK IT.

DO YOU NOT YET PERCEIVE THAT I AM HE, AND THERE IS NO OTHER?

WHAT HAVE YOU GAINED FROM GOING YOUR OWN WAY? WHY DO YOU HARDEN YOUR HEART TOWARD ME? ARE YOU MAD BECAUSE I HAVE NOT GIVEN WHAT YOU HAVE NOT SOUGHT ME FOR?

REFLECT AND TELL ME, HOW MANY TIMES HAVE YOU GONE FORTH AND NEGLECTED MY COUNSEL? HOW MANY TIMES HAVE YOU SOUGHT ME BEFORE PURSUING WHAT YOU BELIEVED TO BE TRUE? IS IT ANY WONDER YOU HAVE BEEN DECEIVED? IS IT ANY WONDER YOUR HEART HURTS?

I AM LOVE, AND WITHOUT ME, THERE IS NO LOVE. BEAUTY IS VAIN, BUT A WOMAN OF ME IS TO BE PRAISED.

YOU COVET AND ARE ENVIOUS OF THOSE WHO HAVE WHAT YOU DESIRE, YET, YOU DO NOT SEE THAT THEY HAVE SOUGHT ME.

SHALL I CONGRATULATE YOU FOR THE LITTLE TIME YOU SPEND WITH ME? WHEN WERE YOU LAST IN MY WORD? FOR HOW LONG?

WHY DO YOU HOLD ANGER AND BITTERNESS TOWARD ME? WHY DO YOU RESENT ME? DO YOU NOT SEE THAT YOUR LIFE AND MIND ARE FILLED WITH MORE OF THE WORLD THAN MY WORD?

YOU KNOW THE LINGO OF THE FAITH, BUT ARE YOU LIVING THE FAITH? I KNOW YOU DO GOOD AND HAVE A KIND AND GENTLE HEART, BUT NO MAN HAS SAVED HIMSELF BY GOOD WORKS. IT IS BY GRACE THROUGH FAITH ALONE, AND YOUR FAITH MUST WORK, BUT YOU ARE TO WORK OUT YOUR FAITH IN FEAR AND TREMBLING.

IT IS NO WONDER WHY YOU HAVE HAD YOUR HEART BROKEN. DO YOU NOT SEE THAT I DESIRE TO MEND IT? DO YOU NOT KNOW THAT I AM THE GREAT COMFORTER, THE ALPHA AND OMEGA, THE ONE WHO IS AND HAS ALWAYS BEEN?

WHAT MAN HAS HELPED YOU THAT HAS NEVER LEFT YOU? WHO CAN YOU SAY HAS BEEN WITH YOU THROUGHOUT ALL SEASONS OF YOUR LIFE? THOUGH MANY HAVE LEFT YOU, YOU HAVE CUT OTHERS OFF. THOUGH YOU HAVE BEEN HURT, YOU HAVE HURT OTHERS.

WHY DO YOU RUN WHEN I TELL YOU TO WALK? WHY DO YOU PREVENT ME FROM ENTERING IN? WHY DO YOU HIDE BEHIND THE FACE OF RELIGION? DO YOU NOT KNOW THAT I AM THE GOD OF ABRAHAM, ISAAC, AND JACOB? DO I NOT KNOW THE THOUGHTS AND INTENTIONS OF THE HEART?

YOU DESIRE TO ACHIEVE WHAT YOU WANT IN YOUR OWN STRENGTH, BUT YOU HAVE NOT ACQUIRED THAT WHICH YOU SEEK. YOU KNOW RIGHT FROM WRONG, BUT WHERE IS YOUR REPENTANCE? WHY DO YOU REBEL AND GO IN THE WAYS OF THE WORLD? WHAT HAVE YOU GAINED FROM BEING WITH THOSE OF THE WORLD?

BETTER TO GO TO THE HOUSE OF MOURNING THAN THE HOUSE OF FEASTING. BETTER IS A LITTLE WITH THE FEAR OF ME THAN INDULGENCE WITH THE WICKED. FOR THEY KNOW NOT WHAT THEY DO. THEIR MOUTHS SPEAK OF WORLDLY THINGS.

TELL ME, DO YOU TRANSFORM THEM WHEN YOU ARE WITH THEM? WHAT HAVE YOU DONE THAT HAS LED THEM TO ME? DO YOU DEMONSTRATE ME TO THEM BY YOUR WORDS? THOUGH YOU MAY SPEAK, IT IS BUT LITTLE. DO YOUR ACTIONS FOLLOW THAT WHICH YOU BELIEVE?

MY SON, BE A DOER OF THE WORD AND NOT A HEARER ONLY, LEST YOU DECEIVE YOURSELF. FOR BAD COMPANY CORRUPTS GOOD MORALS.

I DESIRED TO DO MORE, BUT YOU WOULD NOT LISTEN. YOU HAVE STRAYED FROM THE FAITH AND FROM ME. YOU MUST RETURN TO YOUR FIRST LOVE. YOU MUST ENTER INTO MY LOVING ARMS AND REPENT.

YOUR LIFE IS NOT WHAT YOU DESIRE BECAUSE YOU HAVE NOT MADE ME YOUR FIRST DESIRE. YOU HAVE SOUGHT THE WAYS OF MAN AND THEY HAVE TURNED OUT FLAWED.

WHAT GOOD IS IT IF A MAN GAINS THE WHOLE WORLD, YET LOSES HIS SOUL? WHAT HAVE YOU GAINED WITH THOSE YOU SURROUND YOURSELF WITH? DO YOU REALLY BELIEVE THAT THE WOMEN YOU DESIRE WERE OF ME?

WHY WERE YOU SO EASILY DECEIVED? DO YOU NOT KNOW? THOSE WHO ARE NOT IN MY PRESENCE AND MY WORD LACK DISCERNMENT. THOSE WHO WANT

NOTHING TO DO WITH ME, EXCEPT WHEN IT IS TIME FOR REQUESTING OF ME IN ORDER TO RECEIVE, ARE DECEIVED.

DECEPTION CONTINUES ON AND INCREASES. HOW WILL YOU STAND AGAINST THE NEXT WAVE OF DECEPTION THAT COMES? WILL YOU SO EASILY GO AFTER THAT WHICH SPARKLES AND GLITTERS, BUT IS NOT OF ME? WILL YOU JUDGE SOMEONE BY EXTERNAL BEAUTY AND NOT LOOK WITHIN?

I TELL YOU, WHITE-WASHED TOMBS ARE DEAD. THERE IS NO LONG LASTING BEAUTY FOUND FROM THOSE OF THE WORLD OR THOSE WHO DECLARE THE RIGHT WORDS.

YOU MUST SEEK ME FOR A WOMAN OF ME. YOU MUST DIE TO YOURSELF AND SUBMIT AND SURRENDER ALL.

I KNOW THE VOID IN YOUR SOUL. I KNOW WHAT IS MISSING. WHY DO YOU CONTINUE TO NEGLECT ME DAY AFTER DAY? WHY DO YOU SEEK EVERYTHING AND EVERYONE BUT ME?

I KNOW IT IS DIFFICULT, BUT I WILL MEET YOU WHERE YOU ARE. YOU ARE NOT TOO FAR GONE. CEASE FROM HARDENING YOUR HEART TOWARD ME. FOR WHY SHOULD YOU BE ANGRY AND UPSET AT ME FOR THE VERY THING WHICH YOU INFRINGE UPON YOURSELF?

AM I NOT GOOD, LOVING, GRACIOUS, AND MERCIFUL? HAVE I NOT BEEN CALLING YOU? WHY DO YOU RUN FROM ME? WHERE DO YOU SEEK TO GO THAT I CANNOT SEE OR FIND? WHY DO YOU ATTEMPT EVERYTHING BUT THAT WHICH YOU KNOW TO BE TRUE?

YOU MUST SEEK DELIVERANCE AND SEEK ME WITH YOUR WHOLE HEART.

YOU WILL NOT LAST IN THE DAYS TO COME. YOU WILL FALL BY YOUR OWN HAND IF YOU DO NOT HEED MY WORDS.

I KNOW YOUR THOUGHTS. I KNOW WHAT YOU SPEAK WHEN NO ONE IS AROUND. I HEAR ALL THINGS.

I AM WILLING TO HEAL, BUT YOU MUST REPENT. BELIEVE IN ME, NOT JUST IN MIND BUT WITH YOUR HEART. THROW YOURSELF DOWN AT THE FOOT OF THE CROSS, FOR I AM HE WHO SAVES THOSE WHO ARE LOST.

I NEED NOTHING. I AM COMPLETE IN WHO I AM. NONETHELESS, I CALL THOSE WHO ARE FAR FROM ME OR NOT OF ME.

WHICH ARE YOU? YOU KNOW. DO NOT DECEIVE YOURSELF. IT IS TIME TO SEEK ME WITH ALL YOUR HEART, SOUL, MIND, AND STRENGTH. ONLY THEN WILL YOU HAVE TRUE AND EVERLASTING FREEDOM. CHAINS WILL BE BROKEN. YOU WILL SING A NEW SONG. YOUR SOUL WILL BE UPLIFTED INTO MY PRESENCE AND YOU WILL FIND PEACE AND JOY.

I AM WILLING TO GIVE WHAT YOU DESIRE, BUT YOU MUST HEED MY WORD. REBELLION IS AS WITCHCRAFT, AND I DESPISE THOSE WHO PARTAKE IN SORCERY. IF REBELLION IS AS THE SAME, WILL YOU NOT HEED MY WORDS?

I AM LONG-SUFFERING AND PATIENT, BUT MY PATIENCE RUNS THIN FOR THOSE WHO KNOW THE TRUTH BUT DO NOT LIVE IN IT; FOR THOSE WHO KNOW THE WAY BUT DO NOT WALK IN THE WAY; FOR THOSE WHO KNOW WHAT MUST BE DONE BUT FAIL TO DO WHAT THEY KNOW THEY MUST DO.

HOW LONG WILL YOU CONTINUE IN YOUR WAY? SHOW ME THE PROOF OF YOUR PLANS AND HOW THEY HAVE MADE YOU SUCCEED IN THE WAYS YOU THOUGHT. TELL ME, WHAT GOOD HAS COME FROM YOU NEGLECTING ME?

IT IS TIME TO DETHRONE THE DISGUISE. YOU KNOW WHAT MUST BE DONE. TIME IS SHORT AND ETERNITY IS LONG.

MY WORDS ARE SPOKEN IN LOVE, BUT A CONVICTING TOUGH WORD MUST COME TO THOSE WHO ARE HARD OF HEART AND BITTER. DEPRESSION AND ANXIETY

OCCUR WHEN MAN PLACES THEIR IDENTITY IN ANYTHING BUT ME AND SEEK EVERYTHING ASIDE FROM ME.

DO NOT BASE WHO I AM OFF OF THOSE WHO HAVE HURT YOU. DO NOT THINK I AM ASSOCIATED WITH THOSE WHO PLAY THE GAME OF RELIGION; THOSE WHO SPEAK MY NAME BUT I DID NOT SEND THEM. WHO DECLARE MY WORD, BUT FOR SELF-GAIN.

I AM NOT A MAN THAT I SHOULD LIE. YOU HAVE BEEN WOUNDED AND HURT, BUT I COME TO MEND AND HEAL THE BROKEN HEART.

DO NOT USE YOUR PAST AS AN EXCUSE FOR NEGLECTING TO DO IN THE PRESENT THAT WHICH WILL CHANGE YOUR FUTURE.

THOSE IN HELL HAVE NO RE-RUNS. THEY REMAIN IN THEIR STATE FOR ETERNITY. LET GO, MY SON, AND ALLOW ME TO TAKE THE FULL BLOW OF YOUR PAIN, ANGER, DEPRESSION, GUILT, SHAME, AND SADNESS. I CAN HANDLE IT, FOR WHILE YOU WERE STILL A SINNER I DIED FOR YOU.

ENTER INTO THE FAITH IN FULL. DO NOT BE ONE OF THOSE WHO DEPARTS FROM THE FAITH; WHO TASTED OF ME BUT NEGLECTED ME AND TURNED THEIR BACK AGAINST ME.

WHAT SHALL YOU GAIN BY GOING AGAINST ME, HIM WHO CREATED ALL THINGS? DO I NOT HAVE A PLAN AND PURPOSE FOR YOUR LIFE? DO I NOT PROVIDE THOSE WHO COME TO KNOW ME WITH HOPE?

IT IS TIME TO CHOOSE THIS DAY WHOM YOU WILL SERVE. WILL IT BE ME? OR MAMMON? WILL IT BE THE GOD OF ALL THINGS? OR WILL IT BE GODLESS FRIENDS? DO YOU NOT KNOW BAD COMPANY CORRUPTS GOOD MORALS?

YOU MUST UNDERSTAND THAT THIS ROAD IS DIFFICULT, BUT I PROMISE TO BE WITH YOU. ALLOW ME IN, THAT I MAY CHANGE YOU. I WILL GIVE YOU A NEW

HEART AND A NEW SONG. YOU WILL BE OVERWHELMED WITH MY PRESENCE AND WILL REJOICE IN WHAT I HAVE IN STORE FOR YOU.

NOW IS THE TIME. THIS IS MY WARNING. IF YOU SEEK ME, YOU WILL FIND ME. IF YOU GO TO MY WORD, I WILL MEET YOU THERE. IF YOU POUR OUT YOUR HEART AND SOUL BEFORE ME AND TRULY REPENT, I WILL CHANGE YOU.

NEGLECT TO DO SO, AND I WILL FORSAKE YOU. I WILL CUT YOU OFF FOREVER, AND YOU WILL NOT EXPERIENCE ALL THAT I AM.

KNOW THAT I DESIRE FOR NONE TO PERISH, BUT ALL TO COME TO REPENTANCE. YOUR LIFE IS A GIFT AND YOU ARE MEANT TO BLESS MANY.

I KNOW YOU DESIRE TO DO GOOD AND YOU ARE GENTLE OF SPIRIT, BUT THESE ATTRIBUTES DO NOT OVERRIDE MY CALL TO OBEY MY WORD, HEED MY VOICE, AND REPENT OF SIN.

WHAT WILL YOU DO? I HAVE SPOKEN. MAKE YOURSELF LIKE A MAN AND DO RIGHT. NOT JUST IN PUBLIC OR BY WORD, BUT BEFORE ME. DO RIGHT AND OBEY, AND I WILL BLESS YOU. FOR I AM HE WHO CONQUERED DEATH AND THE GRAVE.

COME NOW, AND ALLOW MY PRSENCE TO FLOW. NEVER AGAIN WILL YOU FEEL HEARTBREAK, FOR I WILL GIVE YOU THE DESIRE OF YOUR HEART. PREPARE YOURSELF AND BE BOLD COMING TO MY THRONE, AND YOU WILL RECEIVE MY GRACE. PREPARE YOURSELF FOR THE FUTURE, AND I WILL BRING IT TO COMPLETION.

FOR THAT WHICH I BEGIN I WILL BRING TO AN END. ALL THINGS WORK TOGETHER FOR GOOD FOR THOSE WHO LOVE ME.

CEASE REBELLION AND REPENT. I WILL TAKE CARE OF THE REST.

I LOVE YOU, AND AS A FATHER DISCIPLINES THE SON

IN WHOM HE LOVES, SO I DISCIPLINE YOU WITH A CORRECTING WORD, ONE THAT BRINGS CONVICTION.
HEAR MY VOICE, TURN AND CHANGE, AND YOU WILL FIND REST.

This was not an easy word to deliver, but it is one God wanted to speak to the individual. There was no denying this was from the Lord. The person I read this to was in tears the whole time. After we left each other and went our way, they followed up via text and thanked me for the word. They knew it was from God.

This is the power of prophecy, and it is why Paul declares, "Therefore, brethren, desire earnestly to prophesy" (1 Corinthians 14:39 NKJV). When God speaks, whether man listens to the word or not, they know, deep down in their spiritual being, that it comes from Him. There is no denying that when God speaks, it is only a matter of obeying or heeding the call.

"For you can all prophesy one by one, that all may learn and all may be encouraged. And the spirits of the prophets are subject to the prophets. For God is not *the author* of confusion but of peace, as in all the churches of the saints" (1 Corinthians 14:31-33 NKJV). God's Word will always bring clarity, never confusion. We are called to test prophetic words from others. We are called to prophesy. Over time, this gift can not only be received but also cultivated into an amazing revealment of God's Love, Power, Compassion, Vision, and Insight in a person's heart and life.

If we ever want to validate whether someone has the gift of prophecy, we must check their prayer life. A person who *prays* to God *hears* from God. Those who have this gift will have it in greater measure the more they seek God to increase it and pray.

There are so many Scriptures that reveal prophecy. It is not just about Christ, though that is the *main* prophecy. When prophetic words are given that are *not about* Christ (but a person's situation or circumstance), they are *from* Him. Prophecy is all about God, but it is important to know that words can be given by Him, through us, to other individuals. We briefly state this, as some say, "There is no such thing as prophecy. It's just about Christ." Once again, this is a belief instilled by man and certain denominations, but it is not led or developed by the Holy Spirit.

Let us take a look at Nathan bringing the prophetic word to David after he fell into adultery and had her husband killed. Nathan comes with a powerful word. 2 Samuel 12:1-12 (NKJV) tells us what occurred:

> "Then the LORD sent Nathan to David. And he came to him, and said to him: "There were two men in one city, one rich and the other poor. The rich *man* had exceedingly many flocks and herds. But the poor *man* had nothing, except one little ewe lamb which he had bought and nourished; and it grew up together with him and with his children. It ate of his own food and drank from his own cup and lay in his bosom; and it was like a daughter to him. And a traveler came to the rich man, who refused to take from his own flock and from his own herd to prepare one for the wayfaring man who had come to him; but he took the poor man's lamb and prepared it for the man who had come to him."
>
> So David's anger was greatly aroused against the man, and he said to Nathan, "*As* the LORD lives, the man who has done this shall surely die! And he shall restore fourfold for the lamb, because he did this thing and because he had no pity."
>
> Then Nathan said to David, "You *are* the man! Thus says the LORD God of Israel: 'I anointed you king over Israel, and I delivered you from the hand of Saul. I gave you your master's house and your master's wives into your keeping, and gave you the house of Israel and Judah. And if *that had been* too little, I also would have given you much more! Why have you despised the commandment of the LORD, to do evil in His sight? You have killed Uriah the Hittite with the sword; you have taken his wife *to be* your wife, and have killed him with the sword of the people of Ammon. Now therefore, the sword shall never depart from your house, because you have despised Me, and have taken the wife of Uriah the Hittite to be your wife.' Thus says the LORD: 'Behold, I will raise up adversity against you from your own house; and I will take your wives before your eyes and give *them* to your neighbor, and he shall lie with your wives in the sight of this sun. For

you did *it* secretly, but I will do this thing before all Israel, before the sun.'"

God was going to give David much more, yet, due to David's sin, the entire course of his future changed. All by two sins. Truly, "'nothing is secret that will not be revealed, nor *anything* hidden that will not be known and come to light'" (Luke 8:17 NKJV).

Nathan spoke a word from the Lord, but set it up in such a way as to bring a sort of parable before him. This allowed David to experience all the emotions that God had toward him. Simultaneously, when 'Nathan said to David, "You are the man!"' (2 Samuel 12:7), David knew he was in the wrong. He understood immediately and listened to the rest of what Nathan had to deliver.

What then was David's response? "So David said to Nathan, "I have sinned against the Lord." And Nathan said to David, "The Lord also has put away your sin; you shall not die. However, because by this deed you have given great occasion to the enemies of the Lord to blaspheme, the child also *who is* born to you shall surely die." Then Nathan departed to his house" (2 Samuel 12:13-15 NKJV).

Nathan brought a very tough word. Nonetheless, it was coupled with God's Mercy. This is what always occurs when a word is received and truly of the Lord. There may be a tough prophecy to hear, but if it is met with the same heart as David, mercy and grace will be shown. We will not die, but rise, when we listen to the voice of a true prophet who *truly* hears from and speaks on behalf of the Lord, by the counsel of the Holy Spirit.

Another Scripture reveals that God spoke to Simeon, telling him he would see the Son of God before passing away. Luke 2:25-35 (NKJV) declares:

> "And behold, there was a man in Jerusalem whose name was Simeon, and this man was just and devout, waiting for the Consolation of Israel, and the Holy Spirit was upon him. And it had been revealed to him by the Holy Spirit that he would not see death before he had seen the Lord's Christ. So he came by the Spirit into the temple. And when the parents brought in the Child Jesus, to do for Him according to the

custom of the law, he took Him up in his arms and blessed God and said: "Lord, now You are letting Your servant depart in peace, according to Your word; for my eyes have seen Your salvation which You have prepared before the face of all peoples, a light to bring revelation to the Gentiles, and the glory of Your people Israel." And Joseph and His mother marveled at those things which were spoken of Him. Then Simeon blessed them, and said to Mary His mother, "Behold, this Child is destined for the fall and rising of many in Israel, and for a sign which will be spoken against (yes, a sword will pierce through your own soul also), that the thoughts of many hearts may be revealed.'"

It is interesting that even after God spoke to Joseph and Mary by various means, letting them know Who Jesus was, they were still amazed to hear Simeon utter the prophecy and prophetic word of the Lord Jesus Christ. This reveals that, though a word may be difficult to grasp in full, another prophetic word at a later time will be given, to keep one encouraged in the original word they heard. This can come directly from God or through those with the gift of prophecy.

God told Simeon what would occur, and it happened. Simeon saw the fulfillment of God's spoken word, and that is what will always transpire when we truly believe God's Word and press into the prophetic word that He has spoken through one of His saints.

Even Isaiah prophesied of the coming of Christ—roughly 700 years before Jesus was born! "Therefore the Lord Himself will give you a sign: Behold, the virgin shall conceive and bear a Son, and shall call His name Immanuel" (Isaiah 7:14 NKJV). When God speaks, it may not happen immediately, but throughout time, His Word will come forth and prove true. He is not a liar, and it is impossible for Him to lie (Hebrews 6:18). When He speaks, we must listen.

Though there is a fantastic amount of prophetic words in the Old Testament, we want to look more in the New Testament as well, as prophecy was not "just for back then". It is for today, and anyone who believes the contrary has been misled, limited God, trusted in man or denomination, or remains stubborn and is unwilling to yield to the truth.

"The next day John saw Jesus coming toward him, and said,

"Behold! The Lamb of God Who takes away the sin of the world! This is He of Whom I said, 'After me comes a Man Who is preferred before me, for He was before me'" (John 1:29-30 NKJV). John declares to the multitude before him Who the Lord Jesus Christ was. In essence, he was saying, "Do you all remember when I declared to you that after me comes One greater than I? This is the moment! Pay attention, as this is the Messiah I spoke of some time ago. See? God spoke through me, and this is the moment the fulfillment of what was spoken is coming to pass."

"And in these days prophets came from Jerusalem to Antioch. Then one of them, named Agabus, stood up and showed by the Spirit that there was going to be a great famine throughout all the world, which also happened in the days of Claudius Caesar" (Acts 11:27-28 NKJV). Here, we see that prophetic words can result in specifics about the future – not just for individuals, but for the world.

There are men whom God has revealed the future (financially, morally, and politically). God does this at His Own discretion, based on a person's heart for Him and the gifts He has given them. The Spirit showed Agabus that a great famine would come across the whole world. Ironically, it happened during the days of Claudius Caesar.

When a prophetic word is about the future from a true man or woman of God, we would do well to listen. God always warns His people and gives them hidden insight into the future, helping them prepare for what lies ahead. Even Jesus describes the End Times in Matthew 24, giving us discernment to recognize the times as they approach.

Acts 27:21-26 (NKJV) reveals a prophetic word to those who were in fear of the tempest that occurred as they sailed. The Scripture is as follows:

> "But after long abstinence from food, then Paul stood in the midst of them and said, "Men, you should have listened to me, and not have sailed from Crete and incurred this disaster and loss. And now I urge you to take heart, for there will be no loss of life among you, but only of the ship. For there stood by me this night an angel of the God to Whom I belong and Whom I serve, saying, 'Do not be afraid, Paul; you

must be brought before Caesar; and indeed God has granted you all those who sail with you.' Therefore take heart, men, for I believe God that it will be just as it was told me. However, we must run aground on a certain island.'"

Paul declares that the men should have listened to him before setting course. This was a word of knowledge Paul received from God, and he prophesied to them what would occur if they sailed from Crete. The men, of course, did not listen, and what Paul warned about happened.

It is in these moments that men figure out who truly walks with God. In their stubbornness, they refuse to heed the warning. However, in the end, they know they would do well to listen to those who walk with God. If they do not, they will continue to sink into darkness, depravity, and deception.

Paul tells them not to be afraid and that God will spare their lives (which He does). Even when people disobey sound guidance and wise counsel, God is willing to show grace and mercy time and time again. Truly, there is none like Him!

Though there are many prophecies of the coming of Christ and what He did in life (found in the Old Testament and the New Testament), let us end with Peter's sermon – a prophetic word led by the Holy Spirit that includes Scripture from the Old Testament, spiritual wisdom, knowledge, and truth, and direction of what to say, when to say it, and what to reference, by the Wisdom of the Holy Spirit. Acts 2:14-36 (NKJV) declares:

> "But Peter, standing up with the eleven, raised his voice and said to them, "Men of Judea and all who dwell in Jerusalem, let this be known to you, and heed my words. For these are not drunk, as you suppose, since it is *only* the third hour of the day. But this is what was spoken by the prophet Joel:
>> 'And it shall come to pass in the last days, says God,
>> That I will pour out of My Spirit on all flesh;
>> Your sons and your daughters shall prophesy,
>> Your young men shall see visions,
>> Your old men shall dream dreams.

And on My menservants and on My maidservants
I will pour out My Spirit in those days;
And they shall prophesy.
I will show wonders in heaven above
And signs in the earth beneath:
Blood and fire and vapor of smoke.
The sun shall be turned into darkness,
And the moon into blood,
Before the coming of the great and awesome day of the LORD.
And it shall come to pass
That whoever calls on the name of the LORD
Shall be saved.'

"Men of Israel, hear these words: Jesus of Nazareth, a Man attested by God to you by miracles, wonders, and signs which God did through Him in your midst, as you yourselves also know— Him, being delivered by the determined purpose and foreknowledge of God, you have taken by lawless hands, have crucified, and put to death; Whom God raised up, having loosed the pains of death, because it was not possible that He should be held by it. For David says concerning Him:

'I foresaw the LORD always before my face,
For He is at my right hand, that I may not be shaken.
Therefore my heart rejoiced, and my tongue was glad;
Moreover my flesh also will rest in hope.
For You will not leave my soul in Hades,
Nor will You allow Your Holy One to see corruption.
You have made known to me the ways of life;
You will make me full of joy in Your presence.'

"Men *and* brethren, let *me* speak freely to you of the patriarch David, that he is both dead and buried, and his tomb is with us to this day. Therefore, being a prophet, and knowing that God had sworn with an oath to him that of the fruit of his body, according to the flesh, He would raise up the Christ to sit on his throne, he, foreseeing this, spoke concerning the resurrection of the Christ, that His soul was not left in Hades, nor did His flesh see corruption. This Jesus God has raised up, of which we are all witnesses. Therefore being exalted to the right hand of God, and having received from the Father the promise of the Holy Spirit, He poured out this which you now see and hear.

"For David did not ascend into the heavens, but he says himself:
'The LORD said to my Lord,
"Sit at My right hand,
Till I make Your enemies Your footstool." '
"Therefore let all the house of Israel know assuredly that God has made this Jesus, Whom you crucified, both Lord and Christ.'"

This is not only a sermon, but a prophetic word. There is Truth and Scripture all within Peter's words as he was led by the Holy Spirit. What was the response of the crowd? "Now when they heard *this*, they were cut to the heart, and said to Peter and the rest of the apostles, "Men *and* brethren, what shall we do?" Then Peter said to them, 'Repent, and let every one of you be baptized in the name of Jesus Christ for the remission of sins; and you shall receive the gift of the Holy Spirit. For the promise is to you and to your children, and to all who are afar off, as many as the Lord our God will call'" (Acts 2:37-39 NKJV).

In declaration and boldness, Peter continued to properly guide them. They softened their hearts, they listened, and "that day about three thousand souls were added *to them*" (Acts 2:41 NKJV).

Prophetic words are meant to guide people to God and allow people to hear directly from Him regarding their specific needs, situations, concerns, worries, future, present, past, and heart posture before God. Of course, this can occur through prayer and God speaking directly. Yet, through the gift of prophecy, God blesses man to be a vessel of the Holy Spirit speaking through them.

Let us forever remember Ezekiel 12:21-25 (NKJV):

And the word of the Lord came to me, saying, "Son of man, what *is* this proverb *that* you *people* have about the land of Israel, which says, 'The days are prolonged, and every vision fails'? Tell them therefore, 'Thus says the Lord God: "I will lay this proverb to rest, and they shall no more use it as a proverb in Israel." ' But say to them, ' "The days are at hand, and the fulfillment of every vision. For no more shall there be any false vision or flattering divination within the house of

Israel. For I *am* the Lord. I speak, and the word which I speak will come to pass; it will no more be postponed; for in your days, O rebellious house, I will say the word and perform it," says the Lord God.' "

"Surely the Lord God does nothing, Unless He reveals His secret to His servants the prophets" (Amos 3:7 NKJV). Let us seek God for the gift to prophesy that we may exhort, bring edification, and encourage others through the prophetic words that God gives us to declare and share.

———

God in Heaven, Who alone is Sovereign and speaks Truth, You cannot lie or deceive. Your Nature is Goodness, Perfection, and Love. You are Holy and can do no wrong. God, we praise You and lift Your Name On High! We declare Your Glory, Power, Might, and Splendor! You alone give good gifts to the humble heart. God, bless us with the gift of prophecy. Teach us to steward the gift well and to speak only what You give. Make us sensitive to Your Voice, O God. Keep us from deception and falsity. May no evil or deceitful thing be upon our tongue or be proclaimed throughout our mouths. Bless us with a holy hatred of lying lips just as You hate. May we desire mercy, truth, grace, and love. God, make us bold and courageous saints who speak Your Word and a prophetic word when You give it to us. May we never fear man but always walk in the fear of You, the Lord God of Heaven and Earth. In Jesus' name, Amen.

The Gift of Discerning of Spirits

"*To another discerning of spirits.*"
  – 1 Corinthians 12:10 NKJV

The gifts of the discerning of spirits have varying levels and come in different proportions. As with any gift of the Lord, the beauty is not merely in the gift, but in the multiplicity of *functions* of each gift.

Only God is Omnificent (unlimited in creativity) and can bring forth a gift that can be exercised in a variety of ways. When it comes to the gift of the discerning of spirits, it is no different.

Notice that this gift is in the plural. It does not say discerning of a spirit (for example, the discernment to recognize the Holy Spirit in someone). Rather, it specifically says "spirits" because there is a multitude of unclean spirits that either roam through dry and desolate places or dwell within people. The Lord Jesus Christ makes this very clear in Matthew 12:43-45 (NKJV):

> "'When an unclean spirit goes out of a man, he goes through dry places, seeking rest, and finds none. Then he says, 'I will return to my house

from which I came.' And when he comes, he finds *it* empty, swept, and put in order. Then he goes and takes with him seven other spirits more wicked than himself, and they enter and dwell there; and the last *state* of that man is worse than the first. So shall it also be with this wicked generation.'"

Here, we see a multitude of unclean spirits. These unclean spirits range in power and function. Clearly, if someone "opens a door" by, for example, perpetually disobeying God by watching pornography, then, by spiritual legal laws, an unclean spirit is (or unclean spirits are) *permitted* by God to enter the individual (whether they are an unbeliever or a believer). This is clearly demonstrated in the life of King Saul.

King Saul perpetually disobeyed God and ignored the Word of the Lord. Instead, he went his own way. Due to his perpetual disobedience, God permitted an unclean spirit to rush into King Saul. Not only did this occur, but God took His Holy Spirit from Him! 1 Samuel 16:14-23 (NKJV) states:

> "But the Spirit of the Lord departed from Saul, and a distressing spirit from the Lord troubled him. And Saul's servants said to him, "Surely, a distressing spirit from God is troubling you. Let our master now command your servants, *who are* before you, to seek out a man *who is* a skillful player on the harp. And it shall be that he will play it with his hand when the distressing spirit from God is upon you, and you shall be well."
>
> So Saul said to his servants, "Provide me now a man who can play well, and bring *him* to me."
>
> Then one of the servants answered and said, "Look, I have seen a son of Jesse the Bethlehemite, *who is* skillful in playing, a mighty man of valor, a man of war, prudent in speech, and a handsome person; and the Lord *is* with him."
>
> Therefore Saul sent messengers to Jesse, and said, "Send me your son David, who *is* with the sheep." And Jesse took a donkey *loaded with* bread, a skin of wine, and a young goat, and sent *them* by his son David to Saul. So David came to Saul and stood before him. And he loved him greatly, and he became his armorbearer. Then Saul sent to

Jesse, saying, "Please let David stand before me, for he has found favor in my sight." And so it was, whenever the spirit from God was upon Saul, that David would take a harp and play *it* with his hand. Then Saul would become refreshed and well, and the distressing spirit would depart from him."

A brief point to note is that when problems arise, and God allows demons and unclean spirits to come, it is always to work out evil for a greater good (Genesis 50:20). Of course, it is due to our perpetual disobedience that unclean spirits can enter us. However, thanks be to God, that it is in the name of Jesus that demons flee!

"'And these signs will follow those who believe: In My name they will cast out demons; they will speak with new tongues; they will take up serpents; and if they drink anything deadly, it will by no means hurt them; they will lay hands on the sick, and they will recover'" (Mark 16:17-18 NKJV).

Many times, people's problems provide the way for God to make us the solution. For King Saul, through his disobedience, we see that "the Spirit of the LORD departed from Saul, and a distressing spirit from the LORD troubled him" (1 Samuel 16:14 NKJV).

It is a grave danger to perpetually sin against God and not repent and want to change from our sin. Of course, there are the prodigal sons who come back from time to time, but there is no such thing as a perpetual prodigal son. When God's Spirit lives in us, we can't continue to keep on sinning. If we do, we will grieve and quench the Holy Spirit and open ourselves up to not only demons, but a Divine Ultimatum – choosing God and seeking His help to conquer sin, or choosing sin for the rest of our lives. Those who have this moment (as I had after being stuck in pornography for 10+ years) know exactly when God speaks. To choose the wrong answer and vouch for our sin is to commit the unpardonable sin. Matthew 12:31-32 (NKJV) states:

"'Therefore I say to you, every sin and blasphemy will be forgiven men, but the blasphemy *against* the Spirit will not be forgiven men. Anyone who speaks a word against the Son of Man, it will be forgiven him; but whoever speaks against the Holy Spirit, it will not be forgiven him, either in this age or in the *age* to come.'"

To blaspheme the Holy Spirit is to make a *conscious, deliberate, intentional* decision to forsake God and choose our way until death. If this is truly a person's desire (and not an emotional outburst or an overzealous anger toward God that is short-lived), God knows the heart and will allow them to go against Him. If He sees that this decision will truly dictate the rest of their lives and that it is their genuine desire, God will have His Holy Spirit depart from that believer (just as He did with King Saul).

This is also evident in the story of Moses and Pharaoh. When you read Exodus carefully, you will find that, for the most part, Pharaoh hardens his heart toward God at the beginning. Eventually, we see a shift where God hardens Pharaoh's heart. In very simplistic terms, Pharaoh has the free will to harden his heart. God is not surprised by this, but there comes a point where God says, "You think that you have the final say and can continue to harden your heart against Me? I am the Sovereign Lord and Maker of Heaven and Earth. I have given you the gift of libertarian free will within the time and boundaries I permit. Do you think you will have the final say and go against me, hardening your heart? No, I will have the final say. I will harden your heart. You perpetually used the gift I gave you in disobedience. I am now taking over and giving you your heart's desire, but I am Omnipotent and will be the one to harden your heart."

This is a very important passage for understanding one of the ways in which human libertarian free will operates amid God's Sovereignty.

Now, does this happen on a wide scale of born-again believers? No, but it is a reality to monitor. That is why the Lord Jesus Christ Himself said, "'But he who endures to the end shall be saved'" (Matthew 24:13 NKJV). Endurance is part of working *out* our salvation (not working *for* our salvation), which can only be done with the help, aid, power, conviction, encouragement, and strength of the Holy Spirit.

Continuing on, we see that God provided David as the answer to the problem Saul was facing. God gave David favor in the sight of King Saul. In a like manner, God will give us favor when we steward well the season He has us in and the gifts He has given. Discerning of spirits is one of these gifts.

From a young age, I have always had discernment. God gifted me with the ability to discern people's true intentions and perceive what their hearts consisted of, and whether they were truly for God or not. This gift began in High School, but it "fully" unlocked on a spiritual level once I got married.

I remember looking at pictures of people and having a word of knowledge or a thought about the person. I didn't know them, but I would look and say, "Oh, this person looks crazy," or "this person is prideful."

Now, it's very easy to cast a stone and believe I was being judgmental. What I was seeing but not understanding was the spirits within the people. I was noticing what they were about on a spiritual level, and I did not even know them.

This is why I have always been able to get along with others (aside from standing for the Truth of God's Word, which many despise) and know what they are truly about – God answers and reveals what He desires at His Own Will.

As I got married, once I received the gift of tongues (which we will discuss in the appropriate Chapter to come), I received this gift.

Speaking in tongues can unlock other gifts. When God truly gives the gift of tongues, it allows one to understand and appreciate spiritual gifts all the more. From my understanding and experience, those with the gift of tongues most certainly possess at least one other gift of the Spirit.

Once you receive the gift, you know God is real. You should know before, but when the gifts come, you know all the more.

Everything that is in Scripture and everything that God does is a means of revealing Himself, drawing us to Him, and giving Him honor, glory, and praise. When demons are cast out by the name of "Jesus", you know the Lord Jesus Christ is the Son of God. There is no guesswork. Demons don't flee at the name of "John" or "James". They are strictly cast out by the Name of Jesus!

As I received the gift of discerning of spirits, I will never forget the first night my journey began (I have written extensively more on stories in the spiritual realm, casting out unclean spirits, encounters with demons, and deliverance in my book *The Realm Beyond*). These sorts of spiritual realities began to occur predominantly after I got married, and there is a reason for that.

I grew up in a Protestant, Baptist home. I had never heard of demons, deliverance, or the gifts of the Spirit until I listened to a deliverance video by Derek Prince. From struggling with masturbation practically every day, praying and wanting to stop but not getting an answer, God led and revealed to me how deliverance is genuine and real. As I write this (01/14/2025), it has been 7+ years since I have masturbated or had the desire. When God set me free through deliverance in the name of Jesus and speaking out against the spirit that was enslaving me to masturbate, everything changed.

Back to the story of when my gift of the discerning of spirits really had awoken. I was in my home office with my wife. She came in, and I began reading her a Chapter of one of my books. She enjoyed me sharing it with her, and was very supportive (as she typically is – I am blessed!). Afterward, we shared our hearts about a particular matter. I will never forget that when I shared my heart about something that hurt my feelings, there was a chuckle. I asked her, "Why did you laugh?" She said, "What do you mean? I didn't laugh." I said, "Yes, you did. I think it's kind of inappropriate to be laughing. It doesn't make sense considering what I just shared." She then just stared at me with a little grin.

As we looked at each other, I saw something almost move in her eyes. It isn't easy to describe to someone who does not possess this gift, but others who do have the gift know precisely what I see. I hunched over, and I said, "I... I feel like I see something." She then said, "What do you mean?" I said, "I feel like I saw something different... something in your eyes." From there, I had my first encounter with an unclean spirit. To know what happens, you will have to get my book *The Realm Beyond*, as the purpose of this book is to bring understanding to each gift.

I share this to make you well aware that I know what I am talking about and that this is not guesswork. This is real, and there are spiritual realities that spring forth when one possesses the Holy Spirit and the Holy Spirit bestows particular gifts.

As a very brief note, I know many will say, "A Christian cannot have an unclean spirit". To that, I briefly reply, "They can." Deliverance is the children's bread (Mark 7:24-30). When we are children of God by becoming born-again through believing Jesus Christ is Lord and Savior and repenting of our sins, deliverance is ours. We don't want demons to hinder, enslave, compel, or make us addicted to that which grieves the heart of God. We must repent, renounce, and rebuke all unclean spirits from within us. As this occurs, we then cast them out by their name and function in the name of Jesus.

Christians can have unclean spirits. Even Mary had to get demons cast out of her after following Jesus for some time. "Mary called Magdalene, out of whom had come seven demons" (Luke 8:2 NKJV). This is not something to write off or shy away from; it is not about being too arrogant, boastful, or proud. Pride keeps demons in, whereas humility opens the door for them to leave.

If a Christian has a season of backsliding or a moment of, for example, fornicating and having sex with someone, they open themselves to receiving unclean spirits. This can happen when we are born again. That is why our bodies are called temples. In a temple, multiple people can dwell. The Holy Spirit may occupy 95% of our temple, but the remaining 5% consists of unclean spirits, so we need to seek God for deliverance. It is not complicated or something to be embarrassed about, as we all have unclean spirits, which also come through generational curses through the bloodline. "For I, the Lord your God, *am* a jealous God, visiting the iniquity of the fathers upon the children to the third and fourth *generations* of those who hate Me" (Deuteronomy 5:9 NKJV). The question is, what will we do about it, and if we are open to deliverance, what spirits need to go? This is where the gift of discerning spirits comes into play.

Those with the gift of discerning spirits can see what demons individuals possess. Though some have spoken on how they see the spiritual realm habitually, I currently do not have that sort of manifestation of the gift. I predominantly see unclean spirits in individuals' eyes and in how their bodies and faces move.

Let us focus on the eyes for a moment. When you have the gift of discerning spirits, you can detect whether someone has a particular spirit. Combined with the gift of the word of knowledge, you can see spirits of pride, lust, anger, death, depression, insanity, witchcraft, greed, and the like. These come in the way of what you see on a spiritual level within the eyes.

Typically, it is found in a range of blackness and in the depth of blackness in people's eyes. Pride usually has a black, grayish glow, whereas the spirit of death is entirely black. Anger, hate, and resentment have a strong sense of murder. If you have ever felt angry to the point of wanting to hurt someone, you feel that in the eyes of who you are seeing. If it comes to lust, such as pornography, it is a lighter tone of darkness that presents a feeling of shame and guilt.

Each regulation of the blackness, associated with the feeling each color emits, brings forth understanding as to what the unclean spirit is that you are viewing.

Again, this is tough to explain to someone without the gift. Nonetheless, it is a potent gift, as you can discern the spirits within individuals and when they manifest. You can know during deliverance what unclean spirits need to be cast out (as, again, you cast out demons by their name and function). This helps in the deliverance process and also serves as a hidden gift to protect oneself from manipulative, deceptive, and the like.

With the gift of discerning spirits, there is a range of intimidation. Some spirits are more intimidating than others. In my work with deliverance, the greater the intimidation, the greater the slant toward spirits of murder or toward revealing the strongman.

It would be helpful to briefly review the Scriptural proof for some of the points we have mentioned. When it comes to casting out demons by name and their function, we see these truths evident in the following Scriptures:

> **Blind and mute spirit**: "Then one was brought to Him who was demon-possessed, blind and mute; and He healed him, so that the blind and mute man both spoke and saw" (Matthew 12:22 NKJV).
>
> **Deceiving spirits**: "Now the Spirit expressly says that in latter times some will depart from the faith, giving heed to deceiving spirits and doctrines of demons" (1 Timothy 4:1 NKJV).

Spirit of fear: "For God has not given us a spirit of fear, but of power and of love and of a sound mind" (2 Timothy 1:7 NKJV).

Legion (many demons): "Jesus asked him, saying, "What is your name?" And he said, "Legion," because many demons had entered him" (Luke 8:30 NKJV). This Scripture is important to understand, as during deliverance sessions, you can speak to them and say, "In the name of Jesus, what is your name?" It may take a few minutes of repeating the question, but eventually, they must fold.

It is also important to know that people can have many demons within them. A legion back then in certain armies was around 4,000-5,000 soldiers! Though we have listed only a few demons, people can have hundreds or thousands. It is no cause for concern aside from seeking deliverance. As this occurs, a feeling of lightness and relief happens. Certain aspects of your personality will change, as demons would latch onto certain aspects of who you are and rise up at opportune moments prior to deliverance. Anger quickly turns into rage when demons are present. Impatience and irritation are sure to follow if someone does something that we are not entirely fond of. Other aspects of control, manipulation, and criticalness can also be led by, or at the very least enhanced by, unclean spirits.

The gift of the discerning of spirits makes these realities known over time. The more you are in the ministry of deliverance, the more you begin to understand these realities.

It is very important to address that many pretend to cast out demons, and they even go so far as to hire people to fake getting delivered! The gift of the discerning of spirits helps one to also discern the thoughts and intentions of people's hearts (as God permits and leads) to show who is truly of Him and who is putting on a show or seeking money. That is why God is explicitly clear that "'Many will say to Me in that day, 'Lord, Lord, have we not prophesied in Your name, cast out demons in Your name, and done many wonders in Your name?' And then I will declare to them, 'I never knew you; depart from Me, you who practice lawlessness!'" (Matthew 7:22-23 NKJV).

We must never fake or pretend what only God can do. Too many people are deceptive and manipulative, and the Holy Spirit will not only expose them but also give individuals discernment to understand the spirit and intent behind others.

The Lord Jesus Christ not only knew the unclean spirits in individuals, but also the positive spirits. Now, what we mean by "positive spirit" is the proper disposition toward life and others. It is not that good spirits are going from place to place. When someone is of a "pure spirit" or a "joyful spirit", this is exercised by the Holy Spirit, but it is an exemplification of what consists within a man or woman.

"Jesus saw Nathanael coming toward Him, and said of him, 'Behold, an Israelite indeed, in whom is no deceit!'" (John 1:47 NKJV). Jesus had a word of knowledge and discernment to see a spirit of truth, with no deceit. He declared what kind of man Nathanael was and the spirit that was in him.

The gift of discerning spirits allows one to recognize the true good in individuals. It gives people the ability to not operate just on nice deeds and acts of service, but to see directly to the true spirit behind specific actions. If someone possesses a particular fruit of the Holy Spirit that is enhanced above others, those with this gift can tell instantly. "But the fruit of the Spirit is love, joy, peace, longsuffering, kindness, goodness, faithfulness, gentleness, self-control" (Galatians 5:22-23 NKJV). When someone possesses one of these fruits in greater measure than the others, discerning of spirits allows an individual to know what others are about and whether they are truly of God and can be trusted.

"And behold, there was a woman who had a spirit of infirmity eighteen years, and was bent over and could in no way raise herself up. But when Jesus saw her, He called her to Him and said to her, "Woman, you are loosed from your infirmity." And He laid His hands on her, and immediately she was made straight, and glorified God" (Luke 13:11-13 NKJV).

Many times, problems in the body, nervous system, bloodstream, and other physical ailments are due to demons. This notion sounds bizarre upon first hearing. I remember hearing Derek Prince speak on this matter and not understanding it, but believing it, nonetheless.

The complete extraction of stories that will give you goosebumps is found in my book *The Realm Beyond*, but this happened to me at the end of some of my deliverances.

I have had my leg grow in line with my other leg (from my Wife's gift of healing). I have had a loosening of perpetual tightness around my neck (due to Leviathan, pride, stubbornness, and being "stiff-necked"). I had the spirit of Lucifer (not Satan, but a spirit that is filled with ego and entitlement), as seen in Isaiah 14. Once I got delivered, the pain and misalignment in my spine went away. When I got the spirit of bitterness and envy out, my continual back pain went away.

All of this occurred because I chose, by faith, to believe the entirety of God's Word and receive deliverance. As this happened, I became healed, set free, and physical ailments and certain infirmities vanished!

This makes sense when you consider that unclean spirits dwell in our bodies. Where specifically, it depends on the function and role the demon takes on. Someone continually filled with lust is going to have a spirit of lust in the mind. Someone who continually gossips will have a spirit of gossip in their mouth or tongue. Those who have partaken in yoga and other "spiritual" practices that appear good and friendly but actually invite a koondalini spirit (a false Holy Spirit) will manifest with their tongue. A spirit of murder can be found near the heart. Greed is found in the cheeks and in how one smiles.

There are many different locations and reasons why spirits reside in certain parts of our bodies. With the gift of discerning spirits, this is learned and made known over time. When spirits dwell in certain parts of our bodies, they affect how we feel, think, act, and move forward in our activities and in life. It is essential to seek deliverance if one suffers from ailments and can recognize and be honest with themselves about, for example, bitterness.

Bitterness will keep one in a hunchback position until deliverance occurs. It may sound somewhat crazy, but the Pharisees thought Jesus to be crazy, but He was the Son of God. The ways of God are not the ways of man, and there are spiritual realities that can only be discerned through spiritual giftings given by the Holy Spirit.

"Now it happened, as we went to prayer, that a certain slave girl possessed with a spirit of divination met us, who brought her masters much profit by fortune-telling. This girl followed Paul and us, and cried out, saying, "These men are the servants of the Most High God, who proclaim to us the way of salvation." And this she did for many days.

But Paul, greatly annoyed, turned and said to the spirit, "I command you in the name of Jesus Christ to come out of her." And he came out that very hour" (Acts 16:16-18 NKJV).

Spirits associated with divination and fortune-telling are very real. They can provide correct answers and offer others a means to make money and gain positions of power. Yet, despite this being the case, we know that He Who is in us is greater than he that is in the world (1 John 4:4).

Some spirits are seen as "good" by wicked and evil men, and they will seek out specific individuals or witches, wizards, and warlocks to perform what they can due to having a particular demon of, for example, "divination" in them.

Paul the Apostle had the discernment to recognize that the slave girl had a spirit in her, and he eventually used his gift to command it to leave in the Name of Jesus Christ. The spirit left, and I am sure her masters were very upset with Paul. She was the means by which they made a lot of money, but now she was unable to do so.

Many people would rather keep demons in them than get them out. Ironically, it is when they get cast out that we grow, mature, become more pure, and are less hindered. We open the doors to God's blessing when we are born again because a demon is no longer keeping us in a particular state of thinking, a bad habit, or a sinful lifestyle. Yes, there is free will and responsibility to do what is right, but demons make the process much more difficult – especially when one wants to stop what they know they should, but they cannot, and it seems like an impossible feat.

It is important to note that when Paul cast the demon out of the girl, the masters did not come after him and kill him. Sometimes, we may think that it is risky business getting demons out, but that is a lie of the Enemy. As long as we are doing the Lord's Will, He will protect us. "When a man's ways please the LORD, He makes even his enemies to be at peace with him" (Proverbs 16:7 NKJV).

"But a certain man named Ananias, with Sapphira his wife, sold a possession. And he kept back *part* of the proceeds, his wife also being aware *of it,* and brought a certain part and laid *it* at the apostles' feet. But Peter said, "Ananias, why has Satan filled your heart to lie to the Holy

Spirit and keep back *part* of the price of the land for yourself? While it remained, was it not your own? And after it was sold, was it not in your own control? Why have you conceived this thing in your heart? You have not lied to men but to God." Then Ananias, hearing these words, fell down and breathed his last. So great fear came upon all those who heard these things. And the young men arose and wrapped him up, carried *him* out, and buried *him*" (Acts 5:1-6 NKJV).

Peter had the gift of discerning of spirits to know that Satan filled the heart of Ananias and that he was lying. What was supposed to be given wholly to God was only shown in part. This is a serious matter and one that cost his life!

It is a grave sin to lie, especially to God. "A false witness will not go unpunished, And *he who* speaks lies will not escape" (Proverbs 19:5 NKJV). "Lying lips *are* an abomination to the Lord, But those who deal truthfully *are* His delight" (Proverbs 12:22 NKJV). "The truthful lip shall be established forever, But a lying tongue *is* but for a moment" (Proverbs 12:19 NKJV).

"These six *things* the Lord hates, Yes, seven *are* an abomination to Him: A proud look, A lying tongue, Hands that shed innocent blood, A heart that devises wicked plans, Feet that are swift in running to evil, A false witness *who* speaks lies, And one who sows discord among brethren" (Proverbs 6:16-19 NKJV).

God hates lying lips, and there are severe consequences for those who perpetually lie. God has a holy and righteous hatred toward Satan, whom Jesus declares is the father of lies. "'You are of *your* father the devil, and the desires of your father you want to do. He was a murderer from the beginning, and does not stand in the truth, because there is no truth in him. When he speaks a lie, he speaks from his own *resources,* for he is a liar and the father of it'" (John 8:44 NKJV).

We cannot expect to lie and prosper. We cannot claim to be of God when we continuously lie to others. Greater still, when we lie to God, very extreme repercussions will occur, as it cost Ananias his life.

Peter had the discernment from God to detect that Ananias was lying and did not give everything. This gifting is very powerful as it keeps individuals from being deceived and manipulated. It leaves no room for others to do us evil. It is a beautiful gift that can be used for much good. For those who have the gift, use it well, in the guidance of the Holy Spirit.

It is important to note that, as with any gift, God is in control of this one. We cannot lose the gift, but it doesn't mean it is always activated. I share this because there were moments I thought I lost my gift of discerning spirits.

The first half of my marriage was marked by a lot of spiritual insight through my gifting and by seeing many spirits. After that occurred, however, there was a brief transition. The gift was still there, and I would notice demons in people's eyes as I would go out, but it wasn't like before. I may have been able to detect unclean spirits in one to two people's eyes, whereas before, I was noticing demons in everyone's eyes. I would come home having witnessed demons in 30, 40, 50+ people!

God began to reveal to me that He is in charge of what He reveals and when the gifting is activated. He showed me that sometimes He will prevent me from seeing, in people's eyes, the spirits they have, because it would be too much.

When the gifting started to settle down, I was going through a tremendous season of change, moving out of State (when we had just moved), Jackie getting pregnant, switching jobs, and going through narcissistic abuse of various kinds from specific individuals (who I will not name at this time to protect them). In all of this, God had finally released me to receive revelation beyond what I could ever fathom. Some of the books are currently out, but I have been working on a multi-volume series on the Characteristics of God that introduces hundreds of new attributes – something only God could reveal and do! This will be one of my lifelong works, and the series is called *The Infinite Omni*.

When we are going through a lot in our lives, God will protect us and help us not see everything. That would have been too overwhelming for me at the time of everything going on. He dialed the gift back, allowed it to remain in use, but, given my current season, made sure I did not continually see demons in people's eyes.

God will do this with every gift out of love, as we are not infinite beings who can take in the full measure of everything. Imagine the person with the word of knowledge gift continually receiving knowledge of everyone they know and knowing everything that will occur.

They would become exhausted and could not live in the present! God is in charge of the gifting, and we need not worry if we lose a gift just because it "is not as strong as it used to be". God is in control, and He does this out of love. "For the gifts and the calling of God *are* irrevocable" (Romans 11:29 NKJV).

It is important to understand that as one grows in the gift of discerning of spirits, they will begin to discern certain spirits over specific environments and groups. When Scripture declares, "For we do not wrestle against flesh and blood, but against principalities, against powers, against the rulers of the darkness of this age, against spiritual *hosts* of wickedness in the heavenly *places*" (Ephesians 6:12 NKJV), we see a range of different roles and functions. Not all demons and unclean spirits are the same. Just as God has a hierarchy of His angels for various roles and functions, so does Satan with those who side with him.

Daniel 10:12-14 (NKJV) reveals the encounter Daniel had with an angel after he had a vision:

> "Then he said to me, 'Do not fear, Daniel, for from the first day that you set your heart to understand, and to humble yourself before your God, your words were heard; and I have come because of your words. But the prince of the kingdom of Persia withstood me twenty-one days; and behold, Michael, one of the chief princes, came to help me, for I had been left alone there with the kings of Persia. Now I have come to make you understand what will happen to your people in the latter days, for the vision *refers* to *many* days *to come.*'"

Here, we see that the prince of the kingdom of Persia withheld the angel from relaying the message for 21 days. This is why prayer is so important: Prayer speeds up the process of what can occur, or a lack of prayer can slow it down. Prayer can provide aid in the spiritual war we do not see, or a lack of prayer can give greater power to the Enemy to steal, kill, and destroy (John 10:10).

After the angel visits Daniel, further along in Daniel 10, verses 20-21 (NKJV) specifically state:

"Then he said, 'Do you know why I have come to you? And now I must return to fight with the prince of Persia; and when I have gone forth, indeed the prince of Greece will come. But I will tell you what is noted in the Scripture of Truth. (No one upholds me against these, except Michael your prince)'" (Daniel 10:20-21 NKJV).

Here, we see there are "princes" over certain nations in the spiritual realm. If Satan is referred to as the god of this world (2 Corinthians 4:4) and ruler of the world (John 12:31, John 14:30), and if there are princes who oversee nations, then it logically follows that there are principalities, powers, rulers of darkness, and spiritual hosts that oversee states, countries, cities, neighborhoods, and households.

Have you ever wondered why there is a commonality in specific locations? It does not take long when you have the gift of discerning spirits to know that there are hidden, underlying spiritual matters behind many aspects. There is a reason why, if you visit specific locations in the world, even those without this gift feel a very dark presence.

When you look at specific neighborhoods, some are extremely dirty. Just as the old saying goes, "birds of a feather flock together", so demons of one accord share similar cohorts.

Why is perversion rampant in some cities, but not in others? Demons. Why are some cities so much more violent and dark than others? Is it the people? No, it is demons. Why do certain groups of friends come together? It is because of the spirits that are in them.

It is not a fascinating wonder why a family of narcissists gets angry and upset at the scapegoat who finally sees reality for what it is, sets up boundaries due to continual abusive behavior, and does not want to partake in a family of abusers, manipulators, gossipers, and slanderers. Though people are responsible for allowing unclean spirits to come forth, there is a vital reality to understand: when you begin to wake up to spiritual matters, the demons within individuals will not be happy. Instead, they are going to ramp up their anger and rage toward you, attempting to make your life ten times more difficult. This is why going no-contact with people who do not respect your boundaries is important.

When your boundaries are appropriate and meant to protect your heart, since we are commanded to, for "out of it *spring* the issues of life" (Proverbs 4:23 NKJV), and they are not respected by others, it is because the demons in them hate that you have perceived their mission. When you call out demons in others, they ramp up one hundredfold. Demons are not for you, and when they are found out in other individuals, and they know you have the gift of discerning spirits, and you call them out, the hate and rage that will come against you will become much more severe.

When these truths begin to open up to you, you will see that these spirits are not just localized to environments but groups of people. There is a reason why certain ethnicities and nationalities have their common ways of speaking and acting, but also have a multitude of bad habits and ways of doing life that seem normal to them but, from a Biblical perspective, are sinful and wrong.

Much of culture is dictated by demonic activity. Have you ever found it peculiar how, not all, but a vast majority of people within a specific ethnicity or community gossip and are all about image? How others are prone to legalism? How some believe it to be okay to be overly sensual? How some find it absolutely okay to partake in witchcraft?

Have you ever found it strange that, within certain groups and locations, many seem to always struggle financially? Many ethnicities buy into the culture and do not allow their children to develop their own identity in Christ Jesus. Rather, they become enmeshed with a parent (or both parents) and are forced to do precisely what the parents want in terms of career and lifestyle. There is no freedom or the ability to follow God, only what the parents want.

Discerning of spirits also opens up greater insight into genders. Is it any wonder why even genders have their own specific struggles (Of course, not everything is universal, and there is overlap in what is to be said, but it is simply to give a basic level of understanding about the reality of what we are discussing)? Men having anxiety in caring for their family? Women having anxiety about how they look? Husbands finding it more difficult to *love* their wives? Wives finding it more difficult to *respect* their husbands?

These realities are not for everyone. However, there is a sort of common theme seen throughout time and from generation to generation. This is due to strongholds that need to be bound in the name of Jesus and demons being cast out!

I have gotten to a point where, when I walk into a building, I feel a dark spiritual presence. I can sense if this place is truly of God or not. I received a word of knowledge about what takes place in certain buildings. The Holy Spirit helps me discern whether I should eat at a particular restaurant.

My wife has this gift in part. We will walk into a restaurant, and both of us will sense whether or not we should be there. There are even restaurants we have eaten in, where I know child-trafficking discussions and wicked business deals have been done... one day, I will speak on this horrific reality in much greater detail. For now, it is important to understand that the Holy Spirit reveals all of this in greater measure as time goes on and we press into the Presence and Word of God.

We who have the gift, and those of us who are born-again and walk with God, must "not believe every spirit, but test the spirits, whether they are of God; because many false prophets have gone out into the world" (1 John 4:1 NKJV). There are too many who "are false apostles, deceitful workers, transforming themselves into apostles of Christ. And no wonder! For Satan himself transforms himself into an angel of light. Therefore it is no great thing if his ministers also transform themselves into ministers of righteousness, whose end will be according to their works" (2 Corinthians 11:13-15 NKJV).

We must desire to be those who possess the most incredible gift outside of God Himself that can only come from God Himself: *Discernment* (I will be writing on this extensively later on in this book at the appropriate Chapter).

Without discernment, we will be tossed to-and-fro, manipulated, deceived, believing whatever fits our lifestyle and opinions, and we will not operate in sound wisdom. This is why Solomon prayed to God, "Therefore give to Your servant an understanding heart to judge Your people, that I may discern between good and evil. For who is able to judge this great people of Yours?" (1 Kings 3:9 NKJV). To receive understanding of the Holy One of Israel is to increase in discernment, and to increase discernment is the wisdom to perceive what is good and evil, what is of God and what is of the Enemy, what is according to the Word and what is against It, what is virtue and what is sinful.

Others can recognize the Holy Spirit in us, whether or not they have the gift. "Now when the sons of the prophets who *were* from Jericho saw him, they said, 'The spirit of Elijah rests on Elisha'" (2 Kings 2:15 NKJV). When the Holy Spirit is fully ruling and reigning within us, others can discern something different about us. It is not just what we do, but it is the Spirit within us that they can discern and sense.

The gift of discerning of spirits is to detect evil, but also to reveal good. It can confirm whether someone is truly born again and who possesses similar mantles. It helps us discern if we should take someone at their word or if there is mischief, deceit, and craftiness behind what is being said and done.

Though all is done by the Holy Spirit, Who is One of the Three in the Holy Trinity, we can nonetheless relate to different people in Scripture. This is because not all of us are called to have the wisdom and wealth of Solomon, or the boldness and martyrdom of Peter. Whatever God chooses for our lives, people with the gift of discerning of spirits will truly detect not just the Holy Spirit within us, but also the similar calling He has placed on our lives, as those of old. For Elisha, the sons of the prophets saw the spirit of Elijah (i.e., the life-giving calling and mantle from the Holy Spirit). Not only was this true, but Elisha received a double portion (2 Kings 2:9-10) and went on to do mighty works.

Let us go to God, requesting of Him this gift, that we might become greater saints who partake in deliverance, bring healing, and help set people free in the Name of Jesus from the bondage of demons!

God in Heaven, Who alone is All-Wise, knowing what shall be before it comes to pass, Who alone is Immortal and Invisible, Who takes in all information and is the Creator of information itself, Who does not grow tired or weary, Whose Understanding is Infinite and Greatness is Unsearchable, Who perceives all things simultaneously and in an instant, You alone are aware of all that was, is, and shall be. You alone are Him Who Was, Is, and will always Be. God, we bless Your Holy Name! God, prepare us to receive and steward well the gift of discerning of spirits. God, grant us this gift to protect ourselves and others. God, we want to help other people. We ourselves want ot be delivered from unclean spirits and demons. We want others to be set free! God, if it is in Your Will, bless us with the gift of discerning of spirits. May we use it only for Your Glory, not for self-gain or for being puffed up. God, we ask that You would give us the gifts of the Spirit to move mountains in this life. O God, we bless You and believe You will answer, according to Your Omniscient, Providential Wisdom, Guidance, and Counsel. May Thy Will be done, on Earth as it is in Heaven. In Jesus' name, Amen.

The Gift of Tongues

"*To another different kinds of tongues.*"
– 1 Corinthians 12:10 NKJV

The gift of speaking in tongues can only come from God. It is not the ability to speak other languages. Though that is a *skill set* that God equips specific individuals with, as He has a purpose for some speaking multiple languages and others excelling with just their native tongue, the gift of speaking in tongues is not speaking a different language, but a heavenly tongue.

"For he who speaks in a tongue does not speak to men but to God, for no one understands him; however, in the spirit he speaks mysteries" (1 Corinthians 14:2 NKJV). The gift of speaking in tongues is not talking to man in a particular language, but in a heavenly language that is directly toward God Almighty.

It is essential to address that there has been a perversion and mockery in the house of God with those who believe they have tongues or can be *taught* the gift. This gift cannot be taught; it is given and performed only by the Holy Spirit.

It is very easy to speak in babble. It is not difficult to make up words. When someone pretends to have the gift or has "been taught the gift of tongues", they severely damage the ability for people to believe that the gift of tongues is truly a Heavenly gift and real.

In many undiscerning Pentecostal circles, there is this notion that one can teach someone this gift. Some common training involves working yourself up to a state of speaking in tongues. Others say, "just start to loosen your tongue" and start babbling. It is nothing more than stupidity and lunacy. These are strong words to describe what is occurring, but they are absolutely true. God is not mocked, and neither will the gifts He gives be mocked (lest we become like the Pharisees).

People are so quick to believe man rather than go to God for an answer or remedy, and it is no wonder that certain denominations dismiss this gift. It is not a justification for their position, but is an understanding of the discernment that other individuals recognize that people are making up the gift of tongues through babble. This is not a means to disregard the Bible entirely; however, it reveals that this is a true gift.

When men such as David Wilkerson, Derek Prince, and A.W. Tozer spoke of having this gift, we can be sure it is genuine. Even above their profession of having this gift, the Scriptures are unambiguous that there is such a thing as a heavenly tongue.

Before we go into the Scripture, it is important to understand that I was in this camp. I would hear other people work themselves up, and the Holy Ghost within me gave me the discernment to recognize that it was fake. People were putting on a show, pretending to have something that they did not.

Despite my discernment, I did not go in the way many do and completely dismiss the gift. I looked at the Word of God and saw very clearly that there is a heavenly tongue. Having grown up in a Baptist/Protestant home, I, of course, had no idea what it actually looked like or sounded like to have the gift. Nevertheless, it was in the Word of God, and I believed, though I did not have the gift.

I began praying for the gift of speaking in tongues when I was 22-to-23 years old. I prayed almost every day for months. Nothing came, and I thought, "Well, I guess God doesn't want me to have the gift. I still believe the gift is real, but it's not for me."

When it comes to praying for gifts, it is important to note that God has a perfect time of answering. Had I received it at that age, I am most certain pride would have begun to take root. I would have been boastful and most likely deceived myself into believing I was favored above others to receive the gift. Sadly, this is what happens for many individuals.

Many people think themselves to be better because they speak in a heavenly tongue, but it is just a revealment of one of the gifts God has given that individual. There is no cause for being puffed up, nor is it a means of truly being saved.

Many charismatics will say, "To be born-again, you have to speak in tongues." This is prominent within certain circles that do not stick to the Word of God but place their own ideology above sound Theology.

You do not need to speak in tongues to be saved. I repeat, you DO NOT need to speak in tongues to be saved. You need to have the Holy Spirit residing in you to be truly saved and born again (which happens through true belief in Jesus Christ as Lord and Savior and genuine repentance of one's sins). Speaking in tongues is simply a gift given by God at His Own discretion.

After some time, I stopped praying for the gift. Years went by, and I would pray maybe a couple of times a year, asking for the gift, but it was no longer a priority for me. When I got married, however, I ended up receiving the gift. It occurred during one of the times my wife and I were doing a deliverance session. After that, I asked her to pray for the gift for me and to impart it to me (as she had the gift).

My wife, Jackie, had never spoken in tongues in front of me prior. This was something I wanted and felt led to ask, as I knew we, as born-again believers, could impart gifts to one another (as the Lord leads and allows). "For I long to see you, that I may impart to you some spiritual gift, so that you may be established— that is, that I may be encouraged together with you by the mutual faith both of you and me" (Romans 1:11-12 NKJV).

As Jackie laid her hands on me and prayed, I began to feel Someone taking over my tongue. I whispered what was being said, as I was embarrassed. It was so new to me, and I wasn't sure if this was it – that I had actually received the gift. "And when Paul had laid hands on them, the Holy Spirit came upon them, and they spoke with tongues and prophesied" (Acts 19:6 NKJV). My wife imparted her gift of speaking in tongues to me through the laying on of hands, and God allowed me to receive the gift.

Within 24 hours, I began speaking louder and more confidently and boldly. I knew how to speak gibberish. It was easy for me to babble, but this was something different and unique. It sounded like a language. It was amazing to have finally received the gift!

Now, it is important to understand that the gift is meant for the edification of oneself *and* for the body *when* there is someone who has the gift of interpretation of tongues (As of writing this Chapter on 01/16/2025, I have yet to receive the gift of interpretation of tongues or meet anyone who has the gift). When I do, it will be extraordinary, as it can only be of God to interpret a heavenly tongue that is different from all worldly languages.

"While Peter was still speaking these words, the Holy Spirit fell upon all those who heard the word. And those of the circumcision who believed were astonished, as many as came with Peter, because the gift of the Holy Spirit had been poured out on the Gentiles also. For they heard them speak with tongues and magnify God" (Acts 10:44-46 NKJV). Pharisees and narcissistic "Christians" will instantly dismiss the gifts of God. Why? They are not truly of God, only pretenders. They are white-washed tombs (Matthew 23:27) and, as my wife puts it, "they harden their hearts against the Holy Spirit and His Voice. If this is the case, how much more His gifts?"

Those who are humble of spirit will marvel at those who *truly* have the gift of speaking in tongues. It will be mysterious and maybe a bit weird to hear at first, but they will be amazed and magnify God! This, of course, should only be done when there is someone to interpret. If no one has the gift of interpretation of tongues, then tongues should not be permitted *in* the church *during* a service.

"If anyone speaks in a tongue, let there be two or at the most three, each in turn, and let one interpret. But if there is no interpreter, let him keep silent in church, and let him speak to himself and to God" (1 Corinthians 14:27-28 NKJV). There are churches out there where, while a pastor is preaching, someone in the back is speaking in tongues, going to and fro across the room. It is very disruptive and distracts people from taking in God's Word.

We gather for multiple reasons, but we all want to hear and grow in the Word of God. If someone —or even a few people —are speaking in tongues during a service, it is a distraction and puffs up the ego of the individual. Scripture is unequivocal on this matter: there should be a person who can interpret tongues, and there should be a dedicated time for this, not a Pastor multitasking by preaching a service out loud while another person is speaking in tongues in the back. The same is true for a Pastor who preaches - they are to preach the Word, not speak in tongues before the congregation (if there is no interpreter). Simple discernment from the Holy Spirit will make this explicitly clear.

The gift of speaking in tongues builds one up by praying in perfect accordance with God's Will. When the Holy Spirit prays in a heavenly tongue through the person, even though we may be unaware of what we are praying, we can nonetheless be equipped for the day and rest in the knowledge that we are praying God's Will. These are the most powerful prayers, and speaking in tongues helps us pray His Will, even when we are unsure of the Perfect Will of God in each and every given day.

Speaking in tongues for extended periods also helps refine our spiritual senses. If we have other gifts of the Spirit, we will be more attuned to them throughout the day or during our time of prayer. Of course, while we pray in tongues, we should be praying in our native language within our minds. It is not difficult, as our body is merely a vessel through which the Holy Spirit prays through us.

When you have the gift of speaking in tongues, you don't have to think about what to say. It just happens on command. While you do this, you can be praying to God about other aspects in your mind. It is almost a "two-in-one" that can be accomplished. It is not difficult; it just takes discipline.

Now, when speaking in tongues for a certain amount of time, you open up the pathway to hearing God's Voice more clearly. This is especially true when one possesses the gifts of knowledge, prophecy, or visions.

When I ask God something specifically in my native tongue and then begin to pray in tongues, after some time, God will give me visions of the very thing I am trying to understand. Other times, I pray, "God, show me what I must know" or "God, show me what You desire to reveal." Then, I will start getting visions. I will speak more about this and how my gift of visions and my wife's gift of interpreting visions go together so wonderfully. Truly, God brought us together!

Speaking in tongues out loud allows us to clear the atmosphere of any demonic activity. We know that "the word of God *is* living and powerful, and sharper than any two-edged sword, piercing even to the division of soul and spirit, and of joints and marrow, and is a discerner of the thoughts and intents of the heart" (Hebrews 4:12 NKJV). When we speak the Word of God out loud, it is more powerful than when we pray in our minds. Of course, it is powerful when we pray in our minds, but if we are coming against the Enemy, the Enemy cannot flee if he cannot hear us declaring, "In the Name of Jesus, devils leave me!". Demons are unable to read our minds (which we will cover in more detail in the Biblical proof about the gift of dreams in the coming chapters).

For now, it is important to know that when the Perfect Will of the Father is prayed aloud, it is the same as praise and worship. The Enemy hates it and wants nothing to do with it! When the Enemy is outside us (meaning, we are not talking about unclean spirits and demons that are in us that need to be cast out), the Enemy flees.

"O Lord, our Lord, How excellent *is* Your name in all the earth, Who have set Your glory above the heavens! Out of the mouth of babes and nursing infants You have ordained strength, Because of Your enemies, That You may silence the enemy and the avenger" (Psalm 8:1-2 NKJV).

This is a very important gift for those called into greater ministry outreach, as the Enemy will continually buffet them. Prayer is of the utmost importance, and the gift of speaking in tongues will keep the Enemy at a distance.

"He who speaks in a tongue edifies himself" (1 Corinthians 14:4 NKJV). When we pray in the heavenly tongue, it is meant to edify us and build us up. If we are down and don't know why, praying in tongues allows the Spirit to pray for exactly what we need and to pray specifically against any hindrances toward us. It edifies us and builds us up, allowing us to move forward in the Power, Might, Strength, Peace, and Joy of the Holy Spirit.

"Even so you, since you are zealous for spiritual *gifts, let it be* for the edification of the church *that* you seek to excel" (1 Corinthians 14:12 NKJV). God will *not* answer the prayer for a spiritual gift from those who want it to boost their ego. The gifts of the Spirit are always meant for the edification of the church, not to make us appear as some sort of "ultra-saint". When this is properly understood, and we set ourselves up in a humble disposition before God and the true, genuine desire to help others, we can be sure that God will answer *as* and *when* He chooses.

When individuals have this specific gift, like all gifts of the Spirit, it varies. When you hear five individuals with the true gift of speaking in tongues, you will notice a differentiation. Each person will be speaking different words in a different tongue. Just as the language of the world has many different tongues (ex: English, French, Spanish), so the language of Heaven has many different tongues.

When we have the gift of tongues, though we speak in the tongue of angels, some tongues are only declared *to* God and known *by* God. Demons cannot perceive the language of what only God gives.

Someone might be able to learn English, French, and Spanish. They are well-versed in many tongues, but they cannot understand German. Likewise, it is with the gift of speaking with tongues.

"And they were all filled with the Holy Spirit and began to speak with other tongues, as the Spirit gave them utterance. And there were dwelling in Jerusalem Jews, devout men, from every nation under heaven. And when this sound occurred, the multitude came together, and were confused, because everyone heard them speak in his own language" (Acts 2:4-6 NKJV).

Though I have not witnessed this, as it is only a move of God that this can be done, the gift of speaking in tongues can fall upon individuals, and God can supernaturally translate it into the native tongue of certain people, groups, and tribes. This is a miracle that I have not witnessed, but which Scripture clearly reveals is possible and can be done.

We must understand that "tongues are for a sign, not to those who believe but to unbelievers; but prophesying is not for unbelievers but for those who believe" (1 Corinthians 14:22 NKJV). Speaking in tongues is for those *outside* the church, whereas prophecy is for those *inside* the church. Sadly, too many people are quick to prophesy over the lives of those who are not born-again. When those prophecies don't come to pass, it is not because God is a liar but because the person who brought the prophetic word did not hear from God and is a false prophet.

For tongues, it is a different matter. Again, when unbelievers truly hear others speaking in tongues (with someone giving the ability to interpret), it is one of the innumerable signs that God exists, that Jesus Christ is Who He said He Was and Is, and that the Holy Spirit is Real. Thus confirming the Trinity is the One, True, Living God.

"I thank my God I speak with tongues more than you all; yet in the church I would rather speak five words with my understanding, that I may teach others also, than ten thousand words in a tongue" (1 Corinthians 14:18-19 NKJV). We must always seek to edify with our giftings, not to boost our ego or image before man. None of us is worthy but the Lord Jesus Christ. He alone deserves all the praise and glory.

The gift of speaking in tongues is a beautiful gift given by God for the edification of oneself, a sign to unbelievers, a means to come together with an interpreter, a way to clear the atmosphere of demons, pray the Father's Will perfectly, receive greater instruction from God, and to bring enhancements, exercising of, or communication through other gifts of the Spirit that we possess.

"But you, beloved, building yourselves up on your most holy faith, praying in the Holy Spirit, keep yourselves in the love of God, looking for the mercy of our Lord Jesus Christ unto eternal life" (Jude 1:20-21 NKJV).

May God forever be glorified for all He has done and is willing to do and give!

God in Heaven, Who alone knows all languages, Who is the Creator of language and has made it work in the way that Thou seest fit, Who alone brings forth languages not known to man, Who reveals Thy creativity in the multitude of gifts and the variations of each gift, You alone are Omnificent. No one possesses creativity like You, Lord God, for by You creativity came. Without You, there is no creativity. In You, is an unlimited supply of creativity. God, we love You and bless Your Holy Name! God, if You see fit, bless us with the gift of speaking in tongues. God, if we are not prepared for such a gift, please cultivate the right spirit within us to receive this gift of the Holy Spirit. We want to commune with You in a deeper way. Draw us to You, and may we continue to press into Thy Goodness, Love, Mercy, and Kindness. Bless us with greater revelation of You, for You are the Unending God, Who has always Been and cannot be overthrown. We worship You, the God Who exists outside, above, and over all language, for by You language works, is differentiated, and provides the means of communicating. Blessed be Thy Name, forevermore, and may Thy Will forever be done. In Jesus' name, Amen.

The Gift of Interpretation of Tongues

"*To another the interpretation of tongues.*"
– 1 Corinthians 12:10 NKJV

While speaking in tongues is *praying* the Will of God perfectly, interpreting tongues is *knowing* what God's Will is perfectly. When we have the interpretation, we can understand precisely what the perfect Will of God is, not only for ourselves but also for others.

The interpretation of tongues, therefore, is a means to have direct understanding of what God desires of a person, group, congregation, couple, or family. When a person understands and receives the interpretation of the Heavenly language of speaking in tongues, they know exactly what God expects and desires at any given time or in a specific moment.

We know God has different wills that extend *from* Him (I have written extensively on this in my book, *God's Will*). For a brief understanding, God has a *Perfect Will*. His Perfect Will is for all to be saved (1 Timothy 2:4, 2 Peter 3:9); however, not all become saved. Therefore,

His Perfect Will is not fulfilled. Nonetheless, His *Ultimate Will* shall come forth.

Even though His Perfect Will of everyone being saved does not occur (because He blessed man with libertarian free will), His Ultimate Will of sending those who despise and reject His Son and want nothing to do with Him will be sent to the Lake of Fire. Again, this is not what God wants, but we know "narrow *is* the gate and difficult *is* the way which leads to life, and there are few who find it" (Matthew 7:14 NKJV).

As we understand these two (of many) Wills of God, we come to find He has different Wills for each of us. There is a *universal, generalized Will* for every born-again believer.

"And Jesus came and spoke to them, saying, "All authority has been given to Me in heaven and on earth. Go therefore and make disciples of all the nations, baptizing them in the name of the Father and of the Son and of the Holy Spirit, teaching them to observe all things that I have commanded you; and lo, I am with you always, *even* to the end of the age." Amen'" (Matthew 28:18-20 NKJV).

God wants all born-again believers to make disciples. From there, God has a *unique, individualized Will* for each of our lives. This is what we know to be our purpose. Namely, the "part of the body" that God calls us to within the Body of Christ. Some of us may be helpers, the hands. Others may be those of clairvoyance, the watchmen with eyes. Some may be the brain, giving wisdom and instruction. Some may be the mouth, preaching, and leading. Others may be the feet, evangelizing and entering the mission field. Whatever the purpose, God has a specific Will for our lives that He calls us to fulfill that others cannot.

As we understand these four wills (which, again, there are more that He possesses that I cover in my book, *God's Will*), we see clearly that God gives us a general understanding of His Will for all believers. However, when it comes to His Will moment by moment, for a season, wanting us to understand and perceive what He wants from us in a month, year, life, or a day by day basis; what we need to practice and seek Him for, and what we need to distance ourselves and depart from, this can be made known through the interpretation of tongues.

"If anyone speaks in a tongue, *let there be* two or at the most three, *each* in turn, and let one interpret" (1 Corinthians 14:27 NKJV). This is the beautiful reality about God – He includes everyone. No one who is born-again is unimportant to the Body of Christ. All are unique, and God can speak through two or three, giving each person speaking in tongues a partial interpretation.

Those who have the gift of interpretation may be listening to one person for a few minutes and gather some information. Another may go, and the person with the gift of interpretation will gain greater understanding. Eventually, the third speaks, and the full interpretation is complete.

This shows the collectivity of God's Spirit working in unison, based on the gifts He has given each person.

I do not yet have this gift, but my Wife and I continue to pray for it. We have yet to meet anyone with this gift, but it most certainly is powerful. To know the Will of God – not just in its substance, but who it is for; not just who it is for, but in understanding what is meant to be known at the current moment of speaking in tongues is a mighty gift.

If God blessed a multitude of us with this gift, can you imagine the division that would be sown in the Enemy's camp? We could know that we are under spiritual attack by witches, wizards, and warlocks. We could know their location and dwelling, and pray specifically against the very curses, hexes, and spells they are placing on us.

God could make known to us which demon keeps harassing us through our spouse. He could reveal what He desires of a particular congregation regarding its finances. He could speak and direct us to know what future opportunities are to come in our lives and how we need to prepare to meet the occasion.

God can do all of this and reveal much more through those who possess the gift of interpretation of tongues.

Of course, God can reveal certain aspects by different measures and other gifts. Nonetheless, we are talking about knowing the Perfect Will of God in a specific season and at all moments.

This is incredible, as, with prophecy, we are to test and weigh words. With the gift of interpretation of tongues, there is no reason to test or weigh the word. Those who *truly* have the gift of interpretation know precisely what the Spirit is praying through the person.

How can we trust the Holy Spirit? Not just because He is God, but because the Spirit of God knows the Will of the Father, instantaneously, perfectly, and entirely. "For what man knows the things of a man except the spirit of the man which is in him? Even so no one knows the things of God except the Spirit of God" (1 Corinthians 2:11 NKJV).

It takes the Holy Spirit giving us the gift not only to pray what is of the Will of God, but also to bring the interpretation. "Now we have received, not the spirit of the world, but the Spirit Who is from God, that we might know the things that have been freely given to us by God" (1 Corinthians 2:12 NKJV).

The Holy Spirit works through each believer in the way He desires. When we witness the Spirit giving the interpretation of three people having their turn to speak in tongues, and the message aligns, it is like putting a puzzle together. Just as the Bible was written by many different individuals but has the same underlying theme, so it is with a multitude of individuals speaking in tongues, each with an interpretation, aligning into a single, understandable, recognizable perception of the Perfect Will of God.

"I wish you all spoke with tongues, but even more that you prophesied; for he who prophesies *is* greater than he who speaks with tongues, unless indeed he interprets, that the church may receive edification" (1 Corinthians 14:5 NKJV). Tongues is beneficial for the individual, but when interpreted, it is valuable to others. When Paul says it is better to prophesy, he means that when God's Holy Spirit prophesies through an individual, it is easily discernible and known. There is no guesswork. The word is given in the native tongue that someone can understand.

When it comes to the gift of speaking in a Heavenly tongue, however, God calls us to pray that we may interpret. "Therefore let him who speaks in a tongue pray that he may interpret" (1 Corinthians 14:13 NKJV). This is further revealment that we can have more than one gift. We can pray for the interpretation, and God is faithful to answer in His timing.

When He blesses someone with the gifts to both speak in tongues and interpret tongues, that person becomes a powerhouse in the Spirit. They can receive whatever God desires to reveal and understand His Perfect Will.

Imagine praying in tongues for a few hours and then knowing everything that God's Spirit is speaking through us and making known to us? We can know the Will of God in just a few minutes, or if we are disciplined and want to hear even further instruction, guidance, counsel, knowledge, insight, and revelation, we can spend more time. It does not just become an exercise of praying the Perfect Will of God and not knowing. Rather, the interpretation can be known and made known to the proper individuals whom God wants to include with the knowledge He gives.

This is a tremendous double gift that can be done in groups or can be done by a single individual. Behind it all, however, is the working, movement, guiding, leading, and directing of the Holy Spirit!

We will include 1 Corinthians 14:13 again in the following passage, but listen to what Paul declares in 1 Corinthians 14:13-17 (NKJV) about speaking in tongues and the interpretation:

> "Therefore let him who speaks in a tongue pray that he may interpret. For if I pray in a tongue, my spirit prays, but my understanding is unfruitful. What is *the conclusion* then? I will pray with the spirit, and I will also pray with the understanding. I will sing with the spirit, and I will also sing with the understanding. Otherwise, if you bless with the spirit, how will he who occupies the place of the uninformed say "Amen" at your giving of thanks, since he does not understand what you say? For you indeed give thanks well, but the other is not edified."

We can pray in tongues over individuals, but without interpretation, it seems mundane to others. We know it is not pointless, but they remain uninformed. It is like telling someone, "I see a blue river with four trees springing forth on each side." Someone with the gift of visions (which we will review in the following chapters) may declare what they see, but without the interpretation, it does not make sense or bring edification. It is not until someone with the interpretation comes along and says, "The blue river signifies the flow of the Holy Spirit. He is about to bring much beauty into your life. The seeds growing are your four family members, for whom you have been praying that they come to know the Lord. God is working on their hearts, and you will soon see them become trees, firmly rooted in the Word of God."

Again, the gifts that require an interpretation can be given to the same individual. However, God often desires to bring edification through groups. When we work together as the Body, we function cohesively as a unit. That which operates as a unit is difficult to shake down. The Enemy hates when the Body of Christ comes together, and the gift of interpretation is a means of not only growing together, but coming together in fellowship.

Paul declares, "I thank my God I speak with tongues more than you all; yet in the church I would rather speak five words with my understanding, that I may teach others also, than ten thousand words in a tongue" (1 Corinthians 14:18-19 NKJV). The church (insofar as a building where gathering for a sermon and growing in God is done through sound, truthful, Biblical teaching) is meant to be done in the native tongue. We want those who are believers and those who come to visit to be taught, not just to throw our gifts around in an attempt to show off and boost our own ego, and to profit nothing from those listening because they do not know what is being said in a Heavenly language.

Every gift given by the Spirit is meant to be used by the Spirit. When we take matters into our own hands, we will always fall short. When we fully trust in the Holy Spirit and pray that He would come forth in a mighty way, He will never cease from performing what only He can do.

Let us all pray for the gift of tongues and the ability to interpret, that we may not wonder what the Will of God is, but always have the capacity and capability of knowing what He desires. Too many are walking around throughout this life in the Body of Christ, saying, "I don't know what God wants from me. I don't understand what I'm supposed to do." They run frantically. Their anxiety and discouragement of not knowing erode their inner being. Stress and worry take root. Eventually, complacency sets in due to uncertainty. They begin to lack any progress because they don't know the Will of God.

When we reach the point of eliminating the suppression of the gifts of the Spirit and begin to embrace and pray for them, we will see many troubles and problems in the Church begin to diminish. People will no longer be able to say, "I don't know what the Will of God is" or "It doesn't matter. Just try your best to figure it out and leave the rest to God." No, to God it matters to Him to make His Will known to us.

He has given us the gifts to know His Will (alongside His Word). The question is, will we press into what He freely offers? If we are quick to receive the free gift of salvation through Jesus Christ, our Lord and Savior, what is keeping us from freely accepting the gifts of the Holy Spirit and embracing them? Is it due to worry? Fear of the unknown? Uncertainty that it is true? When we get out of the way and begin to embrace everything Scripture reveals, and we trust in the Spirit Who now lives in us who are born-again, we will see miracles and wonders occur. We will be amazed and look back and say, "What have I done? O foolish man that I am! Was this accessible to me all this time? These were truths my pastor and church suppressed, telling me they no longer existed. O God, have mercy and bless me as I seek to embrace all that is of You!"

Let us never forget that God's Perfect Will is not only for later on, but for the present moment. God's Will for us is to pray *for* His Perfect Will, both long-term and short-term, and that can only be done perfectly when we possess the gift of interpretation of tongues.

May God make known His Will for each and every one of you, not just through His Word, but by His Spirit; not just by His Spirit, but through the working of the Holy Spirit upon the spiritual gifts of speaking in tongues and interpretation of tongues that He is willing to bestow on those He wills.

God in Heaven, Who desires all to come to the knowledge of the Truth of the Lord Jesus Christ, Who calls all men everywhere to repent, Who is willing and just to forgive us of our sins and to cleanse us from all unrighteousness, You are Love, and there is none like You. God, we thank You for Your willingness to give us Your Holy Spirit. We are blessed to know that He makes known what Your Will is, Heavenly Father. God, we pray that You would touch us in a mighty way. Give us the gift of speaking in tongues and possessing the gift of interpretation of tongues. God, we don't want to limit what You can do. We repent of all the times we have limited You and failed to believe Your Word. Guide us now, in accordance with Your Word, and being led by Your Holy Spirit. Teach us the ways of Christ and how to keep in step with the Spirit. Fill us with faith to believe You can and will do far more than we ever ask or think! Bless us with living a life worthy of the call You have for us. Keep our feet from stumbling, and do not allow us to offset or prolong what You are willing to perform. Give us the strength and power to be holy, just as You are Holy. Above all, may we desire to live godly, uprightly, and righteously before You and men. We bless You, O Lord of Heaven and Earth. In Jesus' name, Amen.

The Gift of Dreams

> "*And it shall come to pass afterward That I will pour out My Spirit on all flesh; Your sons and your daughters shall prophesy, Your old men shall dream dreams, Your young men shall see visions.*'"
> *– Joel 2:28 NKJV*

Dreams occur when we are asleep, whereas visions occur when we are awake.

The gift of dreams is a way the Lord speaks directly to us, helps us understand that He sees us, makes known what is to come, or is a direct way to ask God questions and receive an answer through a dream.

When we think of the Scriptures, the first person who comes to mind is Joseph. Genesis 37:5-10 (NKJV) unpacks the story:

> "Now Joseph had a dream, and he told *it* to his brothers; and they hated him even more. So he said to them, "Please hear this dream which I have dreamed: There we were, binding sheaves in the field. Then behold, my sheaf arose and also stood upright; and indeed your sheaves stood all around and bowed down to my sheaf." And his brothers said

to him, "Shall you indeed reign over us? Or shall you indeed have dominion over us?" So they hated him even more for his dreams and for his words. Then he dreamed still another dream and told it to his brothers, and said, "Look, I have dreamed another dream. And this time, the sun, the moon, and the eleven stars bowed down to me." So he told *it* to his father and his brothers; and his father rebuked him and said to him, "What *is* this dream that you have dreamed? Shall your mother and I and your brothers indeed come to bow down to the earth before you?""

Here, we quickly see that when God reveals the future to us, we must be discerning with whom we share the dream. Of course, our instinct is to share it with those closest to us. Typically, this is our family. We want them to be happy, on board, supportive, and understanding. Rarely, however, does this occur.

Joseph's brothers instantly got upset and angry. As a matter of fact, we are told "they hated him even more for his dreams and for his words" (Genesis 37:8). Joseph's brothers did not want to hear about all the success God was going to give Joseph, much less that they would be bowing to him (as a means of Joseph being above them in status).

We must show some sympathy for the older brothers. Who wants to hear that their younger brother is going to oversee them? Nonetheless, they should not have despised and hated Joseph and sold him into slavery (Genesis 37:28).

We must be discerning when God gives us a dream, for a dream is not meant to be shared with just anyone. We will discuss this further in the chapter on the gift of visions, but it is extremely important not to share our dreams until God gives us the go-ahead. Until then, we must be very cautious.

Joseph must have been extremely excited to receive this dream. He thought that the dream signified what would come soon, but without an interpreter, he did not know when this would come to fruition. Instead, it took roughly thirteen years from the day he had his first dream. Had he had an interpreter, it would have made the acceptance of the dream more realistic and easier to understand that God would work everything out for the greater good.

Since Joseph had no one to interpret his dream, God also trained him in this gifting. Sometimes, God puts us in the wilderness, desert, or prison to give us solitude and time alone with Him for a season. It is in these moments that God is training, preparing, and equipping us to be more and steward more in the Wisdom of the Holy Spirit in the days ahead.

Had Joseph not had those long eleven, unjustifiable years in prison, he would not have found time to be trained in the interpretation of dreams. During that time, God was preparing him for what was to come (we will cover this more in the following chapter on the gift of interpretation of dreams).

For now, it is important to understand that dreams are meant to be shared at a particular time, to a specific person or group, within a given season. If we share outside the boundaries of any of these aspects and neglect to seek God's confirmation, we will not only do more harm than good, but also do more harm to ourselves than we would gain from good, loving, encouraging support.

This is why social media is not the place to share every dream one has. In fact, nowhere in Scripture do we see the call to share every dream. Yet because many do not go to God to confirm whether something is of His Holy Spirit, people are quick to use social media to promote every dream.

"'I have heard what the prophets have said who prophesy lies in My name, saying, "I have dreamed, I have dreamed!" How long will *this* be in the heart of the prophets who prophesy lies? Indeed *they are* prophets of the deceit of their own heart'" (Jeremiah 23:25-26 NKJV). So many on social media claim something they are not, elevate themselves to a position that is not for them, and share what comes from the imagination of their own heart. This is dangerous, as we know "'The heart *is* deceitful above all *things*, And desperately wicked; Who can know it?'" (Jeremiah 17:9 NKJV).

We must be discerning with who we share the dream with, as well as who we listen to who claims to have a dream. The Holy Spirit will bring either conviction or confirmation based on what He speaks within. We must be sensitive to His speaking, lest we get pulled into believing fantasies and fallacies.

"For God may speak in one way, or in another, *Yet man* does not perceive it. In a dream, in a vision of the night, When deep sleep falls upon men, While slumbering on their beds, Then He opens the ears of men, And seals their instruction. In order to turn man *from his* deed, And conceal pride from man, He keeps back his soul from the Pit, And his life from perishing by the sword" (Job 33:14-18 NKJV).

God uses dreams to communicate directly with us. Some of us are so busy throughout the day and rarely take time for Him that God speaks to us in a dream. For many, the fear is of not having any noise. This is due to the insecurity of beginning the process of being comfortable with oneself and dwelling with one's own thoughts in silence. Most people are unable to perform this simple task and would rather be distracted and surrounded by noise than sit in quietness with themselves and God.

God, therefore, will sometimes speak to us in a dream to bring Divine instruction and to keep us from the ways in which we are going. This is where many times Hell testimonies come from; God brings these forth to keep back the soul of man from the Pit (Job 33:18).

Despite what many may believe, God will reveal Hell to whomever He chooses. Though He can do this by way of visions and out-of-body experiences, He can also reveal what Hell is like by way of dreams.

Now, of course, we want to be discerning and not believe every testimony under the sun. Sadly, there are people who see many views with a specific title or topic on the internet. Rather than presenting truth, they want to copycat the specific realm to attract views and revenue. Thankfully, when the frauds come, God's Holy Spirit reveals who they are each time.

The Spirit of Truth has no deceit and, therefore, can expose every lie, since He knows what dwells within man. When people lie on the internet, they will be numbered amongst the transgressors thrown into the Lake of Fire if they continue in the way of deceit and do not trust in Christ and repent of their sins. "'But the cowardly, unbelieving, abominable, murderers, sexually immoral, sorcerers, idolaters, and all liars shall have their part in the lake which burns with fire and brimstone, which is the second death'" (Revelation 21:8 NKJV).

I will now share a dream I had some years ago. I remember waking up instantly and feeling compelled to write it down. I took the next 60-90 minutes to write it down by hand (yes, I am a slow writer). In the middle of the night, God had me record this dream, and I later shared it with others. I did not immediately share, but kept the matter in mind based on what God spoke.

What you will see is the full recording of what I saw, alongside my interpretation. Though I have this gift only in part (it is currently the weakest of those God has given), I will nonetheless receive interpretations at specific points. The true master whom I personally know is my wife. The Holy Spirit makes sense of dreams that make no sense to me. She is able to articulate and piece together everything from the dream. It makes sense every time because the Holy Spirit is giving her the interpretation.

What I experienced in my dream I shall now share. I believe it is a message to all of us on some level, but most certain to the United States of America:

A Dream from God
April 11, 2022
3 AM

Waking up from a dream that I know God revealed, yet I do not know its full meaning. I trust the Holy Spirit will speak as I write this in the middle of the night.

(In my dream) I saw and heard Scripture being read. Yet, Scripture was like a boat. I, as a boy, stood upon each word as Scripture was read from what appeared to be a mother and father. As the words were read (again, I believe they were God's Word) and I safely stood in the boat, the darkness of the sky and water around me began to get darker and darker.

As this happened, eventually black waves consumed the mother and father as they began to read what I believe was Exodus. The moment this occurred, I, whoever I was, had the feeling of wanting to hear more of the Word. I wanted to remain on the Word because they were as a boat that kept me above the thick, black water.

Soon, however, I, in the dream, was consumed by this thick, black water. Somehow, as I entered the water, I was dragged underneath it.

Yet, I did not have to breathe. Maybe I could breathe and did not know it. Nonetheless, I had a special body that survived the long periods of being under water.

As I was pulled under the crashing thick, black waves, I was also in a cave. This cave had rushing black water by which I was able to reach the surface of the water, but soon was swallowed under again. As soon as I could surface, I began to go over what appeared to be mini waterfalls.

At first, I could surface and grasp for air as I was brought into the next descending part of the cave by each mini waterfall. Soon, with each fall, there was no room to surface. This thick, black water was swallowing me alive and I, in the dream, was cast further and further into this cave.

The size of the water ranged, but it felt like this thick, black waterfall spit me out and flowed me into the amount of water ranging from the size of a pool. After being there for some time, the water furthered me towards being thrown from the current height of the cave to a lower level consisting of this same black water.

Each time this occurred, the range of the thick, black water was wider, vaster, and was very cold. The size of the thick, black water felt like going from a pool to a pond, then to a lake, and finally to an ocean. This process did not stop. With each passing time of being tossed into each deeper stage, it was as if the heights of the waterfall of thick, black water became higher, and the water itself got colder.

All this time, everything was black, but could be felt. I wanted to breathe but could not in the way I wanted. I held my breath, feeling as if I was dying and would drown, yet I was surviving and living without air.

Finally, I remember a flash of grey light that allowed me to see through this thick, black water. As this occurred, I saw stars in the form of a circle on the ground underneath the deep water. I don't know the exact amount of the stars when the grey light flashed, but I would estimate there were thirteen.

Again, each waterfall somehow sent me to a deeper stage where I was entirely engulfed by this thick, black water. As I was cast deeper and deeper, there was not one area where I could swim up and breathe for air.

(I am now awake). I woke up from this in silence and remained in bed for some time. Eventually, I got up and began to cry. I felt led to write.

As I write, I believe God has given me understanding into some parts of the dream. I do not recall my current state in the dream before I mentioned what had occurred. I believe, again, the word was God's Word which keeps man afloat from the darkness that would otherwise consume us.

As the man and woman in my dream read the Word, I wanted to hear more, as I was safe from the darkness when the Word was spoken. Yet, somehow, something overtook them. I believe they were martyrs in this story, as they appeared to want to share more with me, but could not, as their lives were taken (although I stated by the thick waves, I am unsure by what they were overtaken by, specifically). When this occurred, I began to be swept away in the dream both by and into this thick, black water.

I believe this thick, black water resembles sin. At first, I thought this dream pertained to sinners in general, but I believe my heart gained understanding (though, I will bring this before my godly group of brothers at my prayer meeting and see what they have to say).

I was not merely a sinner in this dream. I was one who heard the Word by what seemed to be "my family" in the dream – though, it was not my actual family who raised me, as I was somebody else in the dream. I was someone who was raised by the Word, but my faith was not a true, repentant faith in the dream. I was a hearer in the dream, but not a doer.

As the martyr's passed away and were gone, I was left and swallowed up by this thick, black water. I wanted to hear the Words that were spoken just once more, as they were as a boat that kept me above the thick, black water; but I could not. Somehow, those words in the dream were set on fire and then vanished.

The Word of God endures forever, but its hope was burned up from saving me, as I was overcome by sin in this dream.

I believe this resembles many in the church. Many are content with hearing the Word from others and living under the shadow of someone else's faith. They claim to be Christians, but the Word has no place in them. They merely listen to It, thinking that is enough, but they do not obey It, nor do they accept It in Its entirety. Before these self-proclaimed Christians know it, they are quickly swept away by sin.

I believe the different stages of vastness of the thick, black water in the cave signified Hell. There was no one else on my travel downward in the dream. I was alone with no one to answer my call for help.

The fact that I wanted to breathe and felt I needed to take a breath to survive, though I was surviving while under this thick, black water reveals God creating those in Hell with specific bodies.

Man will forever be dying and dead, though alive at the same time in Hell as he drifts further and further from God and is forever overcome and swallowed up by his sin. The water becoming colder with each descension shows the torment of each moment of drifting from the presence of God.

The grey light that flashed and revealed (if my memory serves) 13 stars is unknown to me. It could be symbolic or unrelated, as that is when I woke up.

The theme of this message and dream I believe is that sin damns, and it is sweeping away many of those in the Church who think they are believers but are not born-again. This is meant for us to sound the alarm to congregations who have fallen asleep and pastors who are apathetic or false prophets.

Our power and safety only come from the Word of God. Not merely hearing It but doing It and living It out by the power of the Spirit.

We must not judge, but discern those who profess Christ with righteous judgment. Those who get angry at us in the moment, but later on end up repenting of their sins to God, is a small price to pay to see them saved and not swallowed up by sin and cast into Hell – that place of drifting further from God, being tormented to the point of wanting to die, but having death flee from those who are bound by the pollution of their sin and forever burning in their lusts.

In summary, I believe this dream given by God is this: ***Wake Up Sleepy Church. Repent, for the Kingdom of God is at hand.***

I later took it to my current prayer group at the time. The men provided some additional insight, including how the thirteen stars in a circle are a symbol of the original flag of the United States. They said that the U.S. is being filled with iniquity and going under. Another said, "The burning up of the Word could resemble what happens when a nation does not listen to the Word. Iniquity pours over, uncontrollably."

God gives dreams to issue warnings and sound the alarm. This was one of those dreams, and anyone who is living in the United States of America, who is truly born-again, knows the state of the Church. It is nothing to be proud of, and God is going to clean up and clean out the Church in a relatively short timeframe, in the coming due season.

"John answered, saying to all, 'I indeed baptize you with water; but One mightier than I is coming, Whose sandal strap I am not worthy to loose. He will baptize you with the Holy Spirit and fire. His winnowing fan *is* in His hand, and He will thoroughly clean out His threshing floor, and gather the wheat into His barn; but the chaff He will burn with unquenchable fire'" (Luke 3:16-17 KJV). Truly, God will separate the wheat from the chaff. The time of false prophets and false teachers is coming to an end within God's Church.

Liars will be proven as such, and the Truth will prevail. In God's timing, this will be made clear and evident. In His timing, the Church will be purified, and the wicked will be exposed and brought down.

It is very important to note that demons can *influence how* we dream briefly, but they do *not know* what it is we actually dream. That information strictly belongs to God Almighty. How do we know this? "Now in the second year of Nebuchadnezzar's reign, Nebuchadnezzar had dreams; and his spirit was *so* troubled that his sleep left him. Then the king gave the command to call the magicians, the astrologers, the sorcerers, and the Chaldeans to tell the king his dreams. So they came and stood before the king. And the king said to them, 'I have had a dream, and my spirit is anxious to know the dream'" (Daniel 2:1-3 NKJV).

We will review this more in the following chapter. Still, it is important to note that "The Chaldeans answered the king, and said, "There is not a man on earth who can tell the king's matter; therefore no king, lord, or ruler has *ever* asked such things of any magician, astrologer, or Chaldean. *It is* a difficult thing that the king requests, and there is no other who can tell it to the king except the gods, whose dwelling is not with flesh"'" (Daniel 2:10-11 NKJV).

All those the King called forth could not tell the King what he dreamed. This shows that dreams are known only to God. Not even angels know what we dream (unless God sends an angel to visit us in a dream). Our dreams are hidden from the Enemy, though they can affect them.

Since we know astrologers, magicians, and sorcerers communicate with the spiritual realm of darkness and demonic activity, and if they themselves could not answer the king's request to tell him what he dreamed, then truly the gift of dreams is only given by God. He alone not only speaks to people within dreams and is Sovereign over dreams, but He also will expose dreams of others to His people.

Truly, dreams are unknown to Satan. Sorcerers can only go off of some information that is given or demonic insight, but demons cannot know what men dream; they can only *influence* dreams. The king received a dream from God that demons did not know. This proves that demons cannot read our minds or know our thoughts; only *influence* them.

After the birth of the Lord Jesus, we see that Mary and Joseph were warned not to return to King Herod and to leave their own country. Matthew 2:12-15 (NKJV) declares:

> "Then, being divinely warned in a dream that they should not return to Herod, they departed for their own country another way.
>
> Now when they had departed, behold, an angel of the Lord appeared to Joseph in a dream, saying, "Arise, take the young Child and His mother, flee to Egypt, and stay there until I bring you word; for Herod will seek the young Child to destroy Him."
>
> When he arose, he took the young Child and His mother by night and departed for Egypt, and was there until the death of Herod, that it might be fulfilled which was spoken by the Lord through the prophet, saying, "Out of Egypt I called My Son.""

God knows the means by which He will communicate with His children. Some people are so closed off to the supernatural that you wonder how they are born-again. They easily dismiss that the God of all creation – creating that which is visible out of that which is not seen (Hebrews 11:3) and creating what is both visible and invisible (Colossians 1:16) – is at full liberty to do, speak, move, act, and make known in the ways He sees fit.

For those who truly are born-again, but miss the mark that God is Spirit (John 4:24) and knowing He can do what is spiritual without the physical, they alone carry a knowledge bound within the mind, but not one that leads to full belief, sound counsel, and a child-like faith.

Many denominations have reasoned away spiritual realities to the point where we would think God was physical. This is true for many individuals who refuse to accept the spiritual gifts and believe that God's ways are not our ways, meaning He can bring forth knowledge and greater revelation that man has not known at any time He chooses.

It is time we start believing that, just as with Joseph, God can speak to us in our dreams. When we pray fervently, day and night, God will answer. He will reveal things to come.

Many times, we dismiss our dreams when they are actually footprints to the future or clues to the past. We don't realize it, but God is often speaking, wanting to reveal something. He says this because only He (or those He has given the gift of interpreting dreams) can unravel the mystery of our dreams. For dreams are not always the brain filtering out what must be kept or not, nor are they simply random REM Sleep occurring without any purpose or correlation to our dreams. No, dreams are a means for God to communicate and give interpretation.

For those who have both the gift of dreams and the ability to interpret them, they become lethal. They can see and understand what goes on within their dreams that the Enemy cannot. As we covered, Satan and all of the Enemy do not know what we dream, though they can *affect* what we dream (through whispering thoughts of temptations in our sleep). Of course, the man or woman who prays up sets themselves under the shadow of the Almighty, not permitting the Enemy to cross the hedge of protection set up by Holy Ghost fire!

When we have both the dream and its interpretation, there are huge revelations that we will know in an instant for the future, but we will be guided on when to release them. For not all that is given immediately is meant to be shared immediately. If most people knew this simple principle, they would avoid much harm in the present and future.

God not only gives dreams to the righteous, but also to the wicked; not just to those *of* Him, but also those *apart* from Him. Pilot's wife during the time of Jesus being questioned (before His crucifixion), "sent to him, saying, "Have nothing to do with that just Man, for I have suffered many things today in a dream because of Him"" (Matthew 27:19 NKJV). Pilot's wife warns him not to judge the Lord Jesus and give way to the people. Here, we see that God even worked on behalf of Pilot to allow him the opportunity to escape the judgment he would inflict on the Perfect Godman. Though God knew he would give way to the people and give Christ up, He nonetheless gave Pilot the opportunity.

This is the reality about those in Hell. They did not just receive one chance to come to Christ, but multiple. Those who saw the face of Christ and knew He was innocent still gave way to the fear of man. Though they saw Christ perform great and mighty miracles, possessing wisdom not of this world, they still sought to kill Him. Those in Hell, no matter how many times God reached out to them in this life, still chose their ways, the ways of the world, or operated in the fear of man. In the end, they heaped upon themselves swift destruction.

People are quick to blame God and slow to follow Him. God warned Pilot through his wife, yet he would not listen. God was even gracious to allow Pilot to turn from what he was about to do, but he did not. God truly is for every single person and gives them the chance not to take the path that leads to damnation.

With Pilot's wife, therefore, it was God who spoke to her in a dream. God often speaks to the wicked and those apart from Him in order to lead them to Him. This is happening across the world. Many times, Muslims who will respond to the call of Christ in a dream will receive a dream (or multiple dreams) and be visited by Christ. They respond, and in their proper response, they seek Christ and forsake their religion of Islam.

This is a bold move for those who do so, as they literally put their lives on the line for Christ. Some of us have it so easy and simple in our lives, yet we are afraid to say we believe in Jesus when asked, or to share

Him. This is not the way God desires, and we know that it is those who are cowards who are the first to be cast into everlasting fire (Revelation 21:8).

God's gift of dreams and speaking to the ungodly is to lead them to Him, warn them of their ways, and also provide the opportunity for His people to reveal their gifts of interpretation of dreams. For interpretation only comes by way of God, not man. Man can know in part through divination, but they do not see the whole. For what is of God (the Truth) can only be known in full by God and given by Him in an equal manner.

In Genesis 28:10-15 (NKJV), we see that Jacob has a dream and a visitation from the Lord within his dream:

> "Now Jacob went out from Beersheba and went toward Haran. So he came to a certain place and stayed there all night, because the sun had set. And he took one of the stones of that place and put it at his head, and he lay down in that place to sleep. Then he dreamed, and behold, a ladder *was* set up on the earth, and its top reached to heaven; and there the angels of God were ascending and descending on it. And behold, the Lord stood above it and said: "I *am* the Lord God of Abraham your father and the God of Isaac; the land on which you lie I will give to you and your descendants. Also your descendants shall be as the dust of the earth; you shall spread abroad to the west and the east, to the north and the south; and in you and in your seed all the families of the earth shall be blessed. Behold, I *am* with you and will keep you wherever you go, and will bring you back to this land; for I will not leave you until I have done what I have spoken to you.""

Though it's not the best idea to sleep on a stone, we know that this dream was of the Lord. God made known the future to Jacob, even the future of what would occur years, decades, centuries, and millennia from his time. God sometimes does this because it is the motivation of what is to come and what will occur through us that keeps us going.

God does not reveal everything He will do, for if He did, many of us would not want to inherit the good. If we saw the adversity and suffering we would have to endure, we would not deem it worth it.

Nonetheless, we see that God revealed to Jacob what would come well beyond his years.

Sometimes, God reveals what our lives will bring forth, but not exactly what will be brought forth during our lifetime. What we do is always meant to leave a legacy for Christ. Jacob witnessed and heard all that God would do, even well beyond his lifetime.

Some of us are so earthbound that the only thing we can worry about is the here and now. We are not eternity conscious, and our vision only goes as far as the television at times! We cease from not being able to see beyond ourselves and our lives, and all the while, God wants us to wake up and see what He is willing to do through us.

All that God does has purpose and meaning, and our lives are not meant for us, but for Him. If He desires to see everyone saved (1 Timothy 2:4, 2 Peter 3:9), then certainly He is willing to work through us in a mighty way to reveal His Glory, Goodness, and Name. Truly, He wants us to be vessels through whom He continues to pour out His Power, Wisdom, Love, and blessing, even when we have been caught up into eternity!

It is important to note, then, that dreams reveal the future. Within each dream, the Lord can enter in and choose to speak directly, allowing us to see Him. He also allows us to see the spiritual realm, such as angels. These dreams cannot be fully described, as what is spiritual cannot be fully understood by the natural. Nonetheless, our spiritual senses aid in conceiving what we see, but our vocabulary limits what we can describe, since what we see is unlike anything on Earth.

The gift of dreams is also meant to bring confirmation in times of uncertainty. Now, it is important to take this to the Lord. If the Lord visits us directly, we may believe the dream. However, if it is just a dream, we must pray about the dream. For, again, the Enemy can give us dreams where our wishes and wants desire to have confirmation, but which are not from God.

A simple strategy to ensure a dream is from God is to continue walking with God and staying in fellowship with Him. As this occurs, His Voice is made known, and the Enemy cannot override and deceive us, for we are staying close to the Light and not walking in darkness.

The darkness cannot override the Light, and therefore, the closer we are to the Light, the less likely we are to be deceived.

Also, praying that God alone would give us dreams of instruction, guidance, and counsel, and that the Enemy would be bound from his plots and schemes, is another way to ensure that our dreams are from the Lord.

We note all this because, for those who know my wife, she thought her husband would be another individual (whom she knew before meeting me). She showed me the documents and had over 150 dreams about this person. Of course, this is not who God had for her, and, in the end, he gaslit her.

What we dream can either be from God, of ourselves, or the Enemy. In all cases of dreams, we must stay close to God, praying that He would bless us with the gift of dreams and make known what He desires, while keeping the Enemy at bay.

Before Jesus' birth, Joseph was visited by an angel in a dream. Dreams help lessen the impact of what we see. It is much more intimidating to see an angel in a vision or through our spiritual senses, once they are opened, than in a dream. In a dream, we can manage what we see. In contrast, a vision is much more powerful, as it is us seeing things as they are while we are awake and alert.

"But while he thought about these things, behold, an angel of the Lord appeared to him in a dream, saying, 'Joseph, son of David, do not be afraid to take to you Mary your wife, for that which is conceived in her is of the Holy Spirit. And she will bring forth a Son, and you shall call His name Jesus, for He will save His people from their sins'" (Matthew 1:20-21 NKJV).

Joseph really went through it. I'm sure once he heard from Mary that she was pregnant, his response was something similar to "God impregnated you!? Mary, if you're going to lie to me, I would more well believe an angel did this than God!"

Imagine if you were in Joseph's position. You are to marry a virgin, but God impregnated them and you are to believe that for the first time in all mankind God was the One Who made your bride to carry a Child; not just any Child, but the Son of God! I think all of us men would say, "Yeah, that's a nice try in covering up! I've heard better excuses! What really happened?" We would mock the idea! Yet, this is what occurred, and to help Joseph, God was gracious in bringing confirmation that made sense through a dream.

As a matter of fact, a dream was probably the only way Joseph would listen, as his mind was so wrapped up with "how could you cheat on me", "this didn't happen", "what is my family going to think", "I don't know if I want to marry Mary anymore." His mind was most likely doing mental gymnastics, and the only way to reason with Joseph and let him know he wasn't going mad was to reason with him when he was asleep.

God often speaks in dreams and visions to warn man of what is to come and to bring correction. Let's look at Job 33:14-18 (NKJV) once more:

> "For God may speak in one way, or in another,
>   *Yet man* does not perceive it.
>   In a dream, in a vision of the night,
>   When deep sleep falls upon men,
>   While slumbering on their beds,
>   Then He opens the ears of men,
>   And seals their instruction.
>   In order to turn man *from his* deed,
>   And conceal pride from man,
>   He keeps back his soul from the Pit,
>   And his life from perishing by the sword."

Many times, God will turn people toward His Will or away from their own. He will give them wisdom and instruction, or rebuke them from their own fleshly reason. In all matters, God does this to keep them away from Hell and perishing in this life by their own destruction from sin, evil, and carnality.

Had Joseph not had an angel visit him in a dream, Mary would most likely have been left to herself. This, in turn, would have brought forth a different world of possibilities and outcomes. She would not have a man to protect her, and the way God sought to have things done and accomplished would not have been.

This is why God will warn through dreams—to ensure His Ultimate Divine Will is fulfilled. God knows when to speak and remain silent. He knows when to allow human freedom to do as they please and when to override their freedom with His Sovereignty (insofar as keeping them from consequences, decisions, or circumstances that would arise that do not aid in the overall reality of God's Ultimate Divine Will from being fulfilled). In all aspects, God knows when to intervene and when to refrain.

Let us ask God for the gift of dreams. Let us ask for more than is apparent and dreams we can remember upon waking. Let us have the discipline to write and record what God gives, and seek Him to reveal what it is we have dreamed.

I am blessed that I have dreams, and I have my wife, who has the gift of interpretation. God can do the same for you. He never gives without supplying needs. He will not leave us stranded when we have this gift and do not know what dreams mean. Yes, dreams can be direct, but many times, they are puzzles. The puzzle is an aspect of revealing the greatness of God, as He alone can bring the interpretation or reveal the interpretation to His chosen elect.

May God bless us with this gift, and may we steward it well and take time to begin recording our dreams. They may seem like nothing to us, but to God, they are a means of communicating what only He can reveal.

Blessed be the God and Father of our Lord Jesus Christ, Who by His Spirit reveals great and hidden things that we have not known.

God in Heaven, the Great I AM, the Alpha and Omega, the First and the Last, the Beginning and the End, You are Holy, Just, and Pure. God, You can do no wrong. You are Good to all, and You are Sovereign over all. God, we ask for more dreams from You. Bless us, O God in Heaven, with dreams of instruction. Whatever is keeping us from dreams, reveal this and give us the discipline to seek You for assistance and aid. Give us the strength and financial means to eat well. Bless us with the discipline to go to bed early and get up early. May we be those who partake in the spiritual disciplines necessary to cultivate the gift in which You are willing to give. May we prove ourselves as trusted vessels who seek this gift for none other than Thy Glory and a means to receive instruction, correction, and bring edification to Your Body, the Church. O God, we seek You for this gift, and ask for dreams in a greater measure. Grant us our heart's desire, and lead in all our dreams, Holy Spirit. We lay down our lusts and enticements that would interrupt proper dreaming. We break all legal rights with the lust of the flesh, the lust of the eyes, and the pride of life. Every demon associated with these, we expel you from us in the Name of Jesus and command you to go from us! O God, fill us with more of Your Holy Spirit as we die to the flesh and the world and desire all that is of the Spirit. In Jesus' name, Amen.

The Gift of Interpretation of Dreams

"*And Pharaoh said to Joseph, 'I have had a dream, and there is no one who can interpret it. But I have heard it said of you that you can understand a dream, to interpret it.' So Joseph answered Pharaoh, saying, 'It is not in me; God will give Pharaoh an answer of peace.'"*
– Genesis 41:15-16 NKJV

While the gift of dreams is for speaking and directing, the gift of interpreting dreams is to bring clarity and understanding, and to provide an opportunity for others to be raised up in their gifting.

We know "A man's gift makes room for him, And brings him before great men" (Proverbs 18:16 NKJV). This is how it was for Joseph, and this is how it can be for us who have the gift.

My wife has the gift of this, while I have the gift of dreams. Whenever I share a dream that God gives me, I find it fascinating how she can bring everything together. As she tells me almost every time, "I don't know how I can do this. It's truly God, because when you were speaking, I had no idea what to say."

Those with the gift of interpreting dreams are those who have no idea what is to come of what is to be spoken, but receive the answer at the moment one ends the telling of the dream. This is when the Holy Spirit connects the dots and makes sense of the dream. Of course, there are extensive dreams that require some time for meditation, but overall, it is no more than a few minutes. When the Holy Spirit speaks, He speaks. One does not need to sit there for prolonged periods of time to figure out a dream when they have the gift of interpretation of dreams. It comes directly to them (or after just a few minutes) when one has the gift, is walking with the Lord, and fully trusts in the Holy Spirit to bring forth the understanding.

When we view Scripture and the story of Joseph, while he was in prison for something he didn't do but was accused of trying to lie with Potiphar's wife (Genesis 39:19-23), God built him up in his interpretation of dreams. We will focus much more heavily on this in the following chapters, but watch what happens when Pharaoh has a dream. Genesis 41:1-7 (NKJV) declares:

> "Then it came to pass, at the end of two full years, that Pharaoh had a dream; and behold, he stood by the river. Suddenly there came up out of the river seven cows, fine looking and fat; and they fed in the meadow. Then behold, seven other cows came up after them out of the river, ugly and gaunt, and stood by the *other* cows on the bank of the river. And the ugly and gaunt cows ate up the seven fine looking and fat cows. So Pharaoh awoke. He slept and dreamed a second time; and suddenly seven heads of grain came up on one stalk, plump and good. Then behold, seven thin heads, blighted by the east wind, sprang up after them. And the seven thin heads devoured the seven plump and full heads. So Pharaoh awoke, and indeed, *it was* a dream."

Without reading ahead, if we were to attempt to understand the dream, could we bring the interpretation? It seems somewhat abstract, yet Joseph knew in an instant. He didn't need to sit there and say, "Pharaoh, give me a few days." No, when we permit God to work the gift, the gift happens naturally and instantaneously, without premeditative thought. Joseph brings the answer in Genesis 41:25-32 (NKJV):

"Then Joseph said to Pharaoh, 'The dreams of Pharaoh *are* one; God has shown Pharaoh what He *is* about to do: The seven good cows *are* seven years, and the seven good heads *are* seven years; the dreams *are* one. And the seven thin and ugly cows which came up after them *are* seven years, and the seven empty heads blighted by the east wind are seven years of famine. This *is* the thing which I have spoken to Pharaoh. God has shown Pharaoh what He *is* about to do. Indeed seven years of great plenty will come throughout all the land of Egypt; but after them seven years of famine will arise, and all the plenty will be forgotten in the land of Egypt; and the famine will deplete the land. So the plenty will not be known in the land because of the famine following, for it *will be* very severe. And the dream was repeated to Pharaoh twice because the thing *is* established by God, and God will shortly bring it to pass.'"

In a moment, Joseph correlated that the seven good cows are seven years. This is a crucial point to note, as many dreams bring forth people, animals, environments, and many other aspects that are not to be taken *literally*. A person with the gift of interpretation of dreams knows that these are used in a way to convey a message that could not otherwise be figured out. God does this to allow the Body of Christ to work as the Body of Christ. It brings unity when one person has the gift of dreams and the other a gift of interpretation. It also conveys that what is *from* God can only be understood *by* God. We cannot try to force what a dream means, lest God become angry and furious with us. For many, prophesy and practice divination, deliberately bringing false confirmations of dreams, prophecies, and visions that are not true. In the end, God is angry with these individuals if they do not repent.

We want to understand that we can only have understanding when God gives it to us. Until that occurs, it is out of the vain imagination of our own hearts.

Joseph also knew that the cows resembled whether there would be plenty or famine. Not only did he know this, but he knew who it was for – it was for Egypt! There was no hint that this was for Egypt, but Joseph knew instantly. Additionally, he conveyed that the timeframe was meant to reveal what must be done now for later.

Many dreams are not for today but for a later time. The dreams are meant to encourage, exhort, rebuke, warn, and prepare us for the next stage. God does this so that we might change course of direction or continue going forward, knowing that the harvest is coming. When someone has the gift of interpretation, they can understand not only *what* the dream is but *what it is for.* A person can tell you that what you see is a traffic light, but it is altogether different when you explain what the traffic light is for. Likewise, it is with dreams. Interpretation of dreams is not just for the sake of interpretation, but to provide guidance and counsel as to next steps and actions needed to take place, and what God expects of the individual, people, nation, or world.

Gifts of the Spirit are not hereditary. They are dispersed by the Holy Spirit at His Own discretion. Nonetheless, some gifts overlap within the family that parents can impart to their kids through the confirmation of the Holy Spirit. Let us look at Genesis 37:5-10 (NKJV) for an example:

> "Now Joseph had a dream, and he told *it* to his brothers; and they hated him even more. So he said to them, "Please hear this dream which I have dreamed: There we were, binding sheaves in the field. Then behold, my sheaf arose and also stood upright; and indeed your sheaves stood all around and bowed down to my sheaf." And his brothers said to him, "Shall you indeed reign over us? Or shall you indeed have dominion over us?" So they hated him even more for his dreams and for his words. Then he dreamed still another dream and told it to his brothers, and said, "Look, I have dreamed another dream. And this time, the sun, the moon, and the eleven stars bowed down to me." So he told *it* to his father and his brothers; and his father rebuked him and said to him, "What *is* this dream that you have dreamed? Shall your mother and I and your brothers indeed come to bow down to the earth before you?""

As Joseph shared his dream with his family, they knew the interpretation: they would bow down to him. Of course, any family member would mock or become somewhat upset with this dream. Who wants to think that they, as a big brother, will one day bow before their little brother? His family knew instantly what it meant, but Joseph did not at the time. This is a clear revealment that gifts of the Spirit are to work in a family unit. If you are not understanding, activating, or using your gifts, you are wasting precious time to help bring edification, correction, and encouragement to those around you – especially within your family!

Though the family of Joseph did not have the best approach, there is a reason why Joseph shared the dream. They would be able to interpret, something Joseph did not have at the time. Joseph learned the gift of interpretation later, specifically while in prison. Never find it strange if God "locks you away" in a season of isolation where it is just you and Him. For Joseph, it was over a decade, but look what happened? You must ask the same, "What is God willing to do for me? Does He have me in a season of isolation? If so, what for? What does He desire of me? Am I willing to have it just be Him and I for these next few months and years that I may prepare for what lies ahead?"

Just as singleness is a season of preparation, so it is with a season of isolation. When it seems all we knew is no longer – our friends are gone, family forsakes us, and we are mocked and ridiculed for believing in the LORD God, this is a great place to be. When we really see the value of such a season, we will press into and seek God all the more. "Blessed *are* those who keep His testimonies, Who seek Him with the whole heart!" (Psalm 119:2 NKJV). When we choose to seek God during these times, we not only will receive new gifts, but they will be heightened to such a degree that they will place us before known men. Not for the sake of bringing glory to us, but stewarding well what God has given for His Glory. "Do you see a man *who* excels in his work? He will stand before kings; He will not stand before unknown *men*" (Proverbs 22:29 NKJV). Those who are gifted must grow in their gifting and use it to excel in their work. For gifts are meant to be used in our work, and they will bring us to places we could not reach on our own. Of course, this is all the Holy Spirit, and He honors those who steward well what He gives.

Joseph shows that we can have more than one gift. There is a season of going to others, but eventually we can have the gift ourselves. Of course, we can still seek others' aid with the gifts they have, even if we have the same. I receive much encouragement from those who bring prophetic words to me, though I have the gift as well. What we want to understand, simply, is that we can have as many gifts of the Spirit as we are willing to *continually ask* Him for. There is no limit, and God is willing to do more than we could imagine.

"And when Gideon had come, there was a man telling a dream to his companion. He said, "I have had a dream: *To my* surprise, a loaf of barley bread tumbled into the camp of Midian; it came to a tent and struck it so that it fell and overturned, and the tent collapsed." Then his companion answered and said, "This *is* nothing else but the sword of Gideon the son of Joash, a man of Israel! Into his hand God has delivered Midian and the whole camp." And so it was, when Gideon heard the telling of the dream and its interpretation, that he worshiped. He returned to the camp of Israel, and said, "Arise, for the Lord has delivered the camp of Midian into your hand"" (Judges 7:13-15 NKJV).

The interpretation of the man's dream brought worship to God and confidence from Gideon! It was a means of filling one with greater strength and faith in the Lord. This is one of the ways God speaks to His saints and reveals His Foreknowledge to His saints. Yes, God does this through prophetic words, visions, word of knowledge, and so forth. Still, the interpretation of dreams is simply another way of revealing to us that He has either *declared* what will happen, He Himself will *make* it happen, or He simply *knows* what will happen. In either case, nothing can catch us off guard.

This is a great blessing for us who are going to battle each day. Yes, there are spiritual battles in family homes and at the job, but for some of us, we are going into the bowels of Hell. We are coming against deep, hidden occults as prayer warriors. Some of us are coming against those who partake in sex trafficking. Others of us are trying to save children and help others heal from Satanic Ritualistic Abuse (SRA). In all cases, we want God to speak and declare to us what will happen.

Many times, it is easy to lose sight. Fear can set in, anger and rage, and we can even get in a state of doubting God. It's in these times that we must pray and ask God to bring confidence and assurance. He will, by His Spirit, ultimately, but He also can and is willing (based on His Own discretion) to comfort us by revealing the future before it happens. Truly, we are living in times of victory. A mighty Wind of the Holy

Ghost will be sweeping throughout this world. A revival of repentance and a revival of revelation are on the cusp. God will do this, and He alone will get the Glory.

I am going to make a declared prophecy that I believe is to occur – I believe we are entering into a season (whether it's in the next few years or a few decades) where God is going to have prophets and those who have stewarded the gifts of the Spirit well rise to be at the side of leaders and people in authority. There is going to be one last wave in which the person kings and Presidents want by their side will not be bodyguards, financial elites, or men of military prowess. Yes, they will want and have this already, but above all, they will want a person beside them who hears from the Lord directly! This is what I believe, and time will reveal what has been spoken.

Clearly, this is something that God has done and will continue to do. When the king during Daniel's time had a dream, he knew not what it meant. It strongly bothered him, and he wanted someone to explain what it meant, so much so that he wanted someone to declare the dream that he had as well as its interpretation! Daniel 2:1-6 (NKJV) reveals:

> "Now in the second year of Nebuchadnezzar's reign, Nebuchadnezzar had dreams; and his spirit was *so* troubled that his sleep left him. Then the king gave the command to call the magicians, the astrologers, the sorcerers, and the Chaldeans to tell the king his dreams. So they came and stood before the king. And the king said to them, "I have had a dream, and my spirit is anxious to know the dream."
>
> Then the Chaldeans spoke to the king in Aramaic, "O king, live forever! Tell your servants the dream, and we will give the interpretation."
>
> The king answered and said to the Chaldeans, "My decision is firm: if you do not make known the dream to me, and its interpretation, you shall be cut in pieces, and your houses shall be made an ash heap. However, if you tell the dream and its interpretation, you shall receive from me gifts, rewards, and great honor. Therefore tell me the dream and its interpretation.""

This decree by King Nebuchadnezzar was an impossible task for man, but a simple one for the Holy Spirit. As God set the stage, Daniel was brought forth to declare the dream and its interpretation. Daniel 2:31-45 (NKJV) declares:

> "'You, O king, were watching; and behold, a great image! This great image, whose splendor *was* excellent, stood before you; and its form *was* awesome. This image's head *was* of fine gold, its chest and arms of silver, its belly and thighs of bronze, its legs of iron, its feet partly of iron and partly of clay. You watched while a stone was cut out without hands, which struck the image on its feet of iron and clay, and broke them in pieces. Then the iron, the clay, the bronze, the silver, and the gold were crushed together, and became like chaff from the summer threshing floors; the wind carried them away so that no trace of them was found. And the stone that struck the image became a great mountain and filled the whole earth.
>
> "This *is* the dream. Now we will tell the interpretation of it before the king. You, O king, *are* a king of kings. For the God of heaven has given you a kingdom, power, strength, and glory; and wherever the children of men dwell, or the beasts of the field and the birds of the heaven, He has given *them* into your hand, and has made you ruler over them all—you *are* this head of gold. But after you shall arise another kingdom inferior to yours; then another, a third kingdom of bronze, which shall rule over all the earth. And the fourth kingdom shall be as strong as iron, inasmuch as iron breaks in pieces and shatters everything; and like iron that crushes, *that kingdom* will break in pieces and crush all the others. Whereas you saw the feet and toes, partly of potter's clay and partly of iron, the kingdom shall be divided; yet the strength of the iron shall be in it, just as you saw the iron mixed with ceramic clay. And *as* the toes of the feet *were* partly of iron and partly of clay, *so* the kingdom shall be partly strong and partly fragile. As you saw iron mixed with ceramic clay, they will mingle with the seed of men; but they will not adhere to one another, just as iron does not mix with clay. And in the days of these kings the God of heaven will set up a kingdom which shall never be destroyed; and the kingdom shall not be left to other people; it shall break in pieces and consume all these kingdoms, and it shall stand forever. Inasmuch as you saw that the stone

was cut out of the mountain without hands, and that it broke in pieces the iron, the bronze, the clay, the silver, and the gold—the great God has made known to the king what will come to pass after this. The dream is certain, and its interpretation is sure.'"

Daniel's declaration at the end conveys complete confidence and assurance that what has been revealed will occur. Again, only God could equip Daniel to do such a remarkable feat. Without God, Daniel would have been left to his own devices and would have been executed.

Again, we see that this entire dream makes no sense unless someone has the gift. What is seen in the dream is not to be taken literally; rather, it serves as a guiding pillar for what must be conveyed. God not only provided this moment to raise up a mighty saint in Him who would perform His Will, but He also equipped Daniel to shock those who heard of this gift. As I said before, there are coming days and times where God will select a few to be like Joseph and Daniel – to stand before kings and Presidents and bring forth prophetic words, interpretations of dreams and visions, and provide words of knowledge and wisdom that will baffle them and lead them to wanting those individuals to be by their side. This will occur in God's appointed time.

If we desire to be raised for God's Glory, we must be humble, obedient, and steward well what God has given. These positions are few, but there will be others amongst leaders, government, organizations, and businesses. Nonetheless, if we desire to be among the few called to such positions, the work begins now and must continue. Few there be who are called to such because few there be who endure to the end.

As with all gifts, the interpretation of dreams will always be in demand. Of course, it may not be used every day, but the times when it must come forth, the Holy Spirit is readily prepared to work through the individual. This is evident later on in Daniel (who was given the name of Belteshazzar). Daniel 4:4-27 (NKJV) starts with Nebuchadnezzar speaking:

"I, Nebuchadnezzar, was at rest in my house, and flourishing in my palace. I saw a dream which made me afraid, and the thoughts on my bed and the visions of my head troubled me. Therefore I issued a decree to bring in all the wise *men* of Babylon before me, that they might make known to me the interpretation of the dream. Then the magicians, the astrologers, the Chaldeans, and the soothsayers came in, and I told them the dream; but they did not make known to me its interpretation. But at last Daniel came before me (his name *is* Belteshazzar, according to the name of my god; in him *is* the Spirit of the Holy God), and I told the dream before him, *saying:* "Belteshazzar, chief of the magicians, because I know that the Spirit of the Holy God *is* in you, and no secret troubles you, explain to me the visions of my dream that I have seen, and its interpretation.

"These *were* the visions of my head *while* on my bed:
I was looking, and behold,
A tree in the midst of the earth,
And its height was great.
The tree grew and became strong;
Its height reached to the heavens,
And it could be seen to the ends of all the earth.
Its leaves *were* lovely,
Its fruit abundant,
And in it *was* food for all.
The beasts of the field found shade under it,
The birds of the heavens dwelt in its branches,
And all flesh was fed from it.

"I saw in the visions of my head *while* on my bed, and there was a watcher, a holy one, coming down from heaven. He cried aloud and said thus:

'Chop down the tree and cut off its branches,
Strip off its leaves and scatter its fruit.
Let the beasts get out from under it,
And the birds from its branches.
Nevertheless leave the stump and roots in the earth,
Bound with a band of iron and bronze,
In the tender grass of the field.
Let it be wet with the dew of heaven,
And *let* him graze with the beasts
On the grass of the earth.

Let his heart be changed from *that of* a man,
Let him be given the heart of a beast,
And let seven times pass over him.
'This decision *is* by the decree of the watchers,
And the sentence by the word of the holy ones,
In order that the living may know
That the Most High rules in the kingdom of men,
Gives it to whomever He will,
And sets over it the lowest of men.'

"This dream I, King Nebuchadnezzar, have seen. Now you, Belteshazzar, declare its interpretation, since all the wise *men* of my kingdom are not able to make known to me the interpretation; but you *are* able, for the Spirit of the Holy God *is* in you."

Then Daniel, whose name *was* Belteshazzar, was astonished for a time, and his thoughts troubled him. *So* the king spoke, and said, "Belteshazzar, do not let the dream or its interpretation trouble you."

Belteshazzar answered and said, "My lord, *may* the dream concern those who hate you, and its interpretation concern your enemies!

"The tree that you saw, which grew and became strong, whose height reached to the heavens and which *could be* seen by all the earth, whose leaves *were* lovely and its fruit abundant, in which *was* food for all, under which the beasts of the field dwelt, and in whose branches the birds of the heaven had their home— it *is* you, O king, who have grown and become strong; for your greatness has grown and reaches to the heavens, and your dominion to the end of the earth.

"And inasmuch as the king saw a watcher, a holy one, coming down from heaven and saying, 'Chop down the tree and destroy it, but leave its stump and roots in the earth, *bound* with a band of iron and bronze in the tender grass of the field; let it be wet with the dew of heaven, and let him graze with the beasts of the field, till seven times pass over him'; this is the interpretation, O king, and this is the decree of the Most High, which has come upon my lord the king: They shall drive you from men, your dwelling shall be with the beasts of the field, and they shall make you eat grass like oxen. They shall wet you with the dew of heaven, and seven times shall pass over you, till you know that the Most

High rules in the kingdom of men, and gives it to whomever He chooses.

"And inasmuch as they gave the command to leave the stump *and* roots of the tree, your kingdom shall be assured to you, after you come to know that Heaven rules. Therefore, O king, let my advice be acceptable to you; break off your sins by *being* righteous, and your iniquities by showing mercy to *the* poor. Perhaps there may be a lengthening of your prosperity.'"

Many interpretations are not always easy to give. With each gift comes a straightforward responsibility, and a failure to fulfill it honestly and truthfully will result in one's own demise. The responsibility we are speaking of is easy to understand, but not always easy to do – share the truth. The truth is of the utmost importance, and there is no way of lessening the blow of rebuke that one needs to hear.

When God gives insight into matters that must be addressed, we must speak what has been revealed. After all, we are not out to hurt anyone, and if God is the One Who gives us the interpretation, why must we fear or worry? Why must we be concerned with how that other person might perceive the message or feel? We don't need to, because we are not the ones making up what is revealed! We are just the messengers. "'All that the Lord speaks, that I must do'" (Numbers 23:26 NKJV).

Daniel is very clear toward the end of the passage we just read: "break off your sins by *being* righteous, and your iniquities by showing mercy to *the* poor" (Daniel 4:27 NKJV). When we are stuck in sin, we tend to operate in the fear of being found out. Of course, God shows Grace and Mercy and is not out to bring down those who are struggling. However, when someone is prideful in what they are partaking in, God will expose that individual (if He so chooses). When He does, it is always out of love to wake that person up to the reality that sin is destructive, that Christ can save, that repentance and turning to Him for forgiveness allow God to bring forth transformation.

If we fail to speak what God is revealing, it falls upon our heads. This is made evident when God speaks to Ezekiel in Ezekiel 3:17-19 (NKJV):

"'Son of man, I have made you a watchman for the house of Israel; therefore hear a word from My mouth, and give them warning from Me: When I say to the wicked, 'You shall surely die,' and you give him no warning, nor speak to warn the wicked from his wicked way, to save his life, that same wicked *man* shall die in his iniquity; but his blood I will require at your hand. Yet, if you warn the wicked, and he does not turn from his wickedness, nor from his wicked way, he shall die in his iniquity; but you have delivered your soul.'"

Gifts given by God are meant to be stewarded well, not to be neglected due to fear. We must be courageous and bold, always sharing the truth in love.

As one grows in the interpretation of dreams, it is important to emphasize that the Holy Spirit will connect and make sense of what the dreams entail, but He will also reveal trends. Often, certain images can convey a commonality across the board. For example, some people may say, "crocodiles resemble lying" or "a snake represents deception." They may read books about how to make sense of dreams. This is all fine and well, but we must discern that just because there is a commonality (such as crocodiles in a dream), it does not mean the direction at which the image is revealed is the same. It would be much different to see crocodiles around the White House, for example, as opposed to a person we know who has recently entered our lives. Greater still, around the White House could convey lying in the White House, or that lies are entering the White House, causing an invasion of extra, unnecessary problems. If a dream further reveals specific individuals in the White House, it could suggest that these lies are coming from those around the President, not necessarily the President himself.

We mention all this because we never want to make haste. The Holy Spirit will give the interpretation, but it is the responsibility of the individual with the gift of dreams to share the entire dream. Failure to share the entirety of the dream will either corrupt the interpretation or, most times, prevent the Holy Spirit from giving the interpretation to the person with the gift to interpret. Truly, only God can bring about the complete puzzle that must be solved, by His Holy Spirit speaking to the person with the gift.

It is not until we learn to wholly trust in the Holy Spirit, be trained by Him, and hear His Voice that we will interpret and unpack any and all dreams that God gives to others and to ourselves. Books are great, but reading a book on "how to interpret dreams" only goes so far, as dreams have many components that all the books in the world could not unpack. Reading a book on "how to interpret dreams" will tell us some basic principles of what "such and such" means, but ultimately, one must learn from the Holy Spirit, Who is the Greatest Teacher and the only Teacher we need. "But the anointing which you have received from Him abides in you, and you do not need that anyone teach you; but as the same anointing teaches you concerning all things, and is true, and is not a lie, and just as it has taught you, you will abide in Him" (1 John 2:27 NKJV).

When Pilate had Jesus presented before him (determining whether Jesus should be crucified or not and trading Him in and allowing the prisoner, Barabbas, to go free) and "he was sitting on the judgment seat, his wife sent to him, saying, "Have nothing to do with that just Man, for I have suffered many things today in a dream because of Him""" (Matthew 27:19 NKJV). Sometimes, dreams are so self-evident that the interpretation is understood within the dream. Someone who has the gift of both dreams and interpretations will determine whether something is to be taken literally or needs further interpretation. Of course, if one has the gift of dreams, they can detect, by the Holy Spirit's speaking, if a dream is to be taken literally. However, most of the time, one needs the interpretation of dream. If the dream really means exactly what is conveyed, there will be no hidden meanings. One will wake up in the surety of what they dreamed; they will not sit there wondering what everything means.

It is important to note that God gives gifts to those apart from Him, and He speaks to them for specific reasons. Clearly, Pilate's wife had the gift of dreams and their interpretation. Even though she was not a believer in Christ, she stood up for Him (insofar as she was guided by the dreams God gave her). This reveals that God guides even the ungodly to Him and makes known what is right to them, but that man has free will. In this instance, Pilate's wife did what was right, but Pilate feared man and did what was wrong.

What his wife dreamed exactly, we do not know, but it brought forth great distress. When God wants to wake a person up from spiritual slumber and warn them from doing what is wrong, God will make the dream plain. Pilate's Wife knew exactly what she dreamed, even though it was not conveyed to us. She was an unbeliever, but God chose to speak in such a way. Again, unbelievers can have gifts of the Holy Spirit, but it doesn't mean they are using them by the Power and Guidance of the Holy Spirit. One must be born again for this to occur. Without the Holy Spirit, they may have the gift, but up to a certain point. God gives gifts to all, even when they are in the womb. However, if much of the gifts seems foreign to an individual, it's just because they have not been taught this or know the gifts they have from the Holy Spirit.

Again, I want to emphasize that gifts can be given to people from birth. They may learn to steward the gift, but that does not mean the gift is perfectly used, since the Holy Spirit must be present. God will speak to people in different ways and draw others to Him. He may speak in a dream or vision to unbelievers. Of course, God can give dreams at His Own discretion to those who don't have the gift. Just because we get a dream or vision does not mean we possess the gift. However, when we understand what we see and dream, it shows signs that we have the gift. God will make it plain whether we have a particular gift. These gifts are not meant to be used for our own gain, but by the Spirit's directing. Without Him, we use them in vain. They will not be used appropriately, perfectly, or stewarded well. They will fall into the camp of divination or fortune-telling. Those individuals may have a gift from God since the womb to a certain degree, but they are consulting the Enemy (demons and unclean spirits) rather than God. In the end, partial truths are conveyed, but not the full Truth. This is why we must be born-again to truly understand our gifts and seek guidance and counsel from Him Who is the Gift-Giver! "Every good gift and every perfect gift is from above, and comes down from the Father of lights, with Whom there is no variation or shadow of turning" (James 1:17 NKJV).

Another instance of receiving a dream and understanding its interpretation instantly is found in Matthew 1:18-25 (NKJV) when Jesus is born:

"Now the birth of Jesus Christ was as follows: After His mother Mary was betrothed to Joseph, before they came together, she was found with child of the Holy Spirit. Then Joseph her husband, being a just *man,* and not wanting to make her a public example, was minded to put her away secretly. But while he thought about these things, behold, an angel of the Lord appeared to him in a dream, saying, "Joseph, son of David, do not be afraid to take to you Mary your wife, for that which is conceived in her is of the Holy Spirit. And she will bring forth a Son, and you shall call His name Jesus, for He will save His people from their sins."

So all this was done that it might be fulfilled which was spoken by the Lord through the prophet, saying: "Behold, the virgin shall be with child, and bear a Son, and they shall call His name Immanuel," which is translated, "God with us."

Then Joseph, being aroused from sleep, did as the angel of the Lord commanded him and took to him his wife, and did not know her till she had brought forth her firstborn Son. And he called His name Jesus."

God was willing to speak to Joseph amid his uncertainty, fear, confusion, and not knowing what to do next. God spoke to Joseph in a dream by sending an angel to speak directly and clearly. This was to help Joseph during a very trying time.

Often, dream interpretations are given when someone is in a highly heightened state of stress, fear, doubt, and the like. God does not speak the moment we enter this, nor does He every time we enter a season or period of time like this. God is selective when He speaks and gives interpretation, as He does not want us to depend on the gifts but on Him, knowing that even when it *feels* He is not near, He is. For Joseph, being married to a virgin, yet now the Holy Spirit impregnates her, this man needed further confirmation and clarity that he was not being lied to or deceived. Can you blame the man? I, for one, would want further answers!

This is a blessing to know, as interpretations of dreams not only can be immediate within our own dreams but also can be directly given by God, *sending* an angel to communicate with us. This further confirms the reality of the spiritual realm and of angels. Not only in this life will we entertain angels unaware (Hebrews 13:2), but angels will entertain us knowingly and with our knowledge (by God's Decree). This is exciting, as interpretations can be given not only by the Holy Spirit Himself but also by God, who may send a person or an angel to speak and provide further clarification. People can have the gift of interpretation, but angels can be the direct messengers. In these moments, there is no confusion about the dream's interpretation, for the dream's interpreter serves as a messenger, clarifying to us what must be known within the dream! In the instance of Joseph, he had a dream, but the angel gave instructions and made the next steps clear, making it easy for Joseph to interpret and follow through.

Lastly, we want to understand that in rare cases, dreams can present when one is about to die. This is done so that we might get right with the Lord. I have had to present prophetic words that convey time is short for certain individuals. Though they have been living for a few months since those were delivered, their health is declining at a rapid pace. I am not sure how much longer they have, and within those words that God gave me to give, there was a message of repentance. God sometimes warns by this so that individuals can understand the severity of their sin, how they have continually neglected God and gone their own way, and the current health consequences of their actions. It is in these rare times that God issues a thunderous warning to get people to truly repent and accept Him before it is too late.

Though this is in the Old Testament (before Christ), we see this is what happened with Joseph while in prison. The warning given by Joseph (through interpreting the chief baker's dream) was not meant to make the man sad, though of course he *most likely* became frightened and disheartened at what Joseph revealed. No, it was a means for the man to reflect on his life and get right with God before he drew his last breath. Genesis 40:5-22 (NKJV) tells the story in greater detail:

> "Then the butler and the baker of the king of Egypt, who *were* confined in the prison, had a dream, both of them, each man's dream in one night *and* each man's dream with its *own* interpretation. And Joseph came in to them in the morning and looked at them, and saw

that they *were* sad. So he asked Pharaoh's officers who *were* with him in the custody of his lord's house, saying, "Why do you look *so* sad today?"

And they said to him, "We each have had a dream, and *there is* no interpreter of it."

So Joseph said to them, "Do not interpretations belong to God? Tell *them* to me, please."

Then the chief butler told his dream to Joseph, and said to him, "Behold, in my dream a vine *was* before me, and in the vine *were* three branches; it *was* as though it budded, its blossoms shot forth, and its clusters brought forth ripe grapes. Then Pharaoh's cup *was* in my hand; and I took the grapes and pressed them into Pharaoh's cup, and placed the cup in Pharaoh's hand."

And Joseph said to him, "This *is* the interpretation of it: The three branches *are* three days. Now within three days Pharaoh will lift up your head and restore you to your place, and you will put Pharaoh's cup in his hand according to the former manner, when you were his butler. But remember me when it is well with you, and please show kindness to me; make mention of me to Pharaoh, and get me out of this house. For indeed I was stolen away from the land of the Hebrews; and also I have done nothing here that they should put me into the dungeon."

When the chief baker saw that the interpretation was good, he said to Joseph, "I also *was* in my dream, and there *were* three white baskets on my head. In the uppermost basket *were* all kinds of baked goods for Pharaoh, and the birds ate them out of the basket on my head."

So Joseph answered and said, "This *is* the interpretation of it: The three baskets *are* three days. Within three days Pharaoh will lift off your head from you and hang you on a tree; and the birds will eat your flesh from you."

Now it came to pass on the third day, *which was* Pharaoh's birthday, that he made a feast for all his servants; and he lifted up the head of the chief butler and of the chief baker among his servants. Then he restored the chief butler to his butlership again, and he placed the cup in Pharaoh's hand. But he hanged the chief baker, as Joseph had interpreted to them."

We don't know what the chief baker did, but most likely, Joseph spoke to him of God. This provided him with time to repent and get right with God, which we *hope actually* happened. We don't hear any of his response, but one can be sure that when their life is limited, they will be more compelled to do what is right. This is not always the case, but it most certainly occurs in this life amongst those who are humble enough to honestly reflect, evaluate, and see how they have grieved the heart of God and sinned before Him.

God loves those He made in His image, and He always has the best for us. When He speaks to us in dreams and warns us, may we allow the warning to compel us to do what is right. For God not only warns of a coming death so people can repent, but He also warns us to flee from certain places and people to keep us alive. The interpretation is within the direct message, and God will always give discernment as to whether it is a literal interpretation, a direct message, or something abstract meant to be interpreted.

We see God giving a direct word with a clear understanding and interpretation through what the wise men did when visiting Jesus, and what Joseph did for his family in Matthew 2:7-15 (NKJV):

> "Then Herod, when he had secretly called the wise men, determined from them what time the star appeared. And he sent them to Bethlehem and said, "Go and search carefully for the young Child, and when you have found *Him,* bring back word to me, that I may come and worship Him also."
>
> When they heard the king, they departed; and behold, the star which they had seen in the East went before them, till it came and stood over where the young Child was. When they saw the star, they rejoiced with exceedingly great joy. And when they had come into the house, they saw the young Child with Mary His mother, and fell down and worshiped Him. And when they had opened their treasures, they presented gifts to Him: gold, frankincense, and myrrh.
>
> Then, being divinely warned in a dream that they should not return to Herod, they departed for their own country another way.
>
> Now when they had departed, behold, an angel of the Lord appeared to Joseph in a dream, saying, "Arise, take the young Child and

His mother, flee to Egypt, and stay there until I bring you word; for Herod will seek the young Child to destroy Him."

When he arose, he took the young Child and His mother by night and departed for Egypt, and was there until the death of Herod, that it might be fulfilled which was spoken by the Lord through the prophet, saying, "Out of Egypt I called My Son."'"

We need never worry, for if we lack the understanding of what a dream means, or we are unsure, God will still speak to us directly. He did so with Gideon. Let us view Judges 7:9-15 (NKJV) once more:

"It happened on the same night that the Lord said to him, "Arise, go down against the camp, for I have delivered it into your hand. But if you are afraid to go down, go down to the camp with Purah your servant, and you shall hear what they say; and afterward your hands shall be strengthened to go down against the camp." Then he went down with Purah his servant to the outpost of the armed men who *were* in the camp. Now the Midianites and Amalekites, all the people of the East, were lying in the valley as numerous as locusts; and their camels *were* without number, as the sand by the seashore in multitude.

And when Gideon had come, there was a man telling a dream to his companion. He said, "I have had a dream: *To my* surprise, a loaf of barley bread tumbled into the camp of Midian; it came to a tent and struck it so that it fell and overturned, and the tent collapsed."

Then his companion answered and said, "This *is* nothing else but the sword of Gideon the son of Joash, a man of Israel! Into his hand God has delivered Midian and the whole camp."

And so it was, when Gideon heard the telling of the dream and its interpretation, that he worshiped. He returned to the camp of Israel, and said, "Arise, for the Lord has delivered the camp of Midian into your hand.""

God gives dreams to others on our behalf. Other times, God will tell us that if we are afraid, then we must visit or do such and such to get confirmation. This is why, when it comes to a positive, easy-to-accept prophetic word, we must allow it to be weighed by other prophets. "Do not despise prophecies" (1 Thessalonians 5:20 NKJV). "Let two or three prophets speak, and let the others judge. But if *anything* is revealed to another who sits by, let the first keep silent. For you can all prophesy one by one, that all may learn and all may be encouraged. And the spirits of the prophets are subject to the prophets. For God is not *the author* of confusion but of peace, as in all the churches of the saints" (1 Corinthians 14:29-33 NKJV).

Let us always listen to God's speaking, for He speaks in many ways. If we possess the gift of interpretation of dreams, we must always give God glory and be humble, just as Daniel did in Daniel 2:27-30 (NKJV):

> "Daniel answered in the presence of the king, and said, "The secret which the king has demanded, the wise *men,* the astrologers, the magicians, and the soothsayers cannot declare to the king. But there is a God in heaven who reveals secrets, and He has made known to King Nebuchadnezzar what will be in the latter days. Your dream, and the visions of your head upon your bed, were these: As for you, O king, thoughts came *to* your *mind while* on your bed, *about* what would come to pass after this; and He who reveals secrets has made known to you what will be. But as for me, this secret has not been revealed to me because I have more wisdom than anyone living, but for *our* sakes who make known the interpretation to the king, and that you may know the thoughts of your heart."

May God give us the gift of both dreams and the interpretation of dreams, that we may be more effective saints for His Kingdom. This is why we want to pray to God before each night, "God, bless me with the gift of dreams and interpretation of dreams. Make known to me what must be known on this night. I run to You, Lord Jesus, and I place my family and I under the shadow of Your Wing, acknowledging that You are our Refuge and the righteous run to You and are kept safe. Keep the Enemy and me away from dreams that are not of You. Please speak to me and make clear what must be known. In Jesus' name, Amen." When we pray this, eventually, dreams and interpretations will be unlocked and received. Our duty is to steward these well, which begins by recording them through a document or journal. The more we keep up with this, the more we shall receive from God.

May God bless all of us with greater knowledge, understanding, and discernment, as we pray in all humility for the gift of interpretation of dreams.

God in Heaven, the Alpha and Omega, You are Great and Mighty, and Your years have no end. There is none like You in Heaven or on Earth. You create the stars and know them by name. You know the number of sand on Earth, and You know the number of hairs upon our head. Truly, nothing is too difficult for You. God, You bless man with the ability to think and reason, and we humble ourselves before You, requesting You to bless us with the gift of interpretation of dreams. Bring the increase in this gifting to one hundredfold over the next few months and years. God, keep us from becoming prideful, and do not allow us to take on more than we can bear. Help us to steward well the little You give us that we might steward the much. O God, speak to us in our dreams, and allow us to interpret the dreams of those around us. May they marvel at You, Holy Spirit, and what You are willing to give and do through man. For You deserve all the Glory, and may others who are amazed come to know Jesus as Lord and Savior and receive gifts of the Spirit in a like manner. We trust in You, O God of Heaven and Earth, to perform this, for You alone can do all things. Thy Will be done, Heavenly Father. In Jesus' name, Amen.

The Gift of Visions

"*But this is what was spoken by the prophet Joel: 'And it shall come to pass in the last days, says God, That I will pour out of My Spirit on all flesh; Your sons and your daughters shall prophesy, Your young men shall see visions, Your old men shall dream dreams.'"*
– *Acts 2:16-17 NKJV*

Visions come in a variety of ways, but the end is always the same – to reveal what was, what is, or what will be.

God gives visions to His saints to protect, guide, lead, and bring forth Divine insight. Without visions, we would not see that which can only come from God. We would not have many portions of the Bible. The whole Book of Revelation would not exist. It is because of visions that we, as born-again believers, can know for certainty that God has spoken.

A term you may hear for those who possess the gift of visions is a *seer*. We see this in 1 Samuel 9:9 (NKJV):

"(Formerly in Israel, when a man went to inquire of God, he spoke thus: "Come, let us go to the seer"; for *he who is* now *called* a prophet was formerly called a seer.)"

Just as we can learn to recognize the Voice of God, we can realize what comes from Him. When we walk with God and grow in our knowledge of Him, we begin to understand what is of Him and what is not.

As the gift of the word of knowledge is learned, we come to find that it can be infiltrated (in a wrong and inaccurate manner) by our own knowledge and by the Enemy's knowledge. Simultaneously, when it comes to visions, we must understand that God gives us visions, but the Enemy can also affect our thinking, leading us to perceive and believe that which our minds bring forth, based on certain fears, anxieties, discouragements, and the like.

This is a very important point to address, as many times what people see is not always from God. Likewise, what they hear is not always from the Holy Spirit. It takes discernment to perceive what is of God and what is not. Our discernment increases the more we spend time with God. Truly, "the word of God *is* living and powerful, and sharper than any two-edged sword, piercing even to the division of soul and spirit, and of joints and marrow, and is a discerner of the thoughts and intents of the heart" (Hebrews 4:12 NKJV).

We must take a brief moment to expose the Enemy (I have written more on this in my books, *Waging War* and *Discerning the Devil*). For now, we want to be mindful of how the Enemy can affect our gift of visions and make us believe lies.

Our bodies are temples of the Holy Spirit. "Or do you not know that your body is the temple of the Holy Spirit *Who is* in you, Whom you have from God, and you are not your own? For you were bought at a price; therefore glorify God in your body and in your spirit, which are God's" (1 Corinthians 6:19-20 NKJV).

We are called to glorify God in both our bodies and spirits. There is much to say here, but we want to focus on the call to glorify God with our bodies.

When we do not respect or love God with the temples He has given us, we allow the Enemy to come in and influence how we behave and operate. This is very important to understand, as many have given way to temptation and allowed unclean spirits to enter them. Without even knowing, these demons begin to take over to a certain degree (in how we think, see, operate, speak, carry ourselves, view life, etc.).

Just as there are "black ops" within this life, there is a black OPS in the spiritual realm. Though much can be unraveled by the tactics of the Enemy, we are going to focus very briefly on the OPS of the Enemy, namely, *Oppression*, *Possession*, and *Suppression*.

For unbelievers and believers alike, they can both be *suppressed* by the Enemy. This is where temptation and certain tactics from the Enemy unfold. For the sake of understanding what we are about to address, let us view the aspect of lust.

The closer we are to God, the less likely we are to give way to the Enemy, meditate on a lustful thought (that is from the Enemy), and take the temptation further or act on it. Everyone can receive a thought of lust from the Enemy that attempts to *suppress* and hinder us. This *suppression* (whether we are believers or unbelievers) comes through words. "O, look at her, she's curvy. I wonder what it's like underneath?" or "Wow, he looks like he would be really good in bed."

Though these thoughts can vary from person to person and can be generated in the flesh, many times they come by way of the Enemy. We don't realize it, but our flesh is what *gives in* to the temptation, whereas the temptation itself comes from the Enemy. This was clearly seen in the Garden of Eden (Genesis 3). Satan tempted Adam and Eve, and by using their will in the wrong way, they opened the door to receiving the knowledge of good and evil. It was at that moment that the flesh became weak and sin entered the world. No longer was there just a temptation, but there was a greater pull to give in to temptations.

This is important to understand, as the Enemy will always tempt in order to gain more ground. This happens by *suppressing* us from within our bodies. Once we give in to a temptation, we are either *oppressed* or *possessed*.

For unbelievers, because they do not have the Holy Spirit dwelling within them, they can be *possessed* by demons. This is why you hear prison stories where someone says, "I don't know what happened. It's like something took over," or "Someone told me to do it." These are real instances, and they are incredibly tragic, as, though they are responsible for how they use their free will, in a moment of anger, which turned into hate, which turned into rage, murder occurred. The demons in the unbeliever possessed them to the point where murder was brought forth.

To the extent of the demon and how much of a hold the demon has, terrible murders can occur (beyond just firing a gun). We will not go into detail with this, but it does not take much research to understand how people were killed over the years. When murders are done in gruesome ways, that is entirely the exercising of a demon within an individual who wants to torture and destroy those made in the image of God.

In the example above, this is *strictly* for an unbeliever. They can be possessed to the point where they do something unspeakable. When looking at the topic of lust, a demon can suppress an unbeliever with thoughts. These thoughts are simply words that strive to lead toward a meditation. If the meditation is prolonged and action follows, an open door has just occurred.

That is why when the Enemy comes knocking, we must never allow him in by giving way to the message he is trying to have us believe and the action he wants us to partake in. The moment we do that, a demon can enter our vessel.

In this instant, a silent whisper is given of lust. If the unbeliever gives in by way of action, the demon comes in. As the demon comes into the body, it can also enter *into* the soul or mind. This is very important to understand, as this is where *possession* arises.

I have written extensively on our spiritual makeup in my book, *The Metaphysical Trichotomy of Persons*. For a brief understanding, the soul is our will, whereas our mind is our intellect. If a demon can not just enter our body, but harbor itself within our soul or mind, there can be possession. We will no longer be in control of our intellect and will. Rather, they will be able to do certain things to us that we do not even want to have happen!

Take, for example, the demon that kept throwing the boy into the fire and water. "Then one of the crowd answered and said, 'Teacher, I brought You my son, who has a mute spirit. And wherever it seizes him, it throws him down; he foams at the mouth, gnashes his teeth, and becomes rigid'" (Mark 9:17-18 NKJV). This is not normal behavior, and we see the demon having the power to throw his body wherever he desired.

Now, did this happen all the time? No, but it occurred many times, showing us that this particular demon was *in* both the body and soul.

When it comes to a demon of lust to the unbeliever, we will therefore see this pattern. The demon speaks words that entice a thought that, if meditated on, brings forth a visual. If the visual leads toward an action, the demon enters the unbeliever's body and soul. As the demon enters the unbeliever's body and soul, there is now the ability for the demon to *possess* the unbeliever at certain moments. This can come by way of being a sex addict, perversion, and rape.

When the demon can enter the soul and mind of an unbeliever, there are devastating consequences. They can take legal ground due to disobedient behavior toward God and His Word, and to the lack of the Holy Spirit. There is no one to defend them, as they have invited a demon (or demons) in. As this occurred, they now have an inability to fight, having given way. The only One Who can help them is the Holy Spirit (Whom we receive when we place our hope and trust in Christ and repent of our sins). When this happens, demons cannot *possess* the believer, but they can *oppress*.

When it comes to believers being tempted with a thought from the Enemy, there is a choice. The difference between us, who are born-again believers, and unbelievers is that we have the assistance and aid of the Holy Spirit. The more we grow in the knowledge of the Holy Spirit and cultivate a relationship with Him, the more we will recognize and go to Him to fight the temptations that come our way.

Let us say, in this example, that a believer is *suppressed* by certain thoughts from the Enemy. Again, these are thoughts expressed in words, not visuals. As the believer hears this temptation and, for the sake of this example, they give in, and it leads them to actions of having sex before marriage, watching pornography, etc., a demon enters into them.

When this demon enters the believer, they enter the body, but it *cannot* enter the soul or mind. Why? The Holy Spirit dominates those spiritual realms of a born-again believer's existence. What then does the

Enemy do inside the body? They enter the body and, although they cannot enter our soul or mind, they now have the ability to *oppress* our soul and mind.

Though the Holy Spirit still seals our souls and minds, there is a hindrance from our ability to keep in step with the Spirit and obey God's Word. As a demon of lust enters our body, it makes our flesh all the more weak, and now that the Enemy can oppress a believer, it can tempt us in greater manifestations.

The thoughts a demon gives to those who are believers but have opened doors through acting on suppressing thoughts can now be oppressed much more frequently. The *suppressive* thoughts were original words that could lead to thinking further on what is given. The *oppressive* thoughts are direct visualizations. This allows a demon to offer stronger temptations, but makes them unable to possess us to carry them out.

Whereas unbelievers immediately have little restraint and go full out with certain evils and sins, a born-again believer can be continually *oppressed*, making it more challenging to resist the Devil and knowing he will flee from us when we submit to God (James 4:7). This is why for those who are born-again, yet deny deliverance in the name of Jesus, suffer from a continual heavy burden or struggle with pornography, gluttony, gossip, depression, anxiety, fear, etc. These are not of God, and if someone is born-again, we must ask why there is this habitual struggle. Why is it that, if we want to be set free from these very things and we pray and pray to God to set us free, it still isn't working? It is because we need God's Holy Spirit to deliver us in the name of Jesus.

The OPS of the Enemy, therefore, is *Oppression*, *Possession*, and *Suppression*. For unbelievers, they are *suppressed* and then *possessed*. For born-again believers, they are *suppressed* and, if a door is opened, can be *oppressed*. When addictions, enslavements, and habits are not of God, and we desire to be set free, we now have the proper understanding to know it is a demon of that very aspect that we need to cast out in the Name of Jesus!

Now, how does this relate to the gift of visions? This relates to the standpoint that we often have a visualization or meditation of something that is not of God, but seems to be of God. Other times, it comes from the Enemy or from within our hearts. It is our job to press into the Holy Spirit and discern whether we have this gift. As He makes us aware of our gifting, the more we grow in Him and develop a relationship with Him, the more He will speak, reveal, and make known through visions.

Before we go into some Scriptural insight into the gift of visions and the different types of visions that occur, I shall give two brief testimonies.

Just recently, my Wife and I were going through a lot of spiritual warfare. The Enemy was raining down his strongest attacks, and it was amongst the most intense spiritual warfare I have ever experienced. I will not go into full detail, but I want to point out to you that my wife began to open up about something that happened to her in the past. She said, "I see myself as a little girl wearing a dress." I will not give the rest of what was said as it is private, but I immediately saw that image in my head. I said, "Is the dress red?" She began to weep and said, "Yes." This was a very emotional time that shed light on a lot of what was occurring, and God allowed me to see the instance of when she was a child in this dress and the situation. This is a vision of the *past*.

A vision of both the *present* and *future* occurred during the first week of Jackie and I getting married. Now, mind you, due to pornography from my past, the neurological pathways in my brain suffered greatly. After God set me free, I could see nothing. If someone said, "Think of a blue lion," I couldn't see one.

I used to believe this was a curse by my own doing, but I see now it was God's protection. Due to being stuck in pornography for over 10+ years, starting at the age of nine (due to a seven-year-old introducing it to me), I believe God supernaturally prevented me from visualization, as this protected me from reviewing and bringing to mind everything I saw over those years. My brain was advancing and maturing rapidly but was not fully developed.

Eventually, after a few days of being married to my Wife, I received the gift of tongues. At the time, I did not have the gift of visions, and Jackie did not have the gift of interpretation of visions. We prayed for a while, then both prayed in tongues. As this occurred, Jackie told me to ask God if He would be willing to show us anything. I prayed, "God, if it is Your Will, give me the gift of visions. Help me see only what You want me to see. I rebuke the enemy from planting anything in my mind that is not of God, in Jesus' Name. May it just be You, God. Holy Spirit speak."

After I prayed that, nothing happened for the next ten minutes. I began to think, "Well, it's not the time for me to receive this gift, or it just isn't for me." Then, all of a sudden, certain things started coming forth.

What I am going to share could give me a lot of pushback, but it is one of the many things God has revealed. For whatever reason, these visions that I have are not *dark*. Rather, they expose the *darkness* that pervades this world. After all, we know Satan is the ruler of it (John 12:31).

We actually see God do the same thing with Ezekiel in Ezekiel 8:1-12 (NKJV). The Scripture states:

> "And it came to pass in the sixth year, in the sixth *month*, on the fifth *day* of the month, as I sat in my house with the elders of Judah sitting before me, that the hand of the Lord God fell upon me there. Then I looked, and there was a likeness, like the appearance of fire—from the appearance of His waist and downward, fire; and from His waist and upward, like the appearance of brightness, like the color of amber. He stretched out the form of a hand, and took me by a lock of my hair; and the Spirit lifted me up between earth and heaven, and brought me in visions of God to Jerusalem, to the door of the north gate of the inner *court*, where the seat of the image of jealousy *was*, which provokes to jealousy. And behold, the glory of the God of Israel *was* there, like the vision that I saw in the plain.
>
> Then He said to me, "Son of man, lift your eyes now toward the north." So I lifted my eyes toward the north, and there, north of the altar gate, was this image of jealousy in the entrance.
>
> Furthermore He said to me, "Son of man, do you see what they are doing, the great abominations that the house of Israel commits here, to make Me go far away from My sanctuary? Now turn again, you will see greater abominations." So He brought me to the door of the court; and when I looked, there was a hole in the wall. Then He said to me, "Son

of man, dig into the wall"; and when I dug into the wall, there was a door.

And He said to me, "Go in, and see the wicked abominations which they are doing there." So I went in and saw, and there—every sort of creeping thing, abominable beasts, and all the idols of the house of Israel, portrayed all around on the walls. And there stood before them seventy men of the elders of the house of Israel, and in their midst stood Jaazaniah the son of Shaphan. Each man had a censer in his hand, and a thick cloud of incense went up. Then He said to me, "Son of man, have you seen what the elders of the house of Israel do in the dark, every man in the room of his idols? For they say, 'The Lord does not see us, the Lord has forsaken the land.' ""

Ezekiel saw the darkness that was being done in this vision. God exposed those who were supposed to be of Him. He is at full liberty and discretion to reveal what He wills to reveal to those who have the gift of visions. We would do well not to hide our sin, but to confess and repent. For everything done in private with the thought that one will not be found, will be revealed either in this life or most certainly in the next. For those who *struggle* with certain sins done in private, so long as they are seeking the Lord for deliverance and help, God will refrain from exposing them. For God only exposes the proud and those not humble enough to admit their weakness and seek Him for help to overcome their sins, struggles, addictions, and bad habits.

God has chosen to bless me with the gift of visions to see beautiful realities and understand certain aspects of life. Primarily, He uses it to reveal to me what occurs in darkness. I can tell you that a time is coming very soon when darkness will be brought into the light. This will begin to occur as revival springs forth. People will be tired of evil and sin, and, for a time, revival will occur throughout the land. This will only occur, however, when people truly repent.

"'For nothing is secret that will not be revealed, nor *anything* hidden that will not be known and come to light'" (Luke 8:17 NKJV). This will most certainly occur in Heaven, and there is a coming time when it will happen on Earth. May we be found as children of the Light when this occurs.

The vision was recorded (along with my wife's interpretation). This may offend some people and seem weird, but we will quickly see in Scripture that God speaks in the same way through visions. Sometimes, visions are seen directly. Other times, they are a puzzle. At certain points, they are out of body, and others are out of time. Some consist of the transportation of our soul, others consist of God bringing forth realities to our mind. In all aspects, we see a wide range of visions throughout Scripture in which God bestows the gift of visions.

Let us review both what I saw through the gift of visions that night and what my Wife's interpretation of the vision came to be:

08/21/2023 — Antichrist & Catholic Church
<u>ENCOUNTER</u>

Last night when speaking in tongues, I began to see after 15-20 minutes the upper torso of a man (whose arms were covered with black clothing and hands with black gloves). He was holding a bigger book (I believe the Bible) by one end (all the pages were just being flipped without him touching them.

Later, I saw a man driving. I was looking from the front windshield, and he was behind the steering wheel. Later, I saw something like me looking up and seeing the ceiling of a hospital. After, I saw what looked like to be prism windows (paintings of Mary, specifically - like what you see at the Catholic Church) going around (like a car wheel). I returned to see the man in the car, this time from the side windshield. Something this time, however, entered his eyes, which made them go from being brown to all black.

I later saw red and black. After this, I saw the same man dressed in all black (whose face I could not see) with the Bible turned upside down (the pages were facing the floor). After this, I saw a cave with teeth.

I also saw at some point a pink or red rose surrounded by blackness.

I saw a group of people on horses (I felt they were on my side) running toward a light. The sand they ran on was normal, but after reaching the light, some time passed before I saw a white sky, a white castle, and white sand (and a foot/sandal stepping in the white sand).

(This happened during Jackie and I's time, not in the vision) After,

I began to cry tremendously (in fear) and I wanted to speak out loud to Jackie, but I could not. It was as if someone had their hand on my throat (this happened 3 times). I would be speaking in tongues, sweating, and crying, wanting to say something, but I could not.

When it was done, Jackie began to pray powerfully against the Catholic Church, pedophilia, and that God would open doors for those who are caged and held captive. She and I felt a burden for those within the Catholic Church who were deceived. We both wept in different ways, and we felt a call from God that we were to expose the Enemy and his working within the Catholic Church. The greatest deception is that which closely resembles the truth. We believe the antichrist will be involved in the Catholic Church when the time comes.

As Jackie prayed, I saw a white horse and a blue eye (that seemed all the universe was inside this eye).

After Jackie prayed, she saw a flash of blue light in our room (it was like a sideways "V").

INTERPRETATION (MY WIFE)

The man behind the steering wheel represents people being led astray by the Catholic Church' blasphemous teachings of idolatry and the like.

The car represents the Catholic Church because the wheel of the car had glass prism windows (containing the statues of Mary and Jesus). He got into an accident, and it led to death. Many are being led to a spiritual death by Catholicism. His eyes turned black because he was deceived by false teaching and "blinded by darkness" (1 John 2:11).

The red and black symbolize Satanism. Catholicism is directly tied to Satanism.

The man in black turning the pages of the Bible upside down and handling the Word of God with carelessness was the Antichrist. He twists the Word of God and contradicts it, leading many astray from the infallible Word itself. The Antichrist spirit is already in the world (1 John 4:1-6).

Before speaking on what is seen above, it is important for everyone who has this gift to follow in suite with Habakkuk 2:2-3 (NKJV):

"Then the LORD answered me and said: "Write the vision And make *it* plain on tablets, That he may run who reads it. For the vision *is* yet for an appointed time; But at the end it will speak, and it will not lie. Though it tarries, wait for it; Because it will surely come, It will not tarry."

Only God could reveal the future since He is Timeless. Only God knows what is to occur because He is All-Knowing. We are called to write down the visions He gives us. If we steward well what He gives, He will continue to bring an increase and more visions in greater measure.

It is only God Who could have revealed the vision just mentioned and given its interpretation. There are more weighty visions that must be kept secret, but the point is to know that when God speaks, He speaks. There is a reason why He chooses to reveal what He reveals. For some, His visions are easier on the soul. For others, they can be difficult to digest. God does what He wills with the gifting, and the Holy Spirit makes known its interpretation.

I believe it is very important to emphasize that the vision is speaking to the Catholic *Church*, not necessarily all Catholics. There are Catholics who are born-again. However, when idolatry arises and men are placed on a pedestal, this becomes very problematic.

This book is not a means to put down Catholics in any way. It is to reveal what God is willing to reveal. I have written books (such as *Unraveling Deception: Discerning Darkness*) on how even within Christianity, there are many false prophets, false teachers, lukewarm Christians, and hypocrites. Scripture is unequivocal on these matters, and it is important to address them as the Holy Spirit leads.

Now, visions come in many forms. They are either direct out-of-body experiences, actual sights, puzzles to decipher, or imagery within the mind. All of these spring forth in the way God desires.

Now, someone could say, "Why does God have to make it so hard? Why can't He just give everyone the means to just see what was, is, and shall be? Why do some visions have to be riddles?" God does so because it includes others. It provides a means to show that God is not only the *Giver* of gifts, but the *Supplier* of them. God gives the vision, but He also gives the gift of interpretation, which can supply the meaning.

For my Wife and I, this has been something beautiful that has connected us on a deeper level. Without her, my visions would not make sense. They would seem like a bunch of random compilations of aspects I see but have absolutely no understanding of. Without me, Jackie would have nothing to interpret! Truly, God does a marvelous work and has His reasons for giving to each person as He wills.

Not having the full picture allows us to go to God more to receive understanding. Just look at the prophets of old. For us, their visions don't make any sense! Yet, as we read on, God makes sense of what they see.

We will review much more in-depth the interpretation of visions, but let us look at the vision of Zechariah in Zechariah 4:1-5 (NKJV):

> "Now the angel who talked with me came back and wakened me, as a man who is wakened out of his sleep. And he said to me, "What do you see?"
>
> So I said, "I am looking, and there *is* a lampstand of solid gold with a bowl on top of it, and on the *stand* seven lamps with seven pipes to the seven lamps. Two olive trees *are* by it, one at the right of the bowl and the other at its left." So I answered and spoke to the angel who talked with me, saying, "What *are* these, my lord?"
>
> Then the angel who talked with me answered and said to me, "Do you not know what these are?"
>
> And I said, "No, my lord.""

If you are unfamiliar with the Book of Zechariah, yet have the gift of interpretation of visions, before you read the rest (either in the Word of God or in the following Chapter), ask God for the interpretation. See if He gives it to you (and don't get discouraged if He doesn't. God has His reasons (and plus, it's in the Word, so no need to get disappointed!)).

Notice in the above passage, however, that Zachariah sees some random imagery, but he cannot make sense of it. God eventually gives him the interpretation through an angel throughout the rest of Zachariah 4.

What we see here is that an angel gives him the interpretation (which can still occur). However, now that we have the Holy Spirit (for those who are born again), we can receive both the gift of visions and the interpretation of visions, or, instead of an angel, God can bring us a friend, spouse, or family member to bring their interpretation through their gifting.

One important point to note is that the angel woke Zechariah up. This leads us to distinguish a brief difference between visions and dreams. Dreams occur when we are asleep, whereas visions occur when we are awake. This is a short understanding to help you know which gift you possess. This is not to say that as you dream, God cannot lift your soul out of your body and reveal what He desires through a vision. However, the majority (if not all) of visions *throughout Scripture* occur when a person is awake.

"Jesus saw Nathanael coming toward Him, and said of him, "Behold, an Israelite indeed, in whom is no deceit!" Nathanael said to Him, "How do You know me?" Jesus answered and said to him, "Before Philip called you, when you were under the fig tree, I saw you." Nathanael answered and said to Him, "Rabbi, You are the Son of God! You are the King of Israel!"" (John 1:47-49 NKJV). Here, we see that Jesus had a vision of the *present*.

When we have visions of the present, we can see what is occurring. It doesn't matter where someone is; if God desires to reveal the present to someone, He will reveal the specifics (no matter whether it is a vision of something in another state or another country). It is the same as the gift of the word of knowledge, yet in visions (as seeing). We saw this concept revealed in the gift of the word of knowledge when Elijah heard the King of Syria speaking in his bedroom and made the conversation known to the King of Israel (2 Kings 6:8-14). My Wife has this portion of the gift (though she has visions in this manner as well), whereas mine is typically in the gift of visions and less in the word of knowledge.

We are not in charge of the gift and what is revealed, but the closer we walk with God, the greater measure of the gift will be bestowed as we both exercise and receive more from God through the working of the Holy Spirit upon the gift. Truly, the time is coming when prophets will once again stand by the sides of kings, Presidents, and rulers, and God will work through these men and women to such degrees that they will be indispensable to governing authorities. They will be the people behind the scenes, who are led by Him Who is Unseen: the Eternal God Who is the Holy One of Israel.

"Now it came to pass in the thirtieth year, in the fourth *month*, on the fifth *day* of the month, as I *was* among the captives by the River Chebar, *that* the heavens were opened and I saw visions of God" (Ezekiel 1:1 NKJV). Throughout Ezekiel 1, we see an amazing description of Ezekiel's vision. He saw angelic beings and living creatures. At the end, he saw what "*was* the appearance of the likeness of the glory of the LORD. So when I saw *it*, I fell on my face, and I heard a voice of One speaking" (Ezekiel 1:28 NKJV).

What led him to this conclusion? "And above the firmament over their heads *was* the likeness of a throne, in appearance like a sapphire stone; on the likeness of the throne *was* a likeness with the appearance of a man high above it. Also from the appearance of His waist and upward I saw, as it were, the color of amber with the appearance of fire all around within it; and from the appearance of His waist and downward I saw, as it were, the appearance of fire with brightness all around. Like the appearance of a rainbow in a cloud on a rainy day, so *was* the appearance of the brightness all around it" (Ezekiel 1:26-28a NKJV).

It is incredible how, even today, some have been taken in an out-of-body experience and seen the Lord Jesus Christ. How do out-of-body experiences work? In very simplistic terms, God takes the soul out of the body. The spirit (which is life) of the individual remains with the body, continually giving it life, helping it breathe, keep its heartbeat, etc.

As the soul leaves the body, God allows it to enter different dimensions, with visions differentiated by time and location. John in Revelation had the greatest out-of-body experience of all, seeing the end times and receiving this insight directly from the Lord Jesus Christ! More to be written on this in a bit.

"And a vision appeared to Paul in the night. A man of Macedonia stood and pleaded with him, saying, "Come over to Macedonia and help us." Now after he had seen the vision, immediately we sought to go to Macedonia, concluding that the Lord had called us to preach the gospel to them" (Acts 16:9-10 NKJV). Here, we see that visions don't just include sight; they also include sound. This was also given to Ezekiel in his vision when he saw the living creatures. Ezekiel 1:15-25 (NKJV) states:

> "Now as I looked at the living creatures, behold, a wheel *was* on the earth beside each living creature with its four faces. The appearance of the wheels and their workings *was* like the color of beryl, and all four had the same likeness. The appearance of their workings *was*, as it were, a wheel in the middle of a wheel. When they moved, they went toward any one of four directions; they did not turn aside when they went. As for their rims, they were so high they were awesome; and their rims *were* full of eyes, all around the four of them. When the living creatures went, the wheels went beside them; and when the living creatures were lifted up from the earth, the wheels were lifted up. Wherever the spirit wanted to go, they went, *because* there the spirit went; and the wheels were lifted together with them, for the spirit of the living creatures *was* in the wheels. When those went, *these* went; when those stood, *these* stood; and when those were lifted up from the earth, the wheels were lifted up together with them, for the spirit of the living creatures *was* in the wheels.
>
> The likeness of the firmament above the heads of the living creatures *was* like the color of an awesome crystal, stretched out over their heads. And under the firmament their wings *spread out* straight, one toward another. Each one had two which covered one side, and each one had two which covered the other side of the body. When they went, I heard the noise of their wings, like the noise of many waters, like the voice of the Almighty, a tumult like the noise of an army; and when they stood still, they let down their wings. A voice came from above the firmament that *was* over their heads; whenever they stood, they let down their wings."

Here, Ezekiel not only heard the noise of the living creatures' wings, but he heard a voice. Notice also how Ezekiel attempts to describe what he sees regarding the living creatures. To us, we don't know exactly or fully what he saw.

This is what happens when people are taken up in visions of Heaven or Hell. They cannot fully describe what they see, because words cannot convey the spiritual realm in full (or sometimes, at all). "But as it is written: 'Eye has not seen, nor ear heard, Nor have entered into the heart of man The things which God has prepared for those who love Him'" (1 Corinthians 2:9 NKJV).

Ezekiel uses words and items he knows, but he does not give definitive statements about what he sees. Instead, he uses the phrase "*it was like*". Anyone who has the gift of visions will reach this point when they begin seeing things they cannot explain. They will say what they see, but what they see cannot always be described. So, in their best effort, they clarify using "it is like" or "it was like".

My Wife has this portion of the gift (as it goes along with the gift of the word of knowledge). We will be somewhere, and she will say, "I see (names of people) talking and saying (what she sees and hears)."

This gift of visions most certainly brings forth sight, including sound. Just as Paul received a vision and heard what a man of Macedonia was saying, so we can receive visions of what people are saying from anywhere in the world. Again, God controls what we hear, but this many times can guide us into the following steps or act as a warning sign.

There have been people in my Wife and I's lives where we have had to set boundaries. These boundaries were formed for our protection and were not based solely on what was seen and known in person, but also on what was seen and known when we were not present. In summary, it is a very dangerous matter to gossip and slander others when one is not around.

"Do not curse the king, even in your thought; Do not curse the rich, even in your bedroom; For a bird of the air may carry your voice, And a bird in flight may tell the matter" (Ecclesiastes 10:20 NKJV). Though this can be in regard to monitoring spirits (demons who monitor what you do and say and report back to spread gossip, division, and anger in the spiritual realm amongst individuals), it also reveals the Holy Spirit and how He will warn His people to not go around certain individuals and groups, as reputations have been unfairly damaged due to people's deceptive tongues.

It is important to note that the verse above can be a demon who sows division and strife, whereas the Holy Spirit does so to warn. We know the Holy Spirit is part of this verse, as we are commanded to "not curse the king, even in your thought" (Ecclesiastes 10:20 NKJV). We know that only God can read thoughts (and, therefore, reveal others' thoughts to us). Other than that, demons cannot read our thoughts; they can only influence us to think a certain way. We see this in Matthew 9:1-8 (NKJV):

> "So He got into a boat, crossed over, and came to His own city. Then behold, they brought to Him a paralytic lying on a bed. When Jesus saw their faith, He said to the paralytic, "Son, be of good cheer; your sins are forgiven you."
>
> And at once some of the scribes said within themselves, "This Man blasphemes!"
>
> But Jesus, knowing their thoughts, said, "Why do you think evil in your hearts? For which is easier, to say, '*Your* sins are forgiven you,' or to say, 'Arise and walk'? But that you may know that the Son of Man has power on earth to forgive sins"—then He said to the paralytic, "Arise, take up your bed, and go to your house." And he arose and departed to his house.
>
> Now when the multitudes saw *it*, they marveled and glorified God, who had given such power to men."

Let's now review Acts 10:3-8 (NKJV), which states:

> "There was a certain man in Caesarea called Cornelius, a centurion of what was called the Italian Regiment, a devout *man* and one who feared God with all his household, who gave alms generously to the people, and prayed to God always. About the ninth hour of the day he saw clearly in a vision an angel of God coming in and saying to him, "Cornelius!" And when he observed him, he was afraid, and said, "What is it, lord?" So he said to him, "Your prayers and your alms have come up for a memorial before God. Now send men to Joppa, and send for Simon whose surname is Peter. He is lodging with Simon, a tanner, whose house is by the sea. He will tell you what you must do." And when the angel who spoke to him had departed, Cornelius called two of his household servants and a devout soldier from among those

who waited on him continually. So when he had explained all *these* things to them, he sent them to Joppa."

Here, we see Cornelius receive a vision that includes direct contact of his name being called, a statement that his prayers have been heard, and a declaration of instruction to send for Peter, and where he was located. This vision was of an angel of God, but it was one of instruction.

Sometimes, visions consist of a single entity or Person who directly speaks to us (whether an angel or the Lord Jesus Christ), just as in a conversation with a friend. The vision allows us to speak, see, and understand them while they give us insight and instruction.

"In the year that King Uzziah died, I saw the Lord sitting on a throne, high and lifted up, and the train of His *robe* filled the temple. Above it stood seraphim; each one had six wings: with two he covered his face, with two he covered his feet, and with two he flew. And one cried to another and said: 'Holy, holy, holy *is* the LORD of hosts; The whole earth *is* full of His glory!'" (Isaiah 6:1-3 NKJV).

Those of us who seek God for the gift of visions can be blessed to see what Isaiah received. It is not far-fetched to pray and believe that God will reveal an image of the Lord Jesus Christ and angels in a vision. To receive such a vision when we have the gift, however, we must be humble of spirit. Even Isaiah, after seeing the vision, declared, "'Woe *is* me, for I am undone! Because I *am* a man of unclean lips, And I dwell in the midst of a people of unclean lips; For my eyes have seen the King, The LORD of hosts'" (Isaiah 6:5 NKJV).

God will not give visions to those who are selfish, prideful, arrogant, and haughty. Only the humble and pure in heart will see the Lord. "'Blessed *are* the pure in heart, For they shall see God'" (Matthew 5:8 NKJV).

There are many others throughout the Scriptures who had visions. It would take an entire book (as with all the gifts) to write about every instance in Scripture where there were visions, what we can learn, and so on. For now, we will just bring some extra insight into where you can go in Scripture if you want to see how God worked through visions. Some Scriptures include the following:

- "The words of Amos, who was among the sheepbreeders of Tekoa, which he saw concerning Israel in the days of Uzziah king of Judah, and in the days of Jeroboam the son of Joash, king of Israel, two years before the earthquake" (Amos 1:1 NKJV).
- "Thus the Lord God showed me: Behold, He formed locust swarms at the beginning of the late crop; indeed, it was the late crop after the king's mowings" (Amos 7:1 NKJV).
- "The vision of Obadiah. Thus says the Lord God concerning Edom (We have heard a report from the Lord, and a messenger has been sent among the nations, saying, 'Arise, and let us rise up against her for battle')" (Obadiah 1:1 NKJV).
- "The burden against Nineveh. The book of the vision of Nahum the Elkoshite" (Nahum 1:1 NKJV).
- "On the twenty-fourth day of the eleventh month, which is the month Shebat, in the second year of Darius, the word of the LORD came to Zechariah the son of Berechiah, the son of Iddo the prophet: I saw by night, and behold, a man riding on a red horse, and it stood among the myrtle trees in the hollow; and behind him *were* horses: red, sorrel, and white. Then I said, "My lord, what *are* these?" So the angel who talked with me said to me, "I will show you what they *are*"" (Zechariah 1:7-9 NKJV).
- "Then I turned and raised my eyes and looked, and behold, four chariots *were* coming from between two mountains, and the mountains *were* mountains of bronze. With the first chariot *were* red horses, with the second chariot black horses, with the third chariot white horses, and with the fourth chariot dappled horses—strong *steeds*. Then I answered and said to the angel who talked with me, "What *are* these, my lord?" And the angel answered and said to me, "These *are* four spirits of heaven, who go out from *their* station before the Lord of all the earth. The one with the black horses is going to the north country, the white are going after them, and the dappled are going

toward the south country." Then the strong *steeds* went out, eager to go, that they might walk to and fro throughout the earth. And He said, "Go, walk to and fro throughout the earth." So they walked to and fro throughout the earth. And He called to me, and spoke to me, saying, "See, those who go toward the north country have given rest to My Spirit in the north country"'" (Zechariah 6:1-8 NKJV).

- "The next day, as they went on their journey and drew near the city, Peter went up on the housetop to pray, about the sixth hour. Then he became very hungry and wanted to eat; but while they made ready, he fell into a trance and saw heaven opened and an object like a great sheet bound at the four corners, descending to him and let down to the earth. In it were all kinds of four-footed animals of the earth, wild beasts, creeping things, and birds of the air. And a voice came to him, "Rise, Peter; kill and eat." But Peter said, "Not so, Lord! For I have never eaten anything common or unclean." And a voice *spoke* to him again the second time, "What God has cleansed you must not call common." This was done three times. And the object was taken up into heaven again" (Acts 10:9-16 NKJV).
- "Now I saw when the Lamb opened one of the seals; and I heard one of the four living creatures saying with a voice like thunder, "Come and see." And I looked, and behold, a white horse. He who sat on it had a bow; and a crown was given to him, and he went out conquering and to conquer. When He opened the second seal, I heard the second living creature saying, "Come and see." Another horse, fiery red, went out. And it was granted to the one who sat on it to take peace from the earth, and that *people* should kill one another; and there was given to him a great sword. When He opened the third seal, I heard the third living creature say, "Come and see." So I looked, and behold, a black horse, and he who sat on it had a pair of scales in his hand. And I heard a voice in the midst of the four living creatures saying, "A quart of wheat for a denarius, and three quarts of barley

for a denarius; and do not harm the oil and the wine." When He opened the fourth seal, I heard the voice of the fourth living creature saying, "Come and see." So I looked, and behold, a pale horse. And the name of him who sat on it was Death, and Hades followed with him. And power was given to them over a fourth of the earth, to kill with sword, with hunger, with death, and by the beasts of the earth" (Revelation 6:1-8 NKJV).

- "Now a great sign appeared in heaven: a woman clothed with the sun, with the moon under her feet, and on her head a garland of twelve stars. Then being with child, she cried out in labor and in pain to give birth. And another sign appeared in heaven: behold, a great, fiery red dragon having seven heads and ten horns, and seven diadems on his heads. His tail drew a third of the stars of heaven and threw them to the earth. And the dragon stood before the woman who was ready to give birth, to devour her Child as soon as it was born. She bore a male Child who was to rule all nations with a rod of iron. And her Child was caught up to God and His throne. Then the woman fled into the wilderness, where she has a place prepared by God, that they should feed her there one thousand two hundred and sixty days" (Revelation 12:1-6 NKJV).

As can be seen, many prophets toward the end of the Old Testament had the gift of visions. It is rather sad that many of us tend to overlook them and only view the "famous" stories in the Old Testament, like David, Daniel, and Solomon. Truly, the Bible in Its entirety and collectivity has much to share. Truly, the Holy Spirit desires to reveal deeper revelations within Each Book of the Canon of Scripture.

"After these things the word of the LORD came to Abram in a vision, saying, "Do not be afraid, Abram. I *am* your shield, your exceedingly great reward." But Abram said, "Lord GOD, what will You give me, seeing I go childless, and the heir of my house *is* Eliezer of Damascus?" Then Abram said, "Look, You have given me no offspring; indeed one born in my house is my heir!'" (Genesis 15:1-3 NKJV).

Here, we see Abram having a vision of the Lord. Not only did he hear from the Lord, but he also interacted with Him, spoke to Him, and asked Him a question. Sometimes, in visions from the Lord God, He permits us to speak; to share our hearts, ask questions, and He will answer. If we are ever blessed with the opportunity to have a vision of the Lord God and He permits us to speak, we need not worry about what we will say. God will work in us the questions that we desire to ask.

In Acts 9:1-9 (NKJV), we see the power of a vision when the Lord appears in His Glory in our space-time continuum:

> "Then Saul, still breathing threats and murder against the disciples of the Lord, went to the high priest and asked letters from him to the synagogues of Damascus, so that if he found any who were of the Way, whether men or women, he might bring them bound to Jerusalem.
>
> As he journeyed he came near Damascus, and suddenly a light shone around him from heaven. Then he fell to the ground, and heard a voice saying to him, "Saul, Saul, why are you persecuting Me?"
>
> And he said, "Who are You, Lord?"
>
> Then the Lord said, "I am Jesus, whom you are persecuting. It *is* hard for you to kick against the goads."
>
> So he, trembling and astonished, said, "Lord, what do You want me to do?"
>
> Then the Lord *said* to him, "Arise and go into the city, and you will be told what you must do."
>
> And the men who journeyed with him stood speechless, hearing a voice but seeing no one. Then Saul arose from the ground, and when his eyes were opened he saw no one. But they led him by the hand and brought *him* into Damascus. And he was three days without sight, and neither ate nor drank."

The Lord appeared to Saul (who later would become Paul) in a bright light "that shone around him from heaven" (Acts 9:3). Simultaneously, we see that the men were able to hear the voice of the Lord but did not see anyone (Acts 9:7). God, simultaneously, can have multitudes hear His Voice while secluding the visualization of Himself (or the Light

He dwells within) to a single person. In this Passage, we see it was toward Saul.

Is it any wonder why the Lord told Moses that no one could see His face and live? Exodus 33:20-23 (NKJV) declares:

> "But He said, "You cannot see My face; for no man shall see Me, and live." And the LORD said, "Here is a place by Me, and you shall stand on the rock. So it shall be, while My glory passes by, that I will put you in the cleft of the rock, and will cover you with My hand while I pass by. Then I will take away My hand, and you shall see My back; but My face shall not be seen.""

It is important to note that this is the Lord speaking. It took God to protect Moses from God Himself. Moses could not see the face of the LORD God, lest he die. Likewise, in the vision Saul received, he saw the light coming from Christ, but could not see Christ's face directly.

Now, it could be easy to suggest and say, "Well, then, everyone who claims they have seen Jesus is a liar." On the surface, this may seem wise, but there is a truth that must be conveyed, which will absolve this thinking altogether.

For both Moses and Saul, this vision was within their dimension while they themselves still resided in their bodies. Had they seen the full Glory and face of the Lord while still in their bodies, they would have died. Yet if this vision had not been one in which the Lord entered our dimension, and it had been just a vision in which Moses and Saul were caught up in an out-of-body experience, they would have lived. Why? It would have been just their spiritual man, namely, their soul.

We know one day "that at the name of Jesus every knee should bow, of those in heaven, and of those on earth, and of those under the earth, and *that* every tongue should confess that Jesus Christ *is* Lord, to the glory of God the Father" (Philippians 2:10-11 NKJV). If this is to occur before His Presence, then clearly our soul can see His face without ceasing to be. It is because Moses and Saul's vision was within our dimension that they could not gaze on the face of Christ.

What happened to Saul when viewing the exuding Light from the Holy Presence of the Lord Jesus Christ? He went blind for three days.

That is the magnitude and power of just a few seconds in the Glory of the Lord. The Glowing Light that shines forth for just a few moments can blind us.

To further validate this point, we shall view what John has to say in the Book of Revelation; specifically, Revelation 1:10-20 (NKJV):

> "I was in the Spirit on the Lord's Day, and I heard behind me a loud voice, as of a trumpet, saying, "I am the Alpha and the Omega, the First and the Last," and, "What you see, write in a book and send *it* to the seven churches which are in Asia: to Ephesus, to Smyrna, to Pergamos, to Thyatira, to Sardis, to Philadelphia, and to Laodicea."
>
> Then I turned to see the voice that spoke with me. And having turned, I saw seven golden lampstands, and in the midst of the seven lampstands, *One* like the Son of Man, clothed with a garment down to the feet and girded about the chest with a golden band. His head and hair *were* white like wool, as white as snow, and His eyes like a flame of fire; His feet *were* like fine brass as if refined in a furnace, and His voice as the sound of many glasses of water; He had in His right hand seven stars, out of His mouth went a sharp two-edged sword, and His countenance *was* like the sun shining in its strength. And when I saw Him, I fell at His feet as dead. But He laid His right hand on me, saying to me, "Do not be afraid; I am the First and the Last. I *am* He who lives and was dead and behold; I am alive forevermore. Amen. And I have the keys of Hades and of Death. Write the things which you have seen, and the things which are, and the things which will take place after this. The mystery of the seven stars which you saw in My right hand, and the seven golden lampstands: The seven stars are the angels of the seven churches, and the seven lampstands which you saw are the seven churches."

John was "in the Spirit" and saw the Lord Jesus Christ. He could withstand what he saw because he was "in the Spirit".

To be "in the Spirit" is to be cognitively in the spiritual realm, wholly. Eventually, John would return to his body, but during this vision, and all that the Lord desired to show him, he was taken "in the Spirit," where his soul was extracted.

Even though John could dwell in the presence of the Lord in the Heavenly dimension, he still declares that "when I saw Him, I fell at His feet as dead" (Revelation 1:17). This is the Power, Might, Magnificence, and Majesty of Christ!

John wrote about everything he saw in the Book of Revelation, and it is quite powerful and incredible. Truly, only the Lord could have revealed such Truths that multitudes still do not *fully* understand. Only the Holy Spirit can make known the entirety of the Word of God to us. Though we are limited and will never know everything in Scripture, we can most certainly be led by the Spirit and request that He teach us as much as possible in this life. If this is one of our chief ends, He will answer in a mighty way.

To end, let us review the story of Samuel. "Now the boy Samuel ministered to the Lord before Eli. And the word of the Lord was rare in those days; *there was* no widespread revelation" (1 Samuel 3:1 NKJV). Earlier, we discerned that a "Word of the Lord" can lead to a revelation. This revelation is not just knowledge acquired through a knowing or silent word spoken, but it is also knowledge that can be acquired by *seeing*.

God has always had His people, but sometimes He withdraws for a time when the vast majority are not seeking Him. This is what we find between the Old and New Testaments. In between each, there were roughly 400 years of silence, during which we were not given answers as to what occurred. God did this to reveal that there are moments in the Christian walk when our dependency must be on what has already been given, not on the constant need for revelation.

Now, by revelation we mean a continual need for God to be speaking and His Presence to be felt. There are moments in life where we may be tempted by the *hidden idolatry* of needing the *Presence of God* more than God Himself. There is an idol that can become all about *God continually speaking,* and meanwhile, we are not obeying. That which comes from God must never become an idol ahead of God. God must always be at the forefront. Not even gifts should override our desire for Him.

That is why when God gives us new revelations and Divine truths, rather than rushing to the next thing because we are discontented, we must thank God for revealing what He has given. As we thank Him, we must be content. We can ask for more from Him, but we must do so without angst or impatience. We must be willing to wait on the Lord for the next revelation He desires to bring forth and make known to us.

Samuel went to sleep, and throughout the night he repeatedly heard a Voice calling his name. He thought it was Eli's when it was actually God's. 1 Samuel 3:8-9 (NKJV) declares:

> "And the Lord called Samuel again the third time. So he arose and went to Eli, and said, "Here I am, for you did call me." Then Eli perceived that the Lord had called the boy. Therefore Eli said to Samuel, "Go, lie down; and it shall be, if He calls you, that you must say, 'Speak, Lord, for Your servant hears.'" So Samuel went and lay down in his place. Now the Lord came and stood and called as at other times, "Samuel! Samuel!" And Samuel answered, "Speak, for Your servant hears.""

After the Lord God speaks to Samuel, Samuel sleeps until morning. Though this was an amazing encounter, 1 Samuel 3:15 (NKJV) tells us that Samuel "was afraid to tell Eli the vision." It is never good to hide a vision if God desires us to pass it along to those He wants to hear.

Some people receive visions from God and are so concerned about what others might say that they wait for months and years. I have even heard some individuals wait 10-15 years before they had the courage and boldness to share the vision God gave them! Unless God deliberately makes it known that we should not share a vision, God wants us to share it.

If the Holy Spirit does not speak to us, the vision is often not just for an individual but for the Body of Christ (or for a particular person that God wants us to note and share the vision with). If throughout Scripture we see men having visions and what they saw being recorded, then it is important that we keep a record of what God reveals through the gift of visions and steward what He gives well.

Of course, we don't need to share every vision, but we are called to steward them well and share as the Holy Spirit leads. For the gifts of the

Spirit are not just for ourselves, but for others; not just for others, but ultimately for the Glory of God!

"So Samuel grew, and the LORD was with him and let none of his words fall to the ground. And all Israel from Dan to Beersheba knew that Samuel *had been* established as a prophet of the LORD. Then the LORD appeared again in Shiloh. For the LORD revealed Himself to Samuel in Shiloh by the word of the LORD" (1 Samuel 3:19-21 NKJV).

God always reveals Himself by His Word, and this is how He established Samuel as a prophet. Truly, the office of a person within the Body of Christ will always possess the appropriate gifts of the Spirit, but those who possess the gift don't necessarily hold the office. This is an important distinction.

"Then He said, 'Hear now My words: If there is a prophet among you, *I*, the LORD, make Myself known to him in a vision; I speak to him in a dream'" (Numbers 12:6 NKJV). Here, we see the Lord clearly reveal that those who are truly prophets can and will see Christ in a vision or a dream. If this does not occur, it does not necessarily mean one is not a prophet. However, it can most certainly be a testing ground. For just as there are too many self-proclaimed Christians and not enough born-again believers, so there are too many self-proclaimed prophets and not many true prophets of the Lord.

Again, the office possesses the appropriate spiritual gifts, but the spiritual gifts do not promote one to the office. Some people believe that because they can prophesy, they are a prophet. This is not true. Likewise, just because one has the gift of visions does not instantly make them a prophet. It is only when God appoints a man or woman to an office within the Body of Christ that the person will be adequately equipped and readily able to steward the position —not because of the giftings, but because the Holy Spirit blesses, teaches, and stewards the spiritual gifts through the person.

Let us never forget that visions are given beforehand, so that when they actually happen in the future, we know that God showed us and revealed it beforehand. Acts 9:10-12 (NKJV) states:

> "Now there was a certain disciple at Damascus named Ananias; and to him the Lord said in a vision, "Ananias."

And he said, "Here I am, Lord."

So the Lord *said* to him, "Arise and go to the street called Straight, and inquire at the house of Judas for *one* called Saul of Tarsus, for behold, he is praying. And in a vision he has seen a man named Ananias coming in and putting *his* hand on him, so that he might receive his sight."

God will give a vision to two individuals with different perspectives, but of the same message. This is to bring validation and clarity to both individuals that God is in the midst.

Truly, visions are out-of-body experiences, actual sights, puzzles to be deciphered, or imagery in the mind. In whichever way the vision comes, so long as we are seeking God and asking that God speak to us through visions, it is from Him.

"'I have also spoken by the prophets, And have multiplied visions; I have given symbols through the witness of the prophets'" (Hosea 12:10 NKJV). May God grant us the ability to receive visions from His Word and by His Spirit. May we possess the gift to see in the Spirit, hear visions, increase in discernment, see spiritual truths, understand the past, monitor the present, and know the future. May God bless us with an out-of-body experience if He so chooses to see the realities of Heaven and Hell (for those who can withstand what is seen). May God bless us with visions of angels and, the most incredible vision of all, the Lord Jesus Christ. Let Him be praised forever, for Wisdom, Dominion, and Might are His.

God in Heaven, Who is All-Vision and All-Revelation, Who alone reveals the deep and hidden things but also conceals and protects us from knowing many things, You are the One Who sees all things, instantly. You are the One Who is forever Present with the born-again believer. Truly, it is by Your Holy Spirit that we may be sanctified and continue to become more like Christ. God, we ask that You would bless us with the gift of visions. God, help us to see more clearly that which You are willing to reveal. If we be found pure and humble in spirit, may we see You, Lord

Jesus! We long to be with You and to see Your face. If it is in Thy Holy Will, bless us with Heavenly visions. Reveal the deep and hidden things that must be exposed. God, convict us and lead us to repentance in that which we are living in, and excuse away that which is sin and unprofitable. O God, be our All in All. You alone are worthy of all praise, worship, honor, and glory! May You be Magnified and exalted forevermore. In Jesus' name, Amen.

The Gift of Interpretation of Visions

"*I, Daniel, was grieved in my spirit within my body, and the visions of my head troubled me. I came near to one of those who stood by, and asked him the truth of all this. So he told me and made known to me the interpretation of these things:*"
– **Daniel 7:15-16 NKJV**

The gift of interpretation of visions is meant to reveal deep and hidden mysteries, give God the Glory, bring peace of mind, bring clarity, and help one pray before *revealing* the deep mysteries that could be dangerous if the Enemy were to hear.

There are "monitoring spirits" that continually strive to observe what we do and report back to higher authorities in the spiritual realm. One day, I will write a book on an extensive review of the hierarchy of the Enemy's strategy, warfare, and those in authority. For now, we need only be concerned that "we do not wrestle against flesh and blood, but against principalities, against powers, against the rulers of the darkness of this age, against spiritual *hosts* of wickedness in the heavenly *places*" (Ephesians 6:12 NKJV).

Just as God has His warfare and hierarchy of angels and those in the

Body of Christ (insofar as positions to serve and glorify Him), so Satan mimics exactly what God does, yet he cannot do so perfectly or in full. We see this with the miracles of Moses and the duplication of the Enemy in the sorcerers in Exodus 7:8-12 (NKJV):

> "Then the LORD spoke to Moses and Aaron, saying, "When Pharaoh speaks to you, saying, 'Show a miracle for yourselves,' then you shall say to Aaron, 'Take your rod and cast *it* before Pharaoh, *and* let it become a serpent.' " So Moses and Aaron went in to Pharaoh, and they did so, just as the LORD commanded. And Aaron cast down his rod before Pharaoh and before his servants, and it became a serpent. But Pharaoh also called the wise men and the sorcerers; so the magicians of Egypt, they also did in like manner with their enchantments. For every man threw down his rod, and they became serpents. But Aaron's rod swallowed up their rods."

Truly, the Enemy always strives to copy God but fails in comparison to Him. The Enemy will never come close to overcoming that which is of God and from God.

Monitoring spirits, therefore, are part of the command of Satan's kingdom of darkness. They come to spy, watch, and monitor. As soon as they hear or see something that could be useful, they record it and report it to higher-level entities. "Do not curse the king, even in your thought; Do not curse the rich, even in your bedroom; For a bird of the air may carry your voice, And a bird in flight may tell the matter" (Ecclesiastes 10:20 NKJV). These principalities, rulers, and powers review and quickly assemble a squad to come knocking on the door of a believer. As they do so, they hope to open a door through which many powerful demons can enter, hindering the growth and fulfillment of a prophetic word or interpretation. Matthew 12:43-45 (NKJV) reveals this in greater measure:

> "'When an unclean spirit goes out of a man, he goes through dry places, seeking rest, and finds none. Then he says, 'I will return to my house from which I came.' And when he comes, he finds *it* empty, swept, and put in order. Then he goes and takes with him seven other spirits more

wicked than himself, and they enter and dwell there; and the last *state* of that man is worse than the first.'"

Monitoring spirits do the spying. When they report back, those who once were in the vessel of someone's body (or were not) are now sent to go and wait for an open door (ex, someone falling into a grave sin). If this occurs, it can stunt and prolong what God is willing to perform and do.

As we understand this reality, we can now move on to why interpreting visions is so important. As with all interpretations, when something is given to an individual and made known to a person, group, or congregation, the Enemy finds out at that very moment.

Often, the Enemy does not actually know what God is up to or what will happen. Of course, there are moments (as we saw in the chapter on "the gift of the discerning of spirits") when angels come to relay messages, but sometimes get caught up in battle (Daniel 10:12-17). On a widespread scale, however, God will speak directly to His people with certain gifts by the Holy Spirit. As soon as this is made known by the Enemy, plots and schemes against an individual ramp up significantly (depending on the interpretation).

I experienced this during my name change to Judah Veritas. Once this was made known and released during January 2026 via a YouTube LIVE on my Wife's channel, I experienced some of the strongest warfare. Judah means "praise" and Veritas means "truth" in Latin. My name literally means "(To) Praise (the) Truth." God gave me this name, which He wants me to use moving forward, and you can review some of the story on our social media (I gave an extensive sermon on how God changes and gives new names throughout Scripture). There are many deeper reasons for this, but as of 01/21/2026, God wants this to remain hidden. There is an appointed time, and when that time comes, all will come to understand.

As soon as I made my new name known, I experienced strong oppression from the Enemy, resulting in intense feelings of worthlessness, hopelessness, discouragement, lack of faith, and zero self-confidence. I was even tempted to think that all God has in store for my life and my family, as He has spoken over it, was a lie.

This is why it is important, before every encounter of bringing forth an interpretation of tongues, dreams, or visions, we pray out loud, "In the Name of Jesus, I bind every little bird of the kingdom of darkness that would attempt to monitor and relay feedback to the Enemy. I render your scheme and plans null and void, in the name of Jesus. I rebuke you and, in the name of Jesus, make this conversation and ourselves hidden before you. In the name of Jesus, you shall be deaf to this discussion, and our voices will be mute before you."

As we pray this, demons must flee, and they will be unable to carry out their desires. This is extremely important to remember. Even I forget to pray this, and when a mighty word comes forth, I find myself experiencing tremendous spiritual warfare. My outlook on life changes; I feel a heaviness, and I begin to feel attacks on my mind, which intensify as the word gets closer to fulfillment. When I have prayed a prayer like the one mentioned above, I have noticed that the spiritual warfare does not even come close to what it would have been. This is why we must "pray without ceasing" (1 Thessalonians 5:17 NKJV)!

We must understand that this prayer must be prayed in faith! When this is done, we must realize that it does not mean we will never experience spiritual warfare in the future. There will come a time when the Enemy begins to discern a portion of what is quickly coming forth, and God will send angels to encamp around us. Remember, not everything that occurs is seen. The Enemy can sometimes see more because they are spiritual beings who know when spiritual matters are on the rise. Truly, the spiritual realm is greater than the physical realm.

Interpretation of visions, then, is the ability to solve what is seen. God sometimes makes visions explicitly clear. Other times, He does so by means of including others in the process. Everything He does, He performs on the basis of bringing Him Glory and providing unity. If God gave every single person every gift, we would not need each other (as much). Even mighty men and women of God need companions, friendship, and relationships with those who can bless them in ways they cannot do for themselves.

As we have mentioned repeatedly throughout this book, this is all done by the Holy Spirit. "There are diversities of gifts, but the same Spirit. There are differences of ministries, but the same Lord. And there are diversities of activities, but it is the same God Who works all in all" (1 Corinthians 12:4-6 NKJV).

"In the first year of Belshazzar king of Babylon, Daniel had a dream and visions of his head *while* on his bed. Then he wrote down the dream, telling the main facts" (Daniel 7:1 NKJV). Let us review the visions that came to Daniel. Continuing in Daniel 7:2-8 (NKJV):

"Daniel spoke, saying, "I saw in my vision by night, and behold, the four winds of heaven were stirring up the Great Sea. And four great beasts came up from the sea, each different from the other. The first *was* like a lion, and had eagle's wings. I watched till its wings were plucked off; and it was lifted up from the earth and made to stand on two feet like a man, and a man's heart was given to it.

"And suddenly another beast, a second, like a bear. It was raised up on one side, and *had* three ribs in its mouth between its teeth. And they said thus to it: 'Arise, devour much flesh!'

"After this I looked, and there was another, like a leopard, which had on its back four wings of a bird. The beast also had four heads, and dominion was given to it.

"After this I saw in the night visions, and behold, a fourth beast, dreadful and terrible, exceedingly strong. It had huge iron teeth; it was devouring, breaking in pieces, and trampling the residue with its feet. It *was* different from all the beasts that *were* before it, and it had ten horns. I was considering the horns, and there was another horn, a little one, coming up among them, before whom three of the first horns were plucked out by the roots. And there, in this horn, *were* eyes like the eyes of a man, and a mouth speaking pompous words."

It is important to note that sometimes, God reveals everything within a single vision. Other times, He separates it through a night, a day, a week, a month, or even a year. Having a vision, in part, leads us to seek Him and to pray for the completion and interpretation of the vision.

Daniel continues on in Daniel 7:9-14 (NKJV) of the vision He had of the Ancient of Days:

"'I watched till thrones were put in place,
 And the Ancient of Days was seated;
 His garment *was* white as snow,
 And the hair of His head *was* like pure wool.
 His throne *was* a fiery flame,
 Its wheels a burning fire;
 A fiery stream issued
 And came forth from before Him.
 A thousand thousands ministered to Him;
 Ten thousand times ten thousand stood before Him.
 The court was seated,
 And the books were opened.

"I watched then because of the sound of the pompous words which the horn was speaking; I watched till the beast was slain, and its body destroyed and given to the burning flame. As for the rest of the beasts, they had their dominion taken away, yet their lives were prolonged for a season and a time.

"I was watching in the night visions,
 And behold, *One* like the Son of Man,
 Coming with the clouds of heaven!
 He came to the Ancient of Days,
 And they brought Him near before Him.
 Then to Him was given dominion and glory and a kingdom,
 That all peoples, nations, and languages should serve Him.
 His dominion *is* an everlasting dominion,
 Which shall not pass away,
 And His kingdom *the one*
 Which shall not be destroyed.'"

After the visions, Daniel declares, "'I, Daniel, was grieved in my spirit within *my* body, and the visions of my head troubled me. I came near to one of those who stood by, and asked him the truth of all this. So he told me and made known to me the interpretation of these things'" (Daniel 7:15 NKJV). Notice, Daniel previously had received the interpretation of the dream of the king in a vision in Daniel 2:16-19 (NKJV):

"So Daniel went in and asked the king to give him time, that he might tell the king the interpretation. Then Daniel went to his house, and made the decision known to Hananiah, Mishael, and Azariah, his companions, that they might seek mercies from the God of heaven concerning this secret, so that Daniel and his companions might not perish with the rest of the wise *men* of Babylon. Then the secret was revealed to Daniel in a night vision. So Daniel blessed the God of heaven."

Daniel's gift of visions could reveal the interpretation of a dream, yet here Daniel is, not sure of what his own vision means.

This shows a distinction between the interpretation of visions and the interpretation of dreams. Someone can interpret a dream through receiving a vision, while someone who interprets a vision can outright speak, based on the knowledge God gives. Truly, it is incredible how everything God gives is meant for Him and can work in unison.

God allowed Daniel to interpret the king's dream, but for his vision, Daniel required another interpreter. Sometimes, God will not give someone everything lest they be pompous and puffed up. Let us see what the interpretation of Daniel's vision reveals. Daniel 7:17-28 (NKJV) declares:

> "'Those great beasts, which are four, *are* four kings *which* arise out of the earth. But the saints of the Most High shall receive the kingdom, and possess the kingdom forever, even forever and ever.'
>
> "Then I wished to know the truth about the fourth beast, which was different from all the others, exceedingly dreadful, *with* its teeth of iron and its nails of bronze, *which* devoured, broke in pieces, and trampled the residue with its feet; and the ten horns that *were* on its head, and the other *horn* which came up, before which three fell, namely, that horn which had eyes and a mouth which spoke pompous words, whose appearance *was* greater than his fellows.
>
> "I was watching; and the same horn was making war against the saints, and prevailing against them, until the Ancient of Days came, and a judgment was made *in favor* of the saints of the Most High, and the time came for the saints to possess the kingdom.

> "Thus he said:
> 'The fourth beast shall be
> A fourth kingdom on earth,
> Which shall be different from all *other* kingdoms,
> And shall devour the whole earth,
> Trample it and break it in pieces.
> The ten horns *are* ten kings
> *Who* shall arise from this kingdom.
> And another shall rise after them;
> He shall be different from the first *ones*,
> And shall subdue three kings.
> He shall speak *pompous* words against the Most High,
> Shall persecute the saints of the Most High,
> And shall intend to change times and law.
> Then *the saints* shall be given into his hand
> For a time and times and half a time.
> 'But the court shall be seated,
> And they shall take away his dominion,
> To consume and destroy *it* forever.
> Then the kingdom and dominion,
> And the greatness of the kingdoms under the whole heaven,
> Shall be given to the people, the saints of the Most High.
> His kingdom *is* an everlasting kingdom,
> And all dominions shall serve and obey Him.'
> "This *is* the end of the account. As for me, Daniel, my thoughts greatly troubled me, and my countenance changed; but I kept the matter in my heart.'"

The interpretation is made clear. Had it not been for the person who helped Daniel, he would have been left confused and puzzled.

What Daniel saw has yet to occur. At some point in the future, this vision will manifest. What Daniel saw will actually become prevalent. Until then, it remains for an appointed time.

This is what occurs with visions. Not all of them are for now; they are for the future. Not all of them are for the near future, but for the future generation. Not all of them are for the next future generation, but for future generations from now. Everything that comes by way of a vision and interpretation is not always meant for us, but for an appointed time. It may even be for those who are to proceed from our bloodline. It can be for an entire generation. Maybe it's for a nation or group of people five hundred years from now. Whatever the case, time does not affect the accuracy of interpreting visions, but visions are for an appointed time.

Whether the vision is to occur in six months or six hundred years, the point stands: the interpretation of visions can occur immediately, foretell, or forewarn of what is to come in the future. What an incredible, powerful gift! To have the ability to have insight into understanding visions without seeing the vision oneself. To have the ability to decode and describe a person's vision, though one has not seen everything within the vision.

It is like a vault that has never been made before and is one-of-a-kind. This vault contains the world's most precious gems and jewelry. It is virtually uncrackable. Not even a quantum computer could solve the code within one hundred years! Imagine we walk right up to the vault, know the exact codes (since it is multilayered), and open it without any prior knowledge. This is how the gift of interpreting visions occurs. Those who possess this gift need not worry about the dynamics of the dream, the items, objects, sequence, patterns, or inability of a person to describe what they saw in full. All they need is to trust in the Holy Spirit to bring forth their understanding. When this is truly done in full faith and assurance that God has the answer and will relay it to us who have the gift, there will be a confident peace. At the end of the interpretation, the one who had the vision will know it is from God. Why? The Spirit within the person who had the vision will agree with the Spirit in the person who gave its interpretation. For we know, "There are diversities of gifts, but the same Spirit" (1 Corinthians 12:4 NKJV).

"Then I raised my eyes and looked, and there *were* four horns. And I said to the angel who talked with me, "What *are* these?" So he answered me, "These *are* the horns that have scattered Judah, Israel, and Jerusalem." Then the LORD showed me four craftsmen. And I said, "What are these coming to do?" So he said, "These *are* the horns that scattered Judah, so that no one could lift up his head; but the craftsmen are coming to terrify them, to cast out the horns of the nations that lifted up *their* horn against the land of Judah to scatter it"'" (Zechariah 1:18-21 NKJV).

It is a bewildering reality to ponder how, when we have a dream or vision we do not understand, we do not simply ask God. We do a search on the internet. We go to a friend or a relative. We try to find articles or videos. We ask artificial intelligence. We attempt everything instead of doing what Zechariah continually did: Asking the LORD God, "What are these?"

When we ask the Lord and wait for His speaking, we will get the answer every time. We can even pray for the gift of interpretation for visions and say, "God, I don't know of anyone around me who has this gift. Please, LORD God, make it known to me. Bless me with the gift of interpretation of visions." Will not God bless us with a good gift? Will He not make known that which is confusing us? Of course, if it is a heavy interpretation, God may wait until we are ready for the interpretation. Nonetheless, we worship and serve the Living God Who always answers in His time! We need only wait, be still, and seek to listen.

Earlier today, while having breakfast, I spoke to God in my head. Immediately, He answered back. We had a conversation, and I said, "God, is this what it is like to speak with You?" He said, "Yes." I said, "Why have I not been able to hear Your Voice like this repeatedly?" He said, "You have not taken the time to listen." I am quite ashamed to admit it, and, of course, it is true because God said it! He rebuked me for not spending time listening.

Sometimes, we want to speak to God and not wait for the answer. Other times, we are waiting for an answer, but we never even asked a question! God can give an answer before we ask the question, but we need to ask Him so we know exactly how He is answering. If someone were to randomly tell me, "The game is at 7 PM", and I did not ask them the time of the game, I would be confused.

We must go to God and ask deliberate questions. We must seek Him and ask for the interpretation and say, "Lord, what are these? What does this mean? I had a vision of this, please, tell me, what are You trying to convey? Give me the interpretation." If we pray that in faith, God will make it known. Even if we do not have the gift, the Holy Spirit can make it known. Maybe later throughout the day, we go for a walk, and then all of a sudden, it makes sense. This instant knowledge comes from the Holy Spirit, even if we have not received the gift of interpreting visions.

This is the beautiful reality of the Holy Spirit – He does all the work! If we know He dispenses spiritual gifts and is the Gift-Giver, then obviously He can use His gifts on our behalf to bless us. We may not yet possess the gift, but the Holy Spirit in us is the One Who wields the gifts infinitely, perfectly, and wholly, and He can do and reveal as He pleases. When He gives the interpretation, we don't need the gift to be blessed, for God alone can do anything and everything without prior resources or approval.

"The next day, as they went on their journey and drew near the city, Peter went up on the housetop to pray, about the sixth hour. Then he became very hungry and wanted to eat; but while they made ready, he fell into a trance and saw heaven opened and an object like a great sheet bound at the four corners, descending to him and let down to the earth. In it were all kinds of four-footed animals of the earth, wild beasts, creeping things, and birds of the air. And a voice came to him, "Rise, Peter; kill and eat." But Peter said, "Not so, Lord! For I have never eaten anything common or unclean." And a voice *spoke* to him again the second time, "What God has cleansed you must not call common." This was done three times. And the object was taken up into heaven again" (Acts 10:9-16 NKJV). Though it is not explicitly stated that he was fasting, we see that Peter was hungry. Whether he fasted on purpose or not, he was nonetheless without food for some time. It is important to understand that during moments of fasting, our physical selves are not weighed down. Instead, we uplift our spiritual senses, allowing us to receive more understanding from God.

If we continually eat (which is good and healthy), we will be concerned with feeding the body rather than the soul. "And Jesus said to them, 'I am the bread of life. He who comes to Me shall never hunger, and he who believes in Me shall never thirst'" (John 6:35 NKJV). When we allow God to be our all in all and we take time to fast each week, we will be more attuned to the Voice of God. Just as we cannot hear God's Voice as clearly when we are consumed with movies, conversations, or work, so is it with eating. If we are eating, we are concerned about what we are eating. Our physical senses provide us with input about what we eat. However, when we fast and take time to seek God, we are much more able to receive an enhancement of our giftings, with them being exercised in greater proportion.

Again, it is good to eat healthy food. We must take time to do some form of fasting (God will lead in this, and it doesn't take much time to research what this means).

Continuing with what happened to Peter after his vision in Acts 10:17-23 (NKJV):

> "Now while Peter wondered within himself what this vision which he had seen meant, behold, the men who had been sent from Cornelius had made inquiry for Simon's house, and stood before the gate. And they called and asked whether Simon, whose surname was Peter, was lodging there.
>
> While Peter thought about the vision, the Spirit said to him, "Behold, three men are seeking you. Arise therefore, go down and go with them, doubting nothing; for I have sent them."
>
> Then Peter went down to the men who had been sent to him from Cornelius, and said, "Yes, I am he whom you seek. For what reason have you come?"
>
> And they said, "Cornelius *the* centurion, a just man, one who fears God and has a good reputation among all the nation of the Jews, was divinely instructed by a holy angel to summon you to his house, and to hear words from you." Then he invited them in and lodged *them*.
>
> On the next day Peter went away with them, and some brethren from Joppa accompanied him."

When God gives a vision, it eventually comes to fruition. Not in the way we think, but by the interpretation of it.

We see that the Spirit spoke directly to Peter as he *thought* about the vision. Often, we *receive* the vision but do not take the time to *think* about it. We understand the vision we had; we may record it, but after that, we do not think about its meaning. We cease from going to God and inquiring of Him for its interpretation. When we meditate and reflect on the vision, the Spirit will often give us the answer.

Let's further look at the fulfillment of the interpretation of Peter's vision found in Acts 10:24-33 (NKJV):

> "And the following day they entered Caesarea. Now Cornelius was waiting for them, and had called together his relatives and close friends. As Peter was coming in, Cornelius met him and fell down at his feet and worshiped *him*. But Peter lifted him up, saying, "Stand up; I myself am also a man." And as he talked with him, he went in and found many who had come together. Then he said to them, "You know how unlawful it is for a Jewish man to keep company with or go to one of another nation. But God has shown me that I should not call any man common or unclean. Therefore I came without objection as soon as I was sent for. I ask, then, for what reason have you sent for me?"
>
> So Cornelius said, "Four days ago I was fasting until this hour; and at the ninth hour I prayed in my house, and behold, a man stood before me in bright clothing, and said, 'Cornelius, your prayer has been heard, and your alms are remembered in the sight of God. Send therefore to Joppa and call Simon here, whose surname is Peter. He is lodging in the house of Simon, a tanner, by the sea. When he comes, he will speak to you.' So I sent to you immediately, and you have done well to come. Now therefore, we are all present before God, to hear all the things commanded you by God.'"

God often answers someone's prayer by giving another person a vision. If God wants someone to find a Prophet for them because they are in a position of immense responsibility, God can provide that specific person a vision of the future Prophet's face. He can present what they look like in a dream with instruction to "find this man" or "this man shall be a help to you and speak to you what comes from Me, the LORD of hosts."

God can work in such ways, as we see from the passage above. When Cornelius prayed, God began to move on Peter. Peter spoke based on the vision and interpretation God gave him, and Peter presented it to the appropriate group.

This takes discernment, but when a vision or dream comes, we must not share it with the world. Too often, we see people on social media platforms sharing their dreams or visions when God did not want them to. Other times, people "have many dreams and visions" and continue to share every single one. The trouble is that individuals often do not operate in a spirit of discernment. They are quick to share what they have received because they are zealous or want to reveal how God speaks to them. Ironically, they are those who rarely go to God and say, "Is this dream/vision from You?" or "God, would You like me to share what You showed me (if He in fact did in the first place)?"

Truly, multitudes are led more by passion and zeal than they are by discernment and discretion. We must not be hasty in speaking what God shares with the wrong people, lest we become discouraged, upset, and frustrated.

I have suffered from this in the past. I have been foolish enough to share the long-term vision of what God has revealed to those who, in all respects, put me down, did not believe in me, and discouraged me. I was met with words such as "That will never happen", "I'll believe it when I see it", "you need to be practical", etc. It is devastating when we share what God has given to the wrong voices, for the Enemy often works through voices of discouragement, belittling, and people who are envious, bitter, and lack belief.

Peter knew what to say and when to share, even before Cornelius told him everything. Peter spoke based on the interpretation of the vision God gave him. May we learn to do the same in a like manner.

"The hand of the LORD came upon me and brought me out in the Spirit of the LORD, and set me down in the midst of the valley; and it *was* full of bones. Then He caused me to pass by them all around, and behold, *there were* very many in the open valley; and indeed *they were* very dry. And He said to me, "Son of man, can these bones live?" So I answered, "O Lord GOD, You know"" (Ezekiel 37:1-3 NKJV).

Many times, when God takes us in the Spirit, He commands us to perform certain actions, to look at something specifically, or to answer a question. This is so we can engage with the vision and learn what He is revealing.

The best way to learn something is to teach it. Likewise, the best

SPIRITUAL GIFTS

way to prepare is to bring forth interaction within certain giftings. When the Holy Spirit is speaking or moving, we would do best to listen. If He says, "What do you see?", we must reply. If we say, "I don't know, God. Reveal it to me and make the image clearer. I cannot fully see", God will answer.

Let us see what occurs in the rest of Ezekiel 37:4-14 (NKJV):

> "Again He said to me, "Prophesy to these bones, and say to them, 'O dry bones, hear the word of the LORD! Thus says the Lord GOD to these bones: "Surely I will cause breath to enter into you, and you shall live. I will put sinews on you and bring flesh upon you, cover you with skin and put breath in you; and you shall live. Then you shall know that I *am* the LORD."'"
>
> So I prophesied as I was commanded; and as I prophesied, there was a noise, and suddenly a rattling; and the bones came together, bone to bone. Indeed, as I looked, the sinews and the flesh came upon them, and the skin covered them over; but *there was* no breath in them.
>
> Also He said to me, "Prophesy to the breath, prophesy, son of man, and say to the breath, 'Thus says the Lord GOD: "Come from the four winds, O breath, and breathe on these slain, that they may live."'" So I prophesied as He commanded me, and breath came into them, and they lived, and stood upon their feet, an exceedingly great army.
>
> Then He said to me, "Son of man, these bones are the whole house of Israel. They indeed say, 'Our bones are dry, our hope is lost, and we ourselves are cut off!' Therefore prophesy and say to them, 'Thus says the Lord GOD: "Behold, O My people, I will open your graves and cause you to come up from your graves, and bring you into the land of Israel. Then you shall know that I *am* the LORD, when I have opened your graves, O My people, and brought you up from your graves. I will put My Spirit in you, and you shall live, and I will place you in your own land. Then you shall know that I, the LORD, have spoken *it* and performed *it*," says the LORD.'""

Again, we see that God is giving the interpretation directly to Ezekiel as he has the vision. This shows that God is always behind the interpretation of visions. Sometimes, He prolongs the revealment. Other times, He reveals the meaning to us as we have the vision.

For Ezekiel, God chose to reveal immediately to make sense of what Ezekiel was seeing and to understand what was to come. God can do the same for us and more. We must be willing to humble ourselves, repent of sin, and request of Him the gift for the interpretation of visions. We must seek Him to know and understand what His Will is for our lives.

God is willing to bless us with the gifts of the Spirit. He is willing to reveal what can only come from Him. "Where *there is* no revelation, the people cast off restraint; But happy *is* he who keeps the law" (Proverbs 29:18 NKJV). When we walk in obedience, God brings forth revelations. He gives us insight into what we did not know and what we could not see.

"Then God spoke to Israel in the visions of the night, and said, 'Jacob, Jacob!' And he said, 'Here I am.' So He said, 'I *am* God, the God of your father; do not fear to go down to Egypt, for I will make of you a great nation there. I will go down with you to Egypt, and I will also surely bring you up *again;* and Joseph will put his hand on your eyes'" (Genesis 46:2-4 NKJV). Just as God spoke to Jacob, so He can speak to us. We see this with Samuel: "Now the LORD came and stood and called as at other times, "Samuel! Samuel!" And Samuel answered, "Speak, for Your servant hears"" (1 Samuel 3:10 NKJV). We see this with Isaiah: "Also I heard the voice of the Lord, saying: "Whom shall I send, And who will go for Us?" Then I said, "Here *am* I! Send me""" (Isaiah 6:8 NKJV). Truly, when God calls, we must answer. When we do answer, we open up the door to hearing His Voice more clearly.

God wants to do more than we could ever ask or think. He wants to open the floodgates of blessing. He wants us to come to Him with our requests and bestow upon us what only He can give, for the sake of His Name being glorified through His elect.

May God bless us with the gift of the interpretation of visions, as well as the gift of visions to see the same as John in Revelation 5:1-14 (NKJV):

"And I saw in the right *hand* of Him who sat on the throne a scroll written inside and on the back, sealed with seven seals. Then I saw a strong angel proclaiming with a loud voice, "Who is worthy to open the scroll and to loose its seals?" And no one in heaven or on the earth or under the earth was able to open the scroll, or to look at it.

So I wept much, because no one was found worthy to open and read the scroll, or to look at it. But one of the elders said to me, "Do not weep. Behold, the Lion of the tribe of Judah, the Root of David, has prevailed to open the scroll and to loose its seven seals."

And I looked, and behold, in the midst of the throne and of the four living creatures, and in the midst of the elders, stood a Lamb as though it had been slain, having seven horns and seven eyes, which are the seven Spirits of God sent out into all the earth. Then He came and took the scroll out of the right hand of Him who sat on the throne.

Now when He had taken the scroll, the four living creatures and the twenty-four elders fell down before the Lamb, each having a harp, and golden bowls full of incense, which are the prayers of the saints. And they sang a new song, saying:

"You are worthy to take the scroll,

And to open its seals;

For You were slain,

And have redeemed us to God by Your blood

Out of every tribe and tongue and people and nation,

And have made us kings and priests to our God;

And we shall reign on the earth."

Then I looked, and I heard the voice of many angels around the throne, the living creatures, and the elders; and the number of them was ten thousand times ten thousand, and thousands of thousands, saying with a loud voice:

"Worthy is the Lamb who was slain

To receive power and riches and wisdom,

And strength and honor and glory and blessing!"

And every creature which is in heaven and on the earth and under the earth and such as are in the sea, and all that are in them, I heard saying:

"Blessing and honor and glory and power

Be to Him who sits on the throne,

And to the Lamb, forever and ever!"

Then the four living creatures said, "Amen!" And the twenty-four elders fell down and worshiped Him who lives forever and ever."

God Almighty, Creator of all, Who cannot cease to exist but has always been, Who dwells in Ineffable Light, Who cannot be seen or known in full, to Whom belongs all kingdoms of every generation, Who loves all men and calls all to repentance, Who is the Righteous Judge and Ruler over Heaven and Earth, Great is Thy Faithfulness and Mercies. God, thank You for blessing Your people with gifts of the Holy Spirit. We pray for an increase in revelation and knowledge of Thee. We pray for greater discernment and encouragement. We desire to be vessels filled with You that we may pour out to others. O God, help us to grow in You. Help us to know that You alone are God. You are worthy of worship, praise, honor, and glory! The Heavens themselves declare Your Glory and Your Marvelous, Wonderful Works! There is nothing You cannot do! You are the Great and Mighty I AM, the Sovereign LORD, the Redeemer Who brings restoration to the souls of those saved and sets free those who once were in bondage. O Great and Mighty King, we love You and ask that, if it be pleasing in Your Sight, You would bless us with the gift of the interpretation of visions. Teach us this gift and help us to steward it well. May we always depend and trust in the Holy Spirit with all the gifts You give us. We deserve nothing, O God, but we come boldly to Your Throne, requesting Your help. We love You, and without You, we are nothing. We cannot exist apart from You. Truly, You are the One Who speaks, and it is so; Who declares, and it is done. We lift Your Name On High, O God of our Lord Jesus Christ, Your Blessed Son. In Jesus' name, Amen.

The Gift of Revelation

"*That the God of our Lord Jesus Christ, the Father of glory, may give to you the spirit of wisdom and revelation in the knowledge of Him.*"
– ***Ephesians 1:17 NKJV***

To have a spirit of wisdom, we must have the Holy Spirit and the gift of Wisdom given by Him. Likewise, it is with revelation.

I recently spoke to an individual who, unfortunately, spent the majority of his time bragging about how much he read the Bible. He knew certain doctrines of the faith, but when I asked him if God had revealed any new revelations, he responded with, "Well, it depends on what you mean by revelation." He continued to talk for twenty minutes about that which I'm not going to write down lest you be unable to finish this Chapter!

I am sharing this story before we dive in because many deny that the Holy Spirit can give deeper revelation. It has been made known to me that those who hold this view actually have an impoverished relationship with the Holy Spirit. Rarely, if ever, do they talk about Him. They predominantly speak about the Lord Jesus and "God" in general, but they fail to understand and have a living relationship with the Heavenly Father and the Holy Spirit.

Ironically, those who deny that we can receive greater revelation from God are those who believe all that can be known about Him and His Word already exists. Though this be true, as it is in the Word, it takes the Holy Spirit to bring enlightenment to Divine Truths.

When reading the Word of God, the more you trust the Holy Spirit to teach you, the greater revelations you will receive. As you read, you will understand that each passage is multilayered. There are historical truths to understand. There are basic, fundamental understandings within each Chapter. However, the more you spend time cultivating a relationship with the Holy Spirit, asking Him to lead and trusting Him, the more He will perform mighty works. He will bring to light deeper revelations that could not have been known otherwise.

I know I have mentioned it multiple times, but it must be understood that what the Holy Spirit has revealed to me, He can reveal to you as well. He has shown me hundreds of new attributes never before discussed in all of Theology. How is this possible? It has been 2,000+ years since Christ ascended into Heaven, and we continue to review the same attributes that were present hundreds of years ago.

Why have there not been new attributes about God? If there have been, why have they been so little over the centuries? It is because we do not seek the Holy Spirit and trust Him to reveal deeper truths about the Trinity. We think that what is seen in the Word is all there is. If we just sought the Holy Spirit before reading and said, "God, show me new Attributes and Characteristics of You. I want to know You, God. Not about You, but Who You are – Your Nature, Being, and Existence!", we would be amazed at what He would reveal.

Now, it has taken years for the Holy Spirit to reveal to me the hundreds of new attributes of God that have already begun in my series, *The Infinite Omni: The Unending All Behind All Things*. I am very excited for this and have learned so much from the Holy Spirit! That is when you know He is in control – you learn from what "you produce". However, it is not actually you, but the Holy Spirit in you, speaking, writing, and bringing forth the revelation.

It is therefore extremely important not to hinder God but to seek the Holy Spirit to speak to us through God's Word. As He does so, we will begin to see things that we never would have seen had we not gone to Him. Hidden spiritual truths, metaphysical realities, and spiritual discernment and understanding will be given. We will receive what no man has received because it came from the Holy Spirit.

This is the beautiful reality about God – He is not limited. He is Limitless and Boundless. The Holy Spirit could speak throughout eternity only what is written in the Word of God, and we would not exhaust all the Divine Truths to be known within His Word. It is absolutely incredible to think about this. Not only this, but to meditate on the reality that throughout eternity in Heaven we will be continuing to know and grow more in understanding Who God *Is*, but never coming to a finality of knowing everything. Truly, He alone is Infinite and Transcendent!

We must not be those who think that all to be known from the Word of God is already written down by previous scholars, men, and women. It is time to stop living in the revelation of others and start requesting God's Divine revelation directly from Him! He can do so; the question is, do we believe He can and will?

With this being said, we want to pray for a spirit of wisdom and revelation. We want to ask the Holy Spirit to give us a deeper revelation of Who God Is—not just what He has done or what He can do, but *Who He Is*. When this becomes the forefront of an individual, they are well on their way to living in the fullness of all God has for them and truly seeking nothing but to know God and declare His Might, Magnificence, and Splendor!

Revelation is not just about coming to understand what one did not know previously; it is receiving insight directly from God's Spirit, something that has *never* been known by any man. This is something that, once grasped, should excite each believer and challenge them to dig deep into the Word of God and prayer.

In Matthew 13:11-12 (NKJV), the Lord Jesus answered and said to His disciples when asking Him why He spoke in parables, "'Because it has been given to you to know the mysteries of the kingdom of heaven, but to them it has not been given. For whoever has, to him more will be given, and he will have abundance".

When we look at Jesus' parables, they can sometimes be challenging to understand. As the Holy Spirit speaks, there are multiple different insights and understandings to be had within each given parable. The understanding of a parable is not confined to one interpretation, but an accumulation of revelation given by the Holy Spirit.

God chooses who He will allow others to know the mysteries of Him and His Kingdom. God is in control, and He is the One Who gives individuals a spirit of revelation. To do so, we clearly see that we must not only be found in God by becoming born again, but also be disciples who follow Him each day.

God will not bless the disobedient and those who do not seek Him for greater gifts. God will not give the gifts in greater measure to those who are slothful, lazy, and lethargic. God will bless those with the spirit of revelation when they walk with a pure heart before Him, genuinely wanting to grow in their relationship with Him.

Sadly, many men believe they are saved by the amount of knowledge they can accumulate. Without speaking directly to certain denominations and religions, it is not hard to discern groups (and individuals) who believe they are saved by the amount of information they know. They think intellectualism is a means to salvation, when this could not be further from reality.

To believe one is saved because one knows much is to know everything about someone we respect in history (their childhood and adult years, their family dynamics, career, beliefs, difficulties, failures, successes, favorite food, color, animal, etc.), and to believe that we know that person directly. Just because we know a great deal about an individual from history does not mean we know that person intimately. Likewise, it is with God.

We may read many books about God. We may be well versed in philosophy, reading the Stoics of the past, the Puritans, and the saints of old. We may have a library of thousands of books, but unless we have the Holy Spirit, we do not know God; and when we do not know God, we cannot receive the spirit of revelation.

Revelation is not knowledge and knowing what others have come to know about God. Revelation is God unveiling something that He hides from all (example: attributes about Him not yet revealed).

When a true man or woman of God comes forth with Divine truths never known, it not only challenges others, but it should compel them to seek God for the same spirit of revelation. Unfortunately, many do not take this route but become envious. Little do they know that God is ready and able to give them revelations that someone blessed with revelations does not know. They need only press into the Boundless, Limitless Holy Spirit of God to reveal deeper Divine Truths that are in accordance with His Word.

It is important to know that revelation does not pertain only to what is yet to be known in God's Word and by His Spirit; it can also be something hidden that only a particular individual knows (for example, a person's thoughts).

As we have seen in previous chapters, God can give a word of knowledge about someone that is a revelation to them, but not to the person whose heart God exposes. The gifts of the Spirit can coincide and overlap (as we reviewed at the beginning of this book). The revelation received can serve as a warning and prompt proceeding with caution. Sometimes, it is a means to give greater depth and understanding behind what someone has been thinking or dreaming. It can even be a means of going back and forth with a brother or sister in Christ, understanding life and the future in greater measure.

"When Jesus came into the region of Caesarea Philippi, He asked His disciples, saying, 'Who do men say that I, the Son of Man, am?' So they said, 'Some *say* John the Baptist, some Elijah, and others Jeremiah or one of the prophets.' He said to them, 'But who do you say that I am?' Simon Peter answered and said, 'You are the Christ, the Son of the living God.' Jesus answered and said to him, 'Blessed are you, Simon Bar-Jonah, for flesh and blood has not revealed *this* to you, but My Father Who is in heaven'" (Matthew 16:13-17 NKJV).

Here, we see proof of not only revelation through a word of knowledge being spoken in faith by Peter to Jesus, but we see Jesus being made aware simultaneously of Who brought forth the revelation. Peter knew He was the Christ, and Jesus instantly told him he was blessed because the Heavenly Father revealed this truth.

Remember, the Holy Spirit did not come to live in men until the Lord Jesus Christ ascended into Heaven. That is why the Heavenly

Father spoke to Peter, giving him the revelation of the Lord Jesus, and not the Holy Spirit in this instance. "'Nevertheless I tell you the truth. It is to your advantage that I go away; for if I do not go away, the Helper will not come to you; but if I depart, I will send Him to you'" (John 16:7 NKJV).

What happens after Jesus responds to Peter? We see a continuation of revelation. The Lord Jesus speaks to Peter later in the Book of Matthew and declares, "'And I also say to you that you are Peter, and on this rock I will build My church, and the gates of Hades shall not prevail against it'" (Matthew 16:18 NKJV). The Lord Jesus gave him a revelation of his life and what would occur in the future.

It is always wonderful to receive a revelation through word of knowledge, a prophetic word, or an interpretation of dreams or visions. It is a blessing to receive the spirit of revelation, where we not only can *receive* revelations from God, but also can give revelations to others (through the gift of revelation, directly, or through the gift of revelation exercised and worked through by other gifts of the Spirit). We act as a vessel, able to receive as well as pour into different vessels.

We see the gift of revelation from God working through the gift of dream interpretation with Daniel when it came to the King's dream. Daniel 2:19-23 (NKJV) declares:

> "Then the secret was revealed to Daniel in a night vision. So Daniel blessed the God of heaven. Daniel answered and said: 'Blessed be the name of God forever and ever, For wisdom and might are His. And He changes the times and the seasons; He removes kings and raises up kings; He gives wisdom to the wise And knowledge to those who have understanding. He reveals deep and secret things; He knows what *is* in the darkness, And light dwells with Him. "I thank You and praise You, O God of my fathers; You have given me wisdom and might, And have now made known to me what we asked of You, For You have made known to us the king's demand.'"

God is the One Who "reveals deep and secret things". These secret things are revelations known only to God and can therefore be given by God. If this deep and secret thing is the result of someone's heart,

God has complete control and liberty to reveal what He chooses to reveal.

This is why it is so important that we live holy, not just before God, but also because God can reveal the secrets of men's hearts to man. This will most certainly put the fear of the Lord in some of us who have been sinning without repentance and thinking everything is okay. When that occurs, God will send a Prophet to bring a correcting word.

For Daniel, it was not a matter of what was in the heart of the king, but what type of dream he had. This revelation came through a vision (which we reviewed in more detail in the previous chapters on visions).

Revelations come in a variety of ways, and God chooses the means by which He will reveal what He desires to reveal.

"'However, when He, the Spirit of truth, has come, He will guide you into all truth; for He will not speak on His own *authority*, but whatever He hears He will speak; and He will tell you things to come'" (John 16:13 NKJV). When the Spirit of Truth resides within us, He can give us revelation of what is to come. This is revealed through the Book of Revelation, which has yet to transpire for mankind.

The Holy Spirit speaks what He hears from the Heavenly Father and reveals it as He wills. This is exciting, as we can prepare for the future before it arrives. Of course, God is not going to tell us every detail of what is to come, nor will He always make sure we are prepared. If He continually did so, we would not need faith.

God will reveal the future to those who steward the gift of revelation well. If someone cannot steward the gift well and continues puffing themselves up about what they know, they will not receive the gift.

"Now after six days Jesus took Peter, James, and John his brother, led them up on a high mountain by themselves; and He was transfigured before them. His face shone like the sun, and His clothes became as white as the light. And behold, Moses and Elijah appeared to them, talking with Him. Then Peter answered and said to Jesus, "Lord, it is good for us to be here; if You wish, let us make here three tabernacles: one for You, one for Moses, and one for Elijah." While he was still speaking, behold, a bright cloud overshadowed them; and suddenly a voice came out of the cloud, saying, "This is My beloved Son, in Whom I am well pleased. Hear Him!"'" (Matthew 17:1-5 NKJV).

Revelations can not only come by visions, but also by direct appearances. The Lord Jesus, Peter, James, and John saw Elijah and Moses. This was an appearance that was more than a vision – it was a visible manifestation within our Earth.

It is important to note that direct appearances in this life occur only regarding the Lord Jesus Christ, angels, and demons. "Do not forget to entertain strangers, for by so *doing* some have unwittingly entertained angels" (Hebrews 13:2 NKJV). Unless it consists of Christ and spiritual entities (such as angels and demons), we ourselves will never see dead relatives. When they pass away, that is it. Their finality, whether in Heaven or Hell, is permanent. We will not see them again unless each of us is born again. Then, and only then, will we come in contact with the deceased who are now alive in Heaven. Ecclesiastes 9:5-6 (NKJV) states:

> "For the living know that they will die;
> But the dead know nothing,
> And they have no more reward,
> For the memory of them is forgotten.
> Also their love, their hatred, and their envy have now perished;
> Nevermore will they have a share
> In anything done under the sun."

The most significant revelation of man, which leads to salvation, is the Lord Jesus Christ Himself. For it is from within Him all things unfold. Without Him, we are nothing and would be nothing. He is the One Who spoke all things into existence. He is the One by Whom we receive the Holy Spirit. It is because of Him that we may live and have life more abundantly.

"But I make known to you, brethren, that the gospel which was preached by me is not according to man. For I neither received it from man, nor was I taught *it*, but *it came* through the revelation of Jesus Christ" (Galatians 1:11-12 NKJV). Paul declares it was "by revelation He made known to me the mystery (as I have briefly written already, by which, when you read, you may understand my knowledge in the mystery of Christ), which in other ages was not made known to the sons of men, as it has now been revealed by the Spirit to His holy apostles and prophets" (Ephesians 3:3-5 NKJV).

Again, he declares it is "the mystery which has been hidden from ages and from generations, but now has been revealed to His saints. To them God willed to make known what are the riches of the glory of this mystery among the Gentiles: which is Christ in you, the hope of glory" (Colossians 1:26-27 NKJV). It is sad that many do not know Christ and have not yet heard about Him. Yet, some people hear about Him many times each year and continue to deny and reject Him. Sadly, their portion will be the Lake of Fire if they do not turn from their sin and accept Jesus as Lord and Savior and receive the grace and mercy of God.

"The Revelation of Jesus Christ, which God gave Him to show His servants—things which must shortly take place. And He sent and signified *it* by His angel to His servant John, who bore witness to the word of God, and to the testimony of Jesus Christ, to all things that he saw. Blessed *is* he who reads and those who hear the words of this prophecy, and keep those things which are written in it; for the time *is* near" (Revelation 1:1-3 NKJV). Again, we see that prophecy can be a means of revelation.

When God reveals what is to come to a man or woman, they will write the revelation in ways they can express, but are not entirely sound. This is due to not living in the future, understanding certain generational advancements, for example, in technology, and, when spiritual, not having the right words to express what has never been seen.

The Lord Jesus Christ was willing to reveal much of the future to John. This was an extraordinary blessing from Christ, as this prophecy paved the way for us to speak to us (and to continue receiving revelation within the Book of Revelation!).

A revelation from God continues when we seek the Holy Spirit to make sense of what we read and see.

Let us meditate on the revelation of what is to come in the New Covenant. Hebrews 8:10-12 (NKJV) declares:

> "'For this *is* the covenant that I will make with the house of Israel after those days, says the LORD: I will put My laws in their mind and write them on their hearts; and I will be their God, and they shall be My

people. None of them shall teach his neighbor, and none his brother, saying, 'Know the LORD,' for all shall know Me, from the least of them to the greatest of them. For I will be merciful to their unrighteousness, and their sins and their lawless deeds I will remember no more.'"

Let us never cease from growing in God and desiring a spirit of revelation. Truly, it is a gift given only by God. He will reveal the means by which revelations will be bestowed. It may be knowledge, insight, wisdom, prophecy, visions, or dreams. It may be a deeper understanding of Scripture that no one else has seen. It may be about what lingers within someone's heart or about the future. Whatever the revelation, God is ready and willing to perform and do more than we can ask or think. We must make the request, obey, and have faith that He will answer. In His timing, we will receive and witness that which could only come from Him.

"Now to Him Who is able to do exceedingly abundantly above all that we ask or think, according to the power that works in us, to Him *be* glory in the church by Christ Jesus to all generations, forever and ever. Amen" (Ephesians 3:20-21 NKJV).

God in Heaven, Him Who is All-Vision and the Great Revelation, Who cannot be fully known but can be truly known through Your Son, the Lord Jesus Christ, Blessed Art Thou, O God of all. Who is like You, Who speaks and it is done? Who can stand in Your Holiness and live? Who is the Light of lights and the Life of life? Is it not You, the One and Only Living God? The God of Abraham, Isaac, and Jacob? O Great and Omnipotent Lord, nothing can assail You. Forever, You are Invisible, Eternal, Immortal, and Unseen. By Thy Son we may know Thy true Image, but in the fullness of Who You are, none can see but the Son of God. We praise Thee for revelations from the Holy Spirit. Thank You for looking down on such weak vessels and being willing to provide aid and assistance in our lives. God, we trust in You with all of our tomorrows, as we lean into You all of our present days. Bless us with deeper revelation of Who You are, Your Word, spiritual truths, the future, and greater insight into the spiritual gifts. Guide us, Holy Spirit, into all that is acceptable, loving, pure, and holy. We want to be like You, Christ. Though we shall always fall short in this life, we who are born-again know that Heaven is our promised Home, a Place where there will be no more sorrow or pain, a Place where You will wipe away every tear from our eyes. We look forward to that Day, Lord Jesus, when every knee will bow and tongue will confess You are Lord and Savior. We who are born-again look forward to being with You, learning about You, and being joint heirs with You throughout all of eternity. May all come to salvation through genuine faith in Thee and repentance of sins. May Thy Will forever be done, on Earth as it is in Heaven. In Jesus' name, Amen.

The Gift of Discernment

> "*Therefore give to Your servant an understanding heart to judge Your people, that I may discern between good and evil. For who is able to judge this great people of Yours?*"
> – *1 Kings 3:9 NKJV*

Discernment is the greatest gift needed in the Church today. Amid this generation of deceit and manipulation, we need truth-tellers and Truth-possessors! We need people to start prioritizing what corresponds to reality, and stop attempting to go in the way of what seems right or what we enjoy hearing. We must be grounded in the Bedrock and Foundation of the Word of God and the Lord Jesus Christ. Without God and His Word, we will go in the way of the world – lose sleep, be led astray by carnality, deception, manipulation, and darkness.

Solomon is noted as the wisest man under Christ because He had even the humility and wisdom to request of God that which he could not obtain on his own. He asked God for "an understanding heart". A heart that understands can properly discern. When we operate in God's discernment, we can quickly and easily tell what is of Him and what is not. Yes, we know this by the Word, but even gray can appear as white when its shade resembles more closely what is white than black. The discernment of God helps us distinguish what is of Him and what *appears to be* of Him. It enables us to distinguish between what is true and what is *almost* true. "Then you shall again discern Between the righteous and the wicked, Between one who serves God And one who does not serve Him" (Malachi 3:18 NKJV).

Too many in our day are saying, "This is wonderful" when it is not of God. Too many say, "God is on the move," when it's just the flesh portraying external profits and numbers, but not reaching down to bring transformation within by properly leading others to God. No, many see size and numbers as a means of a powerful ministry. Multitudes are swept away by prophetic words of "You are going to be famous", "You are going to be rich", and "many will know your name." A proper discernment can distinguish, however, that if at the end of such phrases God is not included, these statements can be excluded. They are mere caressing of the flesh, seeking to make us feel more superior than we are.

Many are running to such false prophecies and lack the spiritual maturity to discern them. Their flesh gets in the way, and they are easily manipulated and led astray. They love to hear what gives them a sense of purpose and a massive calling, yet we see that it is better to be lowly and exalted. For not all exalted in this life were exalted by the Hand of God Almighty. In fact, most of those whom we deem to be *of* God will soon be found out that they are not. Their secret sins will rise to the surface, and you will see a massive wave of "Christian influencers" being stripped of what they built. Yes, this is a prophetic word and something to monitor in the years and even decades to come, for God will not allow self to prosper ahead of Him, especially when self is boosting itself in the name of God.

This is why we must never put our faith in people. We must never idolize others. We must never raise them in our minds, but see each of us on level ground before Christ. The difference that will make us rise and ascend is our humility. Too many are inflated with ego, and not enough are led by the Spirit. In our day, we must pray and ask for the discernment of the Holy Spirit to help us distinguish between good and *almost* good; between what is good in the world's eyes and what is good in

God's eyes; between what appears to be of God and what is truly of God. We must have discernment, now more than ever, to detect the wolves in sheep's clothing.

"'Beware of false prophets, who come to you in sheep's clothing, but inwardly they are ravenous wolves'" (Matthew 7:15 NKJV). Wolves aren't just those who preach prosperity or water down the Gospel. No, they are those who talk about how Christ can save you from anxiety and depression, but they refuse to say the word "sin". Christ cannot save us from anxiety and depression until He saves us from our sin, because it is our sin that causes anxiety and depression! Greater still, individuals will speak on how pornography is wrong and its effects. Why? Even the world acknowledges this (insofar as those who are not consumed and in love with it). Most people understand it is wrong and see how it robs us of much. Yes, you will hear people go against this, but not have the discernment to weed out those who are not the actual Body of Christ within their church!

Many churches are filled with unconverted Christians. They are not truly born-again, and we wonder why many are falling away from the Church. They were never of the Church to begin with – they were frauds! They wanted to be part of a community, but they did not want to do what it takes to enter fully into the free gift of salvation. They wanted to volunteer, and in so doing, they brought forth church hurt, or they themselves were taken advantage of because they were babes in *understanding* the Gospel (though, not being covered by the Blood of Christ). They were not mature and unsure how to respond in certain situations or answer questions.

We must begin to ask, "Why are people so quick to volunteer in something that they are not truly fit for, and why are 'leaders' so quick to allow people not born-again in the church to fulfill leadership roles?" Other questions that you begin to ask based on what the Spirit reveals when you have the gift of discernment are: Where did we need to go to school to become a teacher of the Word? A Prophet? A Pastor? When we read the Scriptures, there was no schooling to prepare us for what God alone ordains and calls a man or woman to fulfill. Each position comes with responsibility, and it can only be fulfilled by the Holy Spirit working through a man or woman who is fully submitted to the Will of God.

Man cannot call you to something. He can attempt to prepare you and give you a degree, but a degree means nothing in the eyes of God if He has not called us to be in the position. Truly, positions are only anointed when they are God-appointed. We don't need to go to school and college to then fulfill what we only need the Holy Spirit to prepare, lead, and direct us to, for many professors across colleges today are not born-again. That is why many classes are dead and dry. There is no fresh revelation, just recycling information from other men they have read.

Positions in the Church have become professions rather than being truly born of God. Many professors are intelligent by man's standards, but they are not wise. The wisdom of God is fleeting because God is not present. He is absent, and across many churches today it is the same manifold. There are not as many born-again believers as one may believe within the places that we would deem to have many Christians! In like manner, there are more Christians in the world than we may think, but they are "hidden". Many of those truly living for God are not found on platforms. Instead, man has built many platforms and exalts those who do not *know* God while *claiming* to know Him.

When you begin to walk with the Holy Spirit, the Holy Spirit shows you such things. This is only the beginning, and it is essential to request that God would bless us with Holy Ghost discernment to detect what cannot be seen, is hard to discern, and what otherwise could not be made known had God not revealed it, for He is the Light that exposes the darkness. He is the Truth that conquers deceit. God alone provides the awareness, understanding, and discernment to not be led astray by man, principalities, powers, or demons. Not even Satan himself can lead a man or woman astray who is wholly taken over by the Holy Spirit, being renewed and sanctified day by day, and desires nothing but the Will of God.

We are at war in these dark hours. Many are taken captive by the mighty current of deception. They praise bands more than they praise God. They follow pastors more than they follow God's Word. They are led by emotions rather than the Holy Spirit. In all of this, we are raising "Christians" who are not born-again. As this occurs, the ranks of the

Enemy grow within "the Church". He gets stronger and more powerful because he is placing himself in the camp of God, and there is more of the Enemy blending in with the Church than the Church possessing those who are truly of God.

When such knowledge is made clear by the Holy Spirit, you start to see others and the church building you attend, and you find it is sick. It isn't just about the typical cliché phrase of "the church is for the sick", but you begin seeing that there are pedophiles, Freemasons, Luciferians, and even Satanists blending in within Christian churches. We do not need to go into detail with all these groups, but it must be noted that these are dangerous times. What better way for the wicked to continue in their way than to go to a place where no one would suspect such evil to be occurring? Truly, these people go to God's House during the day, but at night, they participate in what is an abomination. At the proper time, I will be writing extensively on this, but for now, it must be noted that those you see are not always what they claim. What you see at most Churches is not reality. It is fake, and the sooner you wake up to this truth, the sooner you will not be duped, led astray, confused, and unsure. You will see things for what they are.

I do not know the history of how church buildings started, nor do I care to know. The point is simple: the church building is not of God. Yes, good things can happen, but it is a direct, strategic idea of the Enemy to allow those of him to blend in. This will take the wisdom and discernment of the Holy Spirit to grasp fully, but have you ever wondered why we drifted from house churches? Churches nowadays are getting so big —what do we see happening? They are getting filled with pretenders. They are not filled with those born again, and because we have neglected the gifts of the Spirit (which is a doctrine of demons), we have prevented people from discerning and being aware of what should not be in the Church —specifically, *who* should not be in the Church.

The Enemy has built up a perfect system. Aside from the evil that occurs at night and in places where he reigns, it is crucial to understand that, for Satan, the Church *building* is a means of bringing people who worship the Evil One or worship themselves into the camp of God. In so doing, they bring in false doctrine, perversion, corruption, confusion, and sow discord, strife, and partake in evil. They tempt the people of God away, just as the people of the Old Testament tempted the Israelites. In so doing, people begin to go down the path of darkness while blending in with the Light. They can do so by doing this all within the church building. So long as they go to church, they appear as "a good person", and no one would think the worst of them. This is a tremendous problem that not many are aware of, but many need to wake up to, for many are being taken advantage of and led astray.

What would happen if we went back to house churches? What is the benefit? Aside from a more intimate connection, a house church can only get so big. Therefore, when people equipped with the gifts of the Spirit are operating, those who want to "blend in" are unable to do so. They will be loved on in some of the first couple of encounters within a house church, but someone who is directly anti-God but does not want to appear suspicious will not continue attending. They will not be able to put up a front because a house church is small and intimate. Those who genuinely want to know God will stay. Those not of God will leave, specifically after the first encounter.

The importance of keeping the church to a smaller size in a house does not permit those who are evil to remain and blend in, coming in and out, even profiling others as a next victim. Yes, this is real, and it must be monitored. The discernment of the Holy Spirit will wake one up to this reality and encourage others not to pride themselves in megachurches, but to see the tremendous dangers. Much of leadership in those churches involves people who are not born-again. Many of these churches water down the truth, and many lack the proper people to discern who is coming in and who is leaving. This is all a ploy of the Enemy, and it is being exposed within this book. Again, I will be writing another book extensively, but I will leave the title unnamed for now, as the concept will expose a great deal that the Enemy does not want you to know.

Is it any wonder, therefore, why we are commanded, "Beloved, do not believe every spirit, but test the spirits, whether they are of God; because many false prophets have gone out into the world" (1 John 4:1 NKJV)? "But solid food belongs to those who are of full age, that is, those who by reason of use have their senses exercised to discern both good and evil" (Hebrews 5:14 NKJV). Do we desire to be mature in the faith? It is not in the amount of books we read, the pastors we listen to, the number of sermons and podcasts we have heard. Maturity in the faith can only come from Him Who is the Author and Finisher of our faith: The Holy Trinity. Without the Holy Spirit leading us in His Word and growing us in discernment, we merely acquire knowledge that may be deemed admirable by our peers, but is not an effective means of discerning and speaking and acting accordingly.

"And have no fellowship with the unfruitful works of darkness, but rather expose them" (Ephesians 5:11 NKJV). When God gives us discernment about a certain darkness or the Enemy's strategy, it is not meant to be spoken on or shared *immediately*. There is a timing to everything, and the gift of discernment helps us know the *when*, not just the *what*. Some people learn something about a particular group or evil and instantly want to shout it from the rooftops. They deem themselves as being part of a tribe that is "in the know". They find their identity in this and want to be the "first" to share. They want to portray that they know something that others do not. While this may be true, knowledge acquired through discernment must also be adequately discerned as to whether to be shared now or later. Without the Holy Spirit, we will not know the time, whether to share it with the public, or whether it is meant to be shared with us to pray to God by ourselves or with one or two others.

There are realities I know that I cannot write on, because God has not released me to speak on such matters. The *when* is up to Him, but for now, I am tested. Will impulsivity lead me? Will I believe I should do it now, as it will help many others? No, there is a strategic timing to everything. Christ came when He did because that was the appropriate time. A day sooner or later would have offset everything, and the events that should have unfolded would not have come to fruition. We must allow the gift of discernment to be activated by the Holy Spirit and have Him speak the *what* and *when* to us behind all things that He desires to share. Of course, this can only happen the more we spend time in prayer, the Word, and quietness.

The gift of discernment is best understood in quiet. Without silence, we cannot hear God's Voice. The constant noise from people and technology barely allows us to think. If we became disciplined, asked God for the gift of discernment, and took time to be silent, go for a walk, and allow Him to speak, we would grow in discernment each day. The problem is, we always want a distraction. We don't respect ourselves, and we see very little value in "doing nothing". We think this is a waste of time, but if we allow our minds to rest from the noise, we give room for God to speak and for the Spirit to move.

"For the ear tests words as the palate tastes food" (Job 34:3 NKJV). When we learn God's Voice in silence, we can better discern the voice of individuals in the present. We will know whether someone is genuine. We will distinguish between one who not only declares truth, but lives by it, as opposed to a fraud. We will know immediately that something is off about someone else. It will not be due to some trauma we have not worked through, but rather by the Spirit. We may not be able to pinpoint the exact reason why we sense something is off, but sometimes it's not about knowing everything with the gift of discernment; sometimes it's just knowing that something is not in alignment, and we must be cautious and careful.

If someone wants to have us sign something to steal our money, we don't need to know the reason. So long as we have the gift of discernment, we will know something is off when we are asked to sign something that tells one story, but our spirit does not confirm it is true. It senses that something is off, without knowing everything to the fullest, and we therefore do not sign the papers. So it is with everything else in life when one has the gift of discernment.

Truly, we are called to "Test all things; hold fast what is good" (1 Thessalonians 5:21 NKJV). We must "Judge not according to the appearance, but judge with righteous judgment" (John 7:24 NKJV). Righteous judgment is discernment, and proper discernment lines up everything to the Word of God and the Nature of God. If there is no alignment, then something is off, and when something is not as it should be, it is an indication that it is not of God.

Even if something may seem reasonable, but it is not the way we should go, God will make it known. "Consider the work of God; For who can make straight what He has made crooked?" (Ecclesiastes 7:13 NKJV). No one can make a path straight that God has made crooked. It will not align. We may think we can get somewhere faster, but the end will lead to suffering and tragedy. We will be unfulfilled because we refused to listen to the discernment of the Holy Spirit. We thought our way would lead to our end, but our way led to a bend in the road. We did not get to where we thought we would, and we wasted time, money, energy, and resources. Had we listened to the discernment God gave us, we would have refrained from much wasted time and emotional turmoil.

"And this I pray, that your love may abound still more and more in knowledge and all discernment, that you may approve the things that are excellent, that you may be sincere and without offense till the day of Christ" (Philippians 1:9-10 NKJV). The gift of discernment from the Holy Spirit teaches us how to love in all discernment. This universal statement that says "love everyone" does not appropriately convey *how* we are to love each and every person. We are not going to love our enemy the same as we love our wife. We are not going to love an abusive family member the same as a godly friend. With discernment from the Holy Spirit comes the understanding of *how* to love and deal with individuals, based upon the relationship, who they are, how they treat us, and other aspects.

Just because someone is blood does not mean they should be close. God does not put up with abuse from those unwilling to change. Likewise, we must be discerning and love even family who continually gossips, slanders, manipulates, and speaks ill of us for no reason, from a distance. How? By prayer. The Lord Jesus had boundaries, and the Holy Spirit will give us discernment on *who* needs *what* boundaries. If the boundaries are continually crossed, more stringent measures may be required. Above all, we love them as Christ *leads* us to love.

When we have the gift of discernment, we will be approached by others and hear, "I have heard of you, that the Spirit of God *is* in you, and *that* light and understanding and excellent wisdom are found in you" (Daniel 5:14 NKJV). This is what can be known from an individual who dedicates their life to God each day, desiring to be filled with the Spirit and have less of themselves. Those who seek the gift of discernment and are not only blessed with it but also exercise it and continue to seek the Holy Spirit for the increase will be known as those who truly walk with God. Truly, apart from Christ, there is no discernment.

"'Now therefore, let Pharaoh select a discerning and wise man, and set him over the land of Egypt'" (Genesis 41:33 NKJV). Even people around the world will know a man or woman is discerning when they exercise their discernment. It is by the gift of discernment that many are placed in positions to steward the responsibility of helping multitudes. Whatever the position, discernment is needed. Discernment is a means of knowing the difference between good and evil, but also what is godly and *deemed* as merely exemplary (ex: people who *portray* themselves to be perfect). The gift of discernment brings increase in the eyes of man when one fully submits to what God reveals, and has the courage and boldness to speak and operate on what has been revealed.

If a person has the gift of discernment, the path to continual increase in the gift is to "not be conformed to this world, but be transformed by the renewing of your mind, that you may prove what *is* that good and acceptable and perfect will of God" (Romans 12:2 NKJV). Whatever is God's Will will be revealed to one with the gift of discernment. The moment we question and go against what is shown, the Spirit will not exercise the gift through us. We will suffer in the days and weeks ahead, for God does not take lightly those who reject His Voice. He is not overly-sensitive to our disobedience; He simply is God. He will not take time to speak to those who do not want to hear His Voice.

"For the word of God *is* living and powerful, and sharper than any two-edged sword, piercing even to the division of soul and spirit, and of joints and marrow, and is a discerner of the thoughts and intents of the heart" (Hebrews 4:12 NKJV). As one abstains from the world and renews their mind, the renewing of the mind must be met with a continual spending time in the Word of God. The more we spend time in the Holy Scriptures, the more prone we are to obey what God declares.

"Whoever keeps the law *is* a discerning son" (Proverbs 28:7 NKJV). Without the Word, one will not increase in the discernment of the Holy Spirit. They will remain idle, discerning the simple understandings that gossip is wrong, homosexuality is sin, and murder is evil, but they will not advance into the depths that God desires to share with them.

"Counsel in the heart of man *is like* deep water, But a man of understanding will draw it out" (Proverbs 20:5 NKJV). As it is with the man, so it is with God. We can counsel appropriately and effectively, but God must draw that out of us. He does so by drawing us to His Word. If we do not seek God in His Word, we will not hear His Voice, act on what is revealed, or discern the deeper truths of life. We will remain babes in Christ, finishing the race with not much to show. We will have lived a life entirely far from all that *could* have been.

Truly, God is willing and wanting to give many the gift of discernment, but He only provides what is in accordance with one's faith, desire, and want. Suppose we do not have the faith for discernment, and we neglect to have a continual desire and unending want for an increase in discernment. In that case, we shall live an undiscerning life, which, in the economy of God, only gets one so far in being recognized on that Final Day. Yes, one may be saved by the Blood of Christ, but for those destined for Heaven, God is interested in what was done through us by the Holy Spirit. Too many are *only* focused on the Former, when it is Christ Who enters us into the beginning of the faith. For true faith is never-ending, always-increasing, and forever-wanting the Holy Spirit to do more with each passing day.

"The simple believes every word, but the prudent considers well his steps" (Proverbs 14:15 NKJV). Let us strive to be prudent in all things and not be like those who are weak in the faith and believe that we can live without the Holy Spirit. We must seek the discernment of the Holy Spirit in all things, for even now, many of us are believing what is not of God. Many of us have been taken captive by what God does not want us to be taken captive by. We are not seeing deeper truths and greater realities of what is occurring and unfolding around us. We are missing even the ability to see that a child is being trafficked, and we don't even know that they are being abused continually. So much evil is occurring around us, and if we want to fight back against evil, we will go to God, give Him everything, and say, "God, I desire Your discernment alone. Please fill me with the Holy Spirit and reveal to me the idols in my life that must go. Do not let me go in the way of demons, but give me the strength to surrender all that the Holy Spirit may flow fully throughout my life with each passing day. In Jesus' name, Amen."

Let us be like Paul in Acts 20:26-31 (NKJV) and declare:

"'Therefore I testify to you this day that I *am* innocent of the blood of all *men*. For I have not shunned to declare to you the whole counsel of God. Therefore take heed to yourselves and to all the flock, among which the Holy Spirit has made you overseers, to shepherd the church of God which He purchased with His Own blood. For I know this, that after my departure savage wolves will come in among you, not sparing the flock. Also from among yourselves men will rise up, speaking perverse things, to draw away the disciples after themselves. Therefore watch, and remember that for three years I did not cease to warn everyone night and day with tears.'"

We can only follow and know what Paul has declared when the Holy Spirit rules and reigns within us. May God help us to be like Peter in Acts 5:3 (NKJV) when he detected the lies of Ananias, "Then Peter said, 'Ananias, why has Satan filled your heart to lie to the Holy Spirit and keep back part of the price of the land for yourself?'" (Acts 5:3 NKJV). So many are lying for selfish motives, gains, and profits, when God wants us to be part of the wave of unraveling deception. Truly, God is close to exposing many who the common "Christian" deems a believer. What is to come will shock both those in the Church and even the world. God will do this, and He wants us to play a role in discerning who is truly of Him and who merely *appears* to be of Him.

Let us never forget that "the natural man does not receive the things of the Spirit of God, for they are foolishness to him; nor can he know them, because they are spiritually discerned" (1 Corinthians 2:14 NKJV). "For false christs and false prophets will rise and show great signs and wonders to deceive, if possible, even the elect" (Matthew 24:24 NKJV). With deception continually increasing, it is imperative that all of us possess the gift of discernment, which can only come from the Holy Spirit. For if even the elect can be deceived by signs and wonders of false prophets, how much more us when we are not seeking, abiding, and growing in God? "But he who is spiritual judges all things" (1 Corinthians 2:15 NKJV).

"Now I urge you, brethren, note those who cause divisions and offenses, contrary to the doctrine which you learned, and avoid them" (Romans 16:17 NKJV). May God help us all, and bless us with the gift of discernment, to be used for His Glory alone and the edification of ourselves and the Body of Christ. "For God is not the author of confusion but of peace, as in all the churches of the saints" (1 Corinthians 14:33 NKJV).

God in Heaven, Who knows all before all comes to be, Who is the Creator of Life and is the Ultimate Source of Truth, Who alone Is Truth and transcends the physical and metaphysical realm, nothing can escape Your Eye, the Timeless and Boundless God of the Holy Scriptures. There is none like You, nor will there ever be. You alone, O God of Heaven and Earth, rule and reign Supreme, far above the Heavens and the Earth! You bless Your servants with discernment and understanding. You teach them the way they are to go, but only if they are willing to go in such a way. For You bless and exalt the humble, but You bring down the prideful. O God, we request that You prepare us to receive the gift of discernment. Help us to know what is of You and not of You. Give us the ability to distinguish what is Truth and almost Truth, what is Light and nearly Light, what is of You and what appears to be of You. O God, increase our spiritual senses as we submit our spirit to You, requesting that the Holy Spirit do all He has been sent to do through us. Forgive us for our disobedience and sin that has stunted and prevented Your discernment from being bestowed upon us and revealed to us. God, we want to see as You see. Bless us with the ability to know, see, and fight against darkness. In Jesus' name, Amen.

The Gift of Joy

"*For the joy of the Lord is your strength.*" – **Nehemiah 8:10 NKJV**

There is a gift of joy that cannot be obtained other than by God.

Happiness is different from joy. Happiness is temporary, whereas joy is long-lasting. Happiness comes from something external and heightens our feelings for a brief period. Joy, however, comes from God alone and brings forth an inner eruption of gladness. It cannot be contained, and it can be possessed in all seasons, not just in times of prosperity.

Happiness only comes from something working out well. We receive a gift, get blessed by a friend, see a movie we enjoy, or see our investment portfolio rise. These are based on aspects that can fluctuate, and the happiness we receive is derived from the circumstances we are presented. If a friend cancels to go see our favorite movie, our stocks plummet, or someone says, "Just kidding", and they take back the gift, we would not be happy. Joy is different.

With joy, we can rejoice and be glad in any and all seasons. Since joy is a gift of God that can only be given by Him, we can be joyful in any and all circumstances. Why? We see things by the Eternal End, not by their temporary existence and current means. Instead, we see all things through Heaven's Eyes. "My brethren, count it all joy when you fall into various trials, knowing that the testing of your faith produces patience. But let patience have *its* perfect work, that you may be perfect and complete, lacking nothing" (James 1:2-4 NKJV).

"In Your presence is fullness of joy; at Your right hand are pleasures forevermore" (Psalm 16:11 NKJV). Since God is Omnipresent (everywhere at all times), we know that when we are in God's Presence, we can be joyful in any circumstance. We can be going through times of adversity, yet still have the gift of joy, so long as we prioritize God and desire this gift to be given. Yes, joy is a fruit of the Spirit, but it is also a gift. The world does not know this gift because they do not know Him. Someone who is an unbeliever may be genuinely kind, which is another fruit of the Spirit. Of course, their kindness can only go so far apart from God, but it can still be exercised. However, joy can only come from God; hence, it is a gift.

Joy allows us to be grateful for all things. Often, people are ungrateful and unappreciative. I myself have struggled with this much of my life. Being a visionary, I always look ahead. In the current season I am in, God is teaching me to be grounded and present. Through this, I am learning that I can have the gift of joy as I request God to help me have joy in all seasons.

Truly, this is a gift the world does not have, nor can it. Many people live their lives without knowing joy; they only know happiness. Again, this happiness comes from what is going well. The moment something goes wrong, happiness is fleeting. Yet, for us who are born again, when we have this gift, we can shift our perspective to see that God is behind the scenes in all things. Whether directly or not (ex: sin and evil), God is still behind everything *working out* for a greater good. When we recognize this, we may find rest.

"As the Father loved Me, I also have loved you; abide in My love. If you keep My commandments, you will abide in My love, just as I have kept My Father's commandments and abide in His love. These things I have spoken to you, that My joy may remain in you, and that your joy may be full'" (John 15:11 NKJV). The key to increasing all gifts is obedience. God does not honor those who perpetually disobey, but those who strive for excellence and seek the Holy Spirit for assistance to live according to the Word. God is willing to move mountains. He is willing to gift those who place Him first in all areas the desires of their heart, since naturally their desires will be of Him. Why? We tend to request what we prioritize, and what we prioritize, we desire. The gravitation of the heart goes toward that which rules it.

"'Until now you have asked nothing in My name. Ask, and you will receive, that your joy may be full'" (John 16:24 NKJV). Continually, we must go to God to ask Him for what we desire. Too many times, we think we can do something on our own when God is saying, "This will not occur nor prosper unless you seek me with all your heart, soul, mind, and strength." It is at this understanding that we must set ourselves aside and our striving in the flesh, and fully seek God, give it over to Him, and believe He will do it!

When one grasps these simple concepts, possibilities begin to open! We no longer live a lethargic, self-willed faith, but one that is led and directed by the Holy Spirit as we seek God in all things. The more we do this, the greater our faith will be, since God will answer our prayers along the way. Each answer brings forth more faith, and the greater the faith, the greater the joy.

There is a gift of joy that we must seek God to bless us. We don't want to live a life that is idle, down, depressed, or gloom-and-doom. No, we want a faith that moves mountains and that is filled with joy in the Lord! Not joy in circumstance, but joy in knowing we know the One Who can deliver us out of the circumstance and change our hearts within the current situation!

"This is the day the Lord has made; we will rejoice and be glad in it" (Psalm 118:24 NKJV). "Rejoice always, pray without ceasing, in everything give thanks; for this is the will of God in Christ Jesus for you" (1 Thessalonians 5:16-18 NKJV). As we possess the gift of joy, it can be increased through thankfulness. The less we are inclined to thank God, the more we are likely to be led by externals, which either bring happiness or sadness. When we are continually thankful to God for all He has done and will continue to do, our joy shall be increased.

"You have put gladness in my heart, more than in the season that their grain and wine increased" (Psalm 4:7 NKJV). Joy and gladness are of the same, and they exude from one who has been in the Presence of God. Without cultivating a relationship in prayer with our Heavenly Father, we will miss the mark on much. We will not be joyful or glad, but rather feel something is missing. This "missing" is revealment of a lack of going to God to find true joy. As we go to Him, we will be filled with more joy. Greater still, the more we obey Him, we will increase in joy, since the joy of the Lord is our strength (Nehemiah 8:10)!

There is a difference between joy and being optimistic. Many of the world are optimistic. They can be optimistic on how life will unfold and believe in the best. Yet again, optimism comes by way of circumstance. Joy, however, comes from the Lord.

When we start living our lives not being ruled by externals or by how other things in life unfold, we will receive greater rest, peace, and joy. We will not be easily angry or depressed. We will not fear what is to come. Instead, we will look to God and see Him in the midst. This is the answer to receiving the gift of joy – not just praying for it, but choosing to see God in every circumstance and event. The more this occurs, and we are grounded in the truth of Who God Is (of which you can learn more in my ongoing life-series, *The Infinite Omni: The Unending All Behind All Things*), we will not only receive the gift of joy, but learn the art of cultivating it. As this is done, the Holy Spirit will be more active throughout our being, for He is the One Who draws us to meditate and contemplate the Beauty, Majesty, and Might of God Almighty.

"The Lord your God in your midst, the Mighty One, will save; He will rejoice over you with gladness, He will quiet you with His love, He will rejoice over you with singing" (Zephaniah 3:17 NKJV). "The ransomed of the Lord shall return, and come to Zion with singing, with everlasting joy on their heads. They shall obtain joy and gladness, and sorrow and sighing shall flee away" (Isaiah 35:10 NKJV). When we are found in God, this is the promise for every born-again believer. We will go to a place where "'God will wipe away every tear from their eyes; there shall be no more death, nor sorrow, nor crying. There shall be no more pain, for the former things have passed away'" (Revelation 21:4 NKJV).

With this promise in mind for us who are born-again, we can

rejoice! We can live in joy, and request God for the gift of joy and an ever-increasing day by day! God is willing and able. We need only request and do as He expects. As this occurs, we will find a newness and a freshness within our spirit. We will not be as prone to old habits, mindsets, and ways. We will not be easily offset by circumstance. Instead, we will learn to say, "In prosperity and adversity, I will serve and trust the Lord."

"Now may the God of hope fill you with all joy and peace in believing, that you may abound in hope by the power of the Holy Spirit" (Romans 15:13 NKJV).

God in Heaven, Him Who Was, Is, and Always shall Be, Who cannot refrain from existing, but is Existence Himself, Who brought forth all by the Word of Truth, Who Wills all that is good and true, You alone are the Alpha and Omega, the Great God above the Heavens and Earth, the One Who guides His servants, protects His saints, and speaks through His Prophets. Blessed Art Thou, O God of Heaven and Earth. God, we seek You this day for the gift of joy and a greater increase in all the gifts You have given. Teach us the way of You that we may walk humbly before You. God, may we never cease from believing, for by faith it can be accounted to us as righteousness, for You see those who have faith in You as the greatest of saints. For in believing You, we do not allow ourselves to be tempted, overruled, or defeated by circumstance, events, people, the Enemy, or ourselves. O God, fill us with joy from You! Deepen our understanding that the joy of You is our strength! May we never cease from obeying You, but always strive to listen to Your Voice in all matters. God, help us be the Light that shines in the darkness, which the darkness cannot overcome. May we forever be illuminated by the Holy Spirit, revealing to the world what true joy is in You. Bless us, O God of Heaven and Earth, with this gift, that we might bring Life and Love wherever we go, for the Joy within is You, Holy Spirit. Gift us with more of You coming forth on this day, and in the days to come. In Jesus' name, Amen.

The Gift of Encouragement

> "And let us consider one another in order to stir up love and good works, not forsaking the assembling of ourselves together, as is the manner of some, but exhorting one another, and so much the more as you see the Day approaching."
> – *Hebrews 10:24-25 NKJV*

There is a gift of encouragement that comes from God, which is differentiated from the encouragement of the world.

What is of God directs us to the Will of God, whereas what is of the world directs us to the world. When we are encouraged in something we do or accomplish by the world, it is through being earth-bound. It is not with any intrinsic worth or meaning, nor is it derived by God. It is an encouragement to produce what does not last.

Someone may praise us for getting first in a race. Others may say "well done" when we turn a startup into a million-dollar company. Whatever we do, we tend to be praised by men through their authentic encouragement. Of course, there is the opposite end, which is falsified in nature. There is an encouragement that may appear as genuine, but it is mere flattery, and flattery is that which God hates.

"A man who flatters his neighbor Spreads a net for his feet" (Proverbs 29:5 NKJV). God's Wisdom will help us speak as Elihu in Job 32:21-22 (NKJV) and declare:

> "'Let me not, I pray, show partiality to anyone;
>   Nor let me flatter any man.
>   For I do not know how to flatter,
>   *Else* my Maker would soon take me away.'"

God punishes a flattering tongue, and for a holy man or holy woman to flatter is a grave sin and serious offense. Elihu understood it could cost him his reputation and life. This is why we must follow the words of Paul in Romans 16:17-20 (NKJV):

> "Now I urge you, brethren, note those who cause divisions and offenses, contrary to the doctrine which you learned, and avoid them. For those who are such do not serve our Lord Jesus Christ, but their own belly, and by smooth words and flattering speech deceive the hearts of the simple. For your obedience has become known to all. Therefore I am glad on your behalf; but I want you to be wise in what is good, and simple concerning evil. And the God of peace will crush Satan under your feet shortly.
> The grace of our Lord Jesus Christ *be* with you. Amen."

Deception always arises from flattery. When we are naïve and believe every word we hear, we walk in the way of foolishness, neglecting to see the evil to come, and, like the simple, we accept it, continue on, and are punished. We do not foresee or discern the evil behind individuals' words; instead, we merely accept them as truth when, in fact, they are not.

This is an important aspect to note: one can declare something true, but enhance it to the point where it becomes a lie. Take, for example, a corrupt cop. The cop may do one bad thing, but though there are corrupt cops, not all cops are bad. Someone who is easily triggered, naïve in understanding, and full of zeal without knowledge will begin their pursuit of saying, "All cops are corrupt." This, of course, is foolishness and a lie. Just because there are corrupt cops does not mean that *all* cops are bad.

In a like manner, when it comes to flattery, one may say, "You did so well with your investment. I'm so proud of you, that's amazing! You'll have to teach me sometime. I can't believe you knew to invest in that stock at that moment. You really are good at what you do. I don't know anyone like you when it comes to stocks. Great job!" On the surface, this may seem encouraging. Of course, there is truth to the statement, but it begins to be over-enhanced to the point where there is flattery. The truth, though there, begins to fade, and, through overembellishment, a hidden agenda, mockery, envy, jealousy, and anger emerge. For it is not what a person says that matters, but the spirit behind what is said. If the Holy Spirit is not there, it is not authentic encouragement.

Encouragement of the world is rightly that — of the world. It comes from how the world views life and meaning. For those who have the gift of encouragement from the Holy Spirit, there is genuineness and authenticity. It isn't just saying the right words, but meaning what is said. It isn't just about what they do, but about who they are. It isn't just encouragement in who they are, but also in aiding them in the current season they find themselves in, and in recognizing that God is either permitting or putting them through it.

Someone who is single may desire to get married. The people of the world will say, "It's okay, it'll happen in time." Of course, more can be said, but in the essence of what can be said, it does not go much further. For those who are born-again and have the gift of encouragement, however, they will say, "I know this season is tough, but God sees you. He is having you single during this time as a means to prepare. You need to prepare for the other person and get rid of your trauma, triggers, and become more self-aware as you grow in God. Above all, God wants your heart and for you to prioritize Him at all times and in all areas of your life. God loves you and will not give you a wonderful blessing of one of His children to steward when you are not in a state to steward it well. God will help you, and know that every day you grow, you are preparing. The process will speed up as you do what God commands you."

Which exemplifies more encouragement? Of course, the one who has the gift of encouragement from the Spirit. True encouragement is not just about the person; it is also about helping direct them to see God amid what they are going through. If one is not encouraged in the Lord, can encouragement be long-lasting? No, there will always be a need to have more. However, those who have the gift of encouragement bring a word in due season, fit for the proper occasion. "Pleasant words are like a honeycomb, sweetness to the soul and health to the bones" (Proverbs 16:24 NKJV).

Those with this gift speak what is from God and guide others to God. This encouragement is a channeling and a directing to God. Once the person clings to God, the one who has the gift of encouragement does their work. They did what God declared: that the individual who received their words would hear them, accept them, and run to God. Then, when they go to God, the encouragement is long-lasting, because true encouragement is only found in the Lord.

"The Lord God has given Me the tongue of the learned, that I should know how to speak a word in season to him who is weary" (Isaiah 50:4 NKJV). Only the Lord God can give us this gift, which is of the Holy Spirit. There is no other way to be one who encourages not only *in* truth, but guides others always within the encouragement to Him Who *Is* Truth.

"But exhort one another daily, while it is called 'Today,' lest any of you be hardened through the deceitfulness of sin" (Hebrews 3:13 NKJV). Exhorting is a form of encouragement, but when it comes to the gift of encouragement, exhortation naturally follows. Strong enforcement and an urge for someone to do something can awaken them out of a state of depression and spiritual slumber.

Some of us are bound by mindsets we got from parents who are not of God. Others of us are stuck in mundane routines, asking God to move, but not discerning why He isn't. We are complaining that He isn't doing what we ask, but we fail to see that we aren't doing what He is commanding! When someone with the gift of encouragement comes forth, they bring a word of exhortation that helps us see where we have been blind. They show and share what is of God and what we need to change. Those of us who are truly born-again and understand that the Christian walk is one of continual growth and an ever-sanctifying work, they will immediately say, "You are right. I did not see this. Thank you, and thank You, Lord, for speaking through this person! I needed to be woken up."

That is why wherever we go we must "Preach the word! Be ready in season and out of season. Convince, rebuke, exhort, with all longsuffering and teaching" (2 Timothy 4:2 NKJV). We are called to "comfort each other and edify one another" (1 Thessalonians 5:11 NKJV) and "warn those who are unruly, comfort the fainthearted, uphold the weak, be patient with all" (1 Thessalonians 5:14 NKJV). For "Anxiety in the heart of man causes depression, but a good word makes it glad" (Proverbs 12:25 NKJV). When we have the gift of encouragement, even the most depressed souls can awaken and be filled with the joy of the Lord and the joy of their salvation!

Words carry weight, and the greatest are from the Holy Spirit Himself, speaking to us and through us to reach others. When we are in disbelief, battling temptations, feeling weak and tired, lacking energy and the motivation to carry on, the Holy Spirit comes forth and we are awakened, rejuvenated, and ready to walk into all that God has for us!

"A man has joy by the answer of his mouth, and a word spoken in due season, how good it is!" (Proverbs 15:23 NKJV). Those with the gift of encouragement will have joy in their mouth. There will be a satisfaction that the Holy Spirit spoke through them. They will reflect on and be grateful for how the Holy Spirit gave them the exact words to say to encourage a brother or sister in the Lord. Even those of the world, the Holy Spirit is reaching out to them through us. God gives encouraging words to believers and to those who have yet to know Him. God is always reaching out, and often He reaches out to others through us.

This is why we must "Let no corrupt word proceed out of your mouth, but what is good for necessary edification, that it may impart grace to the hearers" (Ephesians 4:29 NKJV). Those who are perverse in speech, speak inappropriate, sexual jokes, and have dark humor will not possess this gift. They will be those who are of the world, finding humor in the ways of the world. No, those who have the gift of encouragement will continually allow the Holy Spirit to speak through them and monitor their words. They may fall at times, as "we all stumble in many things. If anyone does not stumble in word, he *is* a perfect man, able also to bridle the whole body" (James 3:2 NKJV), but their words will be filled with truth, purity, and authenticity. None is perfect, however, in the Power of the Holy Spirit, we who are born-again can most certainly be transformed each day.

"But no man can tame the tongue. *It is* an unruly evil, full of deadly poison. With it we bless our God and Father, and with it we curse men, who have been made in the similitude of God. Out of the same mouth proceed blessing and cursing. My brethren, these things ought not to be so" (James 3:8-10 NKJV). Those who desire this gift must cover their mouth and seek God's assistance and aid to deliver them from any perversity and wickedness that comes from the mouth. Proverbs 13:2-3 (NKJV) declares:

"A man shall eat well by the fruit of *his* mouth,
 But the soul of the unfaithful feeds on violence.
 He who guards his mouth preserves his life,
 But he who opens wide his lips shall have destruction."

When we are quick to speak wickedly, we are revealing to others the depravity within. When we are wise in speech, both in public and private, we will be blessed with the gift of encouragement as we seek the Holy Spirit to bless us with such a beautiful gift.

Acts 2:38-40 (NKJV) declares:

"Then Peter said to them, "Repent, and let every one of you be baptized in the name of Jesus Christ for the remission of sins; and you shall receive the gift of the Holy Spirit. For the promise is to you and to your children, and to all who are afar off, as many as the Lord our God will call."

And with many other words, he testified and exhorted them, saying, "Be saved from this perverse generation.""

God wants us to be saved from this perverse generation. A man may be encouraging, but if we could monitor the silent words uttered within his mind, behind closed doors, or with those closest to him, we would be appalled. We would see that they are those who flatter and may even be genuine in their encouragement, but still cannot be trusted. For trust can only come from those walking in the Truth and those who know Him Who Is Truth. Without such, integrity within an individual in the world can only go so far. Yes, it can be there, but again, it can only go so far.

Let us therefore "consider one another in order to stir up love and good works" (Hebrews 10:24 NKJV). Let us "Bear one another's burdens, and so fulfill the law of Christ" (Galatians 6:2 NKJV).

"Strengthen the weak hands, and make firm the feeble knees. Say to those who are fearful-hearted, 'Be strong, do not fear! Behold, your God will come with vengeance, with the recompense of God; He will come and save you" (Isaiah 35:3-4 NKJV).

God in Heaven, Him Who is our Hope, Encouragement, and Who is the Bedrock of Truth, You alone are Pure and Perfect. You alone are Holy and Just. You alone, O God of Heaven and Earth, can do no wrong. Bless us this day with the gift of encouragement. Clean up our speech and make us speak words that edify, build up, and declare Your Truth! O God, fill us with the faith to receive all of the gifts of the Spirit. Bless us as You see fit, according to the Spirit Who is at work within us. May our efforts always be to align with Thy Will, that nothing may interfere with Your desire to bless us. God, may all that You give us be stewarded well for Thy Glory alone. May we never take credit for what only You can do. Give us the humility to not speak of ourselves, for we are called to let another man praise us and not our own lips. Many will declare their goodness, but who can find a faithful man? Only You, O Lord, can create a faithful, humble man. Do this to us, we pray, and may Your Name be glorified by how we live, move, and have our being. In Jesus' name, Amen.

Gift Blockers & Consequences of Using the Gifts of the Spirit Wrongly

"Thus says the Lord God: 'Behold, I am against the shepherds, and I will require My flock at their hand; I will cause them to cease feeding the sheep, and the shepherds shall feed themselves no more; for I will deliver My flock from their mouths, that they may no longer be food for them.'"
– *Ezekiel 34:10 NKJV*

Using the gifts of the Spirit wrongly is a sure sign of a coming judgment. God will not allow us to use what is of Him or from Him for selfish ambition and succeed. Instead, He will lead us to repentance and bring us to our knees. If we do not heed the call to repent, then He will bring swift justice and judgment. If He relents on swift justice and judgment, then it is prolonged for a greater judgment that is to come.

"Therefore put to death your members which are on the earth: fornication, uncleanness, passion, evil desire, and covetousness, which is idolatry. Because of these things the wrath of God is coming upon the sons of disobedience, in which you yourselves once walked when you lived in them" (Colossians 3:5-7 NKJV). When we are led by carnality, we will not live spiritually minded. We will go in the way that will lead us astray. Eventually, when we continually neglect the call to crucify the flesh and take up our cross daily, we will seek to raise ourselves up daily. In doing so, we will misuse the gifts of the Spirit.

God is not mocked, nor does He take lightly those who use the gifts for self-gain. Micah 3:5-7 (NKJV) declares:

> "Thus says the Lord concerning the prophets
> Who make my people stray;
> Who chant "Peace"
> While they chew with their teeth,
> But who prepare war against him
> Who puts nothing into their mouths:
> 'Therefore you shall have night without vision,
> And you shall have darkness without divination;
> The sun shall go down on the prophets,
> And the day shall be dark for them.
> So the seers shall be ashamed,
> And the diviners abashed;
> Indeed they shall all cover their lips;
> For *there is* no answer from God.'"

God will rebuke, correct, chastise, discipline, and ultimately pour out His wrath on those who choose to declare what is not of Him and pretend to possess gifts of the Spirit they do not have.

Too many are running around pretending to be someone, desiring to feed a need, want, or desire that they cannot obtain on their own. People want to claim they see when they do not see. People want to claim a word when one has not been given. They want to make themselves appear that way because, inwardly, they lack much. The Spirit of God is not in them, and wherever the Spirit of God is not, there is both death and vanity.

This is imperative to know and act accordingly, for to lie about possessing something that can only come from God is to pretend to be God. In turn, we will be proven liars, and our end will be destruction if we seek to do what is of God *apart* from Him.

"'Son of man, these men have set up their idols in their hearts, and put before them that which causes them to stumble into iniquity. Should I let Myself be inquired of at all by them?'" (Ezekiel 14:3 NKJV). Will God listen to the inquiry of those who set up idols upon their hearts? These idols are the desire to have what is of God without God. They want the benefits that can be given or obtained with certain spiritual giftings, without the inner healing and the hidden crucifixion that takes place within. Every day we cease to die to the flesh, we put to rest God's best. Every day we proceed with wanting to be something in this life apart from Him, Who is Life, is a cause for concern that will lead to a life of strife.

Truly, we must meditate on our hearts and see if we are even in the right to go to God. For God does not answer the call of those who seek to do what they want and only go to Him as a means to grant their inner desires. No, God is deaf to the fake as much as He is to the unrepentant unbelievers who want to go their own way. Isaiah 30:8-11 (NKJV) declares:

> "Now go, write it before them on a tablet,
> And note it on a scroll,
> That it may be for time to come,
> Forever and ever:
> That this *is* a rebellious people,
> Lying children,
> Children *who* will not hear the law of the Lord;
> Who say to the seers, "Do not see,"
> And to the prophets, "Do not prophesy to us right things;
> Speak to us smooth things, prophesy deceits.
> Get out of the way,
> Turn aside from the path,
> Cause the Holy One of Israel
> To cease from before us.""

Just as the world wants nothing to do with God, so those who just *want* from God what can only come from Him, but do not want Him for Who He is, treat Him all the same. They refuse to repent and relent in their selfish pursuits. When this occurs, one is guaranteed not to receive what they request from the Lord, for the Lord God Almighty grants requests only to those who prioritize Him above all things.

The way of those who seek the gifts for wrong reasons is evident, but those who use the gifts in a wrong manner and neglect the weightier matters of God's Word and call to repent must receive even greater rebuking. Ezekiel 22:25-28 (NKJV) speaks on this further:

> "The conspiracy of her prophets in her midst is like a roaring lion tearing the prey; they have devoured people; they have taken treasure and precious things; they have made many widows in her midst. Her priests have violated My law and profaned My holy things; they have not distinguished between the holy and unholy, nor have they made known *the difference* between the unclean and the clean; and they have hidden their eyes from My Sabbaths, so that I am profaned among them. Her princes in her midst *are* like wolves tearing the prey, to shed blood, to destroy people, and to get dishonest gain. Her prophets plastered them with untempered *mortar,* seeing false visions, and divining lies for them, saying, 'Thus says the Lord God,' when the Lord had not spoken."

Many people who even have gifts of the Spirit but use them in the wrong way tend to lead many astray. They idolize money, prestige, wealth, and status. They are respecters of persons and see people as a means to their end. There is no love, and they lack any desire to truly give God the glory. In the end, these people will be found out. In the end, all their works will burn on the Final Day, even if they *repent later for* misusing the gifts.

Truly, what is given *by* God is meant to be used *for* Him. If we do not seek to use what He has given for His Glory, then He will give to another, and we will pervert our story. We will not allow God to be the Author of what He wanted to write over our lives. O yes, He may have spoken, but if the call upon our lives does not fulfill the likewise path we are to go down that meets God in what He has spoken, then we will live a ghostly life. It will be a fragmented life that goes unfilled. We will be known for the believer who used what God gave for ourselves, not as the humble servant who stewarded well what God gave for God alone!

The blockage of the gift being truly used is simply due to self. The consequences of not using the gifts appropriately are eventually a ministry that is torn down. We will be exposed by other discerning born-again believers, and we will be stripped of everything God was willing to give. Even if we acquired many things by using the gifts for self-gain, what was gained for self will be brought down, for any idol ahead of God shall be smashed and broken. It will be brought low, and it will not succeed.

Those with a discerning heart will know that many are using the gifts of God inappropriately. They claim to be something they are not. They pretend to have gifts when they do not. They dabble more in witchcraft and new age practices, rather than in God's Word and allowing the Spirit to lead. These people, sadly, will have lived their lives in vanity, leading toward a self-created defeat.

God is extremely serious about what He gives. He expects us to steward it well before Him with all reverence and humility. One may start out well, but it is not how we start that matters; it is how we finish. "The end of a thing *is* better than its beginning; The patient in spirit *is* better than the proud in spirit" (Ecclesiastes 7:8 NKJV).

Let us never let pride, ego, or self get in the way of the gifts God has given us. For if we do, there will be tremendous consequences. If we fail to heed this word of warning, we will be as many before us, pretending to be and possess what we do not have, or using what we do have in a way that is for self-gain and gratification. In any case, God will not endure such distorted practices and ways for long. Eventually, He will reveal to all, and the Truth will prevail.

Let us use well all God has given for His Glory, for in seeking the Spirit to use the gift through us, we will grow in our gifting, and as we grow, we will truly be mighty saints in the Lord. For it will not be by our own power or might, but by God's Spirit.

God in Heaven, Who is Almighty and Sovereign, Who is a Jealous God and will not be mocked, You alone are Holy, Righteous, and Good. O God, cleanse us of our evil ways. Set us free from demonic mindsets and keep the

Enemy far from us. Let us live under the banner of Thy Love and the shadow of Your wing. O God, protect us, even from ourselves. Do not allow us to be deceived. Do not allow us to pretend or fake what we do not have or possess. God, grow us in humility, that we might be saints who are entrusted with all the gifts of the Spirit. Above all, let us serve You with what You have given, seeking You to ever bring the increase, for we alone plant the seed and water. Only You, O God, bring forth the increase and in proportions we could not do if we lived one hundred times over. Blessed be You, the Only Sovereign, Omnipotent God. In Jesus' name, Amen.

Conclusion

"But one and the same Spirit works all these things, distributing to each one individually as He wills."
   – *1 Corinthians 12:11 NKJV*

The Holy Spirit gives what He wills, based on what He sees within us. If our will is in alignment with the Heavenly Father, there is nothing that can be prevented from His Divine Hand. When we request all the gifts of the Spirit from Him, He can and will do so in His timing, if we remain continually aligned with Him and His Word. If we are perpetually in disobedience, then we come out of agreement with what He has declared and expects of us. In the end, we will live mediocre lives that fulfill only a small part of the full call God had for us. In the end, we will only receive a small portion of what God wanted to bless us with.

When we follow God, we can be like Samuel in 1 Samuel 3:19 (NKJV), where "Samuel grew, and the Lord was with him and let none of his words fall to the ground." God can help us live lives so attuned to His Voice and speaking that, if we talk, we will be as an oracle of God before man. God will allow all our words to be fulfilled because we have spent time in the Word of God, seeking the Spirit to speak and to make sense of It. The more we do this, the more we will naturally speak what is of God. As we mature, God will have us work from His Word but speak based on the Spirit's leading. We will have a word in due season for every moment.

As we seek God, He can give us the wisdom and the prudence to know what to say, when to say it, and how to speak it. As this is done, we will be a blessing beyond measure, as God blesses those who obey and seek Him with all their heart, soul, mind, and strength.

"*You who are* named the house of Jacob: 'Is the Spirit of the Lord restricted? *Are* these His doings? Do not My words do good To him who walks uprightly?'" (Micah 2:7 NKJV). God's Word is good to those who walk uprightly. God's Word is good all the time, but it *does* good to those who are good in God's sight. "For *God* gives wisdom and knowledge and joy to a man who *is* good in His sight; but to the sinner He gives the work of gathering and collecting, that he may give to *him who is* good before God" (Ecclesiastes 2:26 NKJV).

"As each one has received a gift, minister it to one another, as good stewards of the manifold grace of God" (1 Peter 4:10 NKJV). Whatever gift(s) we have been given, let us steward them well. Let us seek God continually and request that His Spirit work through us to exercise the gift in a godly, upright, truthful manner. For in all things, God must lead, and for God to lead, we must go to Him before doing. When we learn this simple art of godly counsel, God's Will shall be done. For what is not sought for God to do is done by our own doing. We will operate based on how we think, but the more we spend time with God, the more naturally we will do what He desires. Of course, even when this occurs, we must always go to Him, for in going to Him shows humility and full dependence on the responsibility of His Spirit to move, lead, guide, direct, speak, and do all the Father's Will. Truly, when we do this, "Your ears shall hear a word behind you, saying, "This *is* the way, walk in it," Whenever you turn to the right hand Or whenever you turn to the left." (Isaiah 30:21 NKJV).

"When Jesus came into the region of Caesarea Philippi, He asked His disciples, saying, 'Who do men say that I, the Son of Man, am?'" (Matthew 16:13 NKJV). The proportion of the Spirit ruling our vessels and doing the Father's Will begins with our mindset and disposition of Christ. If we know that He is God and we have accepted Him as Lord and Savior and repented of our sins, there is no stopping the flow of the Holy Ghost. Only our sin and self can get in the way, but if we continually die to self each day, the same Power that raised Christ from the grave will not only reside in us, but He will manifest His Power through us. This is the Way that God desires for all who are born again. This is His will for every believer – "for he who comes to God must believe that He is, and *that* He is a rewarder of those who diligently seek Him" (Hebrews 11:6 NKJV).

"'For I say to you, among those born of women there is not a greater prophet than John the Baptist; but he who is least in the kingdom of God is greater than he'" (Luke 7:28 NKJV). How can the least in the Kingdom of God be greater than John the Baptist? It is due to having the Holy Spirit. John the Baptist was the greatest man to live apart from the Holy Spirit, just as Solomon was the wisest man to live without the Holy Spirit. Of course, the Holy Spirit would come *upon* these men, but it was not until the crucifixion and resurrection of Christ that the Holy Spirit would dwell in man as the Seal and Validation that one is saved.

The Lord Jesus Christ declares, "'Nevertheless I tell you the truth. It is to your advantage that I go away; for if I do not go away, the Helper will not come to you; but if I depart, I will send Him to you'" (John 16:7 NKJV). "In Him you also *trusted,* after you heard the word of truth, the gospel of your salvation; in whom also, having believed, you were sealed with the Holy Spirit of promise, Who is the guarantee of our inheritance until the redemption of the purchased possession, to the praise of His glory" (Ephesians 1:13-14 NKJV).

When we have the Holy Spirit, we can surpass these men. Not because of who we are, but due to how lively and active the Holy Spirit is through us. For God is greater than man, and if we have less of us and more of the Holy Spirit in us, then He will exercise the Father's Will. The Spirit of God will rule our spirit, leading toward a cohesive union between God and ourselves. Though we won't be perfect in this life, the times we are humble and courageous enough to die to self, we will see God move in mighty and miraculous ways.

God is seeking a holy remnant that will be part of a revival of repentance and a revival of revelation of the knowledge of Him. God is readily prepared to exercise the working of miracles and move in ways not seen before. In the day of artificial intelligence, God will not call up His Church until He proves to the world that His Spirit is greater than what man can create; that the spiritual is greater than the technological.

When this occurs, what side will we be on? I know where my Wife and I will be, and my hope and prayer is that you seek God with all your heart, soul, mind, and strength. For the time is coming soon within our generation where not only mountains will move, but we will see "planets move." What once was in reference to mountains in times past will now be small compared to what God is going to do.

Fresh revelation is upon us, and my hope and desire is that you seek all God has for you – not for your sake or for you, but for the sake of those around you and for the Glory of God Almighty.

May God's Spirit fill you, restore you, sanctify you, heal you, change you, empower you, grow you, stretch you, and shape you more into the image of Christ.

Revival is upon us, and the gifts of the Spirit are going to shake and shatter this Earth. When the Spirit moves, the world will truly know that "He Who is in you is greater than he who is in the world" (1 John 4:4 NKJV).

———

God in Heaven, Him Who is Spirit, Truth, and Life, Whose Light shines in the darkness and the darkness has not overcome it, Who is the God and Father of the Lord Jesus Christ, Him Who is the only Begotten Son, Who alone is the Revealed Image of the Invisible God, Whom no weapon can be formed against, Who cannot be overcome, Who cannot be instructed, and in which no counsel can go against, You alone are the Sovereign Omnipotent, the Only Supreme, Independent Ruler Who is the Righteous Ruler and Just Judge. Only You, O God, deserve all the glory, honor, and praise. Dominion is Yours, and we are but vessels to be worked in and through by Your Spirit. God, bless us with a deeper hunger and desire for You. Draw us to Your Word that we might not be distracted by this world. God, You alone are Almighty and can change us. You are willing and wanting to reveal to mankind Your Might and Power. Prepare us, O Lord, to be vessels readily prepared and able to exercise the gifts of the Spirit by the

Spirit's leading. God, do not allow darkness to prevail. Let Your Light shine brighter than the noonday through our lives and Your people. Show the world the foolishness of following in the way of technology and the flesh. God, we are greater and mightier in You than a thousand soldiers. We can fight against principalities and rulers of darkness when we possess Him Who is Greater than any. Holy Spirit, we yield, submit, and surrender our all to You. Prepare us for Divine illumination, as You guide us through the Holy Scriptures. Reveal to us deeper revelations of God, and instill in us the faith that moves mountains. Do not let us cower or become complacent in our faith, but motivate and compel us to more. For in God, there is always more. Teach us the way we are to go, and when we sin, lead us to repentance. Do not allow anything to come between our relationship, and bless us with Your gifts and an ever-increasing in them. Teach us how to use them for the Glory of the One and Only LORD God, we pray. In Jesus' name, Amen.

Afterword

I appreciate you taking the time to read through *Spiritual Gifts: What Can Only Come From The Holy Spirit*.

If this were a blessing, it would be greatly appreciated if you took a few minutes to write a review on the platform you purchased the book (e.g., Amazon).

An honest review can go a long way toward making the book more visible to future audiences.

If you feel led to do so, I genuinely appreciate it.

Judah Veritas

Author

Let's Connect

If you would like to connect with Judah Veritas, you can find him on the following platforms:

For All Relevant Social Media, Linktree: https://linktr.ee/judahandjackieveritas

For Judah's Services: https://stan.store/ascendwithveritas

About Judah Veritas

Judah Veritas came to a more profound knowledge of God when he realized it was only Jesus Christ Who could break the chains of sin that kept him bound.

He is passionate about diving deeper into the study of Who God is, His Attributes, His Nature, and His Being, and sharing the revelations he has received with all who have an ear to hear. His desire is for others to know God intimately. Not only as Father, Son, and Holy Spirit, but as Creator of the Universe.

His testimony is impactful, as it reveals God as the Deliverer. He was supernaturally set free from an addiction to pornography and masturbation at age 23, as a Non-Denominational Christian, and received the gift of tongues and discerning of spirits upon getting married.

Since the age of 25, Judah has consistently posted one video each day on YouTube containing apologetic, theological, or philosophical insight. He is an Entrepreneur, a dedicated Author, a husband to his wife, Jackie Veritas, and a grateful father.

Also by Judah Veritas

Spiritual Gifts is Veritas's eighth book. He has multiple books in the works, expected to launch this year and in the years ahead.

Some of the books to be released soon (or are already published) that were mentioned throughout this book are the following:

- *Ineffable Attributes: Understanding the Inconceivable Characteristics of God* (pg. 8)
- *The Infinite Omni: The Unending All Behind All Things* (pg. 8)
- *Theology of Work* (pg. 11)
- *Unraveling Deception: Discerning Darkness* (pg. 64)
- *The Unknown Known: From God's Simplicity to His Infinity* (pg. 86-87)
- *Absolute Supremacy: The Ascendency of God Almighty* (pg. 86-87)
- *The Realm Beyond* (pg. 97, 130)
- *The Infinite Omni* (pg. 138)
- *God's Will* (pg. 155)
- *The Metaphysical Trichotomy of Persons* (pg. 196)
- *Waging War* (pg. 204)
- *Discerning the Devil* (pg. 204)

We hope *Spiritual Gifts* was an edifying read that benefited your growth in understanding the gifts of the Holy Spirit.

God bless you, keep you, guide you, and continue to lead you in His Will, according to His Word.

www.ingramcontent.com/pod-product-compliance
Lightning Source LLC
Chambersburg PA
CBHW070137100426
42743CB00013B/2734